4

7

5

6

8

A QUITE REMARKABLE FATHER

A Quite Remarkable

Father / Leslie Ruth Howard

HARCOURT, BRACE AND COMPANY

NEW YORK

FOR MY MOTHER, *"the indispensable one"*

Contents

Preface

In collecting material for this book I have been helped by many people—both friends and co-workers of my father. To each who has given me his time and thought, I say thank you.

This book is dedicated to my mother, but that alone will not thank her for the hours of "brainwashing" she underwent at my hands. Nor will it express my gratitude at her complete lack of interference in what is, after all, her life story too.

My brother made all his personal material available to me and I have drawn upon it freely. I thank him for unselfishly permitting me to do this and to use direct quotations from his own work.

My immediate family know full well that this is their book too. My daughters have put up with me, and listened to me read aloud; they have helped me whenever possible, and hardly grumbled at all. My thanks to my husband is simple and brief: without him this book could never have been written.

L.R.H.

A QUITE REMARKABLE FATHER

Prologue / A Daughter's Assessment

On a clear, sunlit morning in June 1943, a commercial airliner took off from Lisbon, Portugal, and headed toward England. It was on a routine daily flight; it moved steadily over Portugal and the tip of Spain and out across the Bay of Biscay. At 12:45 P.M. the aircraft's crew sighted eight German fighters; but this was not unusual. Enemy aircraft were frequently seen and there had been surprisingly few attacks made on the commercial flights. The airliner continued on course but increasingly aware that the eight fighters were still behind. The pilot radioed England: "We are being followed," and took his plane down to wave-top level in an attempt to shake off the fighters. Being unarmed, there was nothing they could do but fly on and pray. Thirty minutes later the English base received a brief message: "We are being attacked." Brief and final. For at that moment six of the German fighters attacked in turn, riddling the helpless, slow-moving plane. It burst into flames and dived into the sea. It was carrying a full load of passengers, tragically including two small children. Among the passengers was my father, Leslie Howard, returning from a lecture tour in Portugal and Spain undertaken for the British Council and, through them, for the Government. Spain was still a neutral country, but that neutrality was in the balance and some weight on the Allied side was of urgent importance. He had gone out officially to speak of the theater but really to speak of England. There has been much conjecture about the reasons behind the attack on this one aircraft. Sir Winston Churchill has given his view in *The Hinge of Fate*. He had been at a Big Three conference in Algiers and was flying back at the same time. He suggests that the Germans thought he was on the aircraft.

The Air Ministry, quoting from the contemporary Luftwaffe operational report, records a different tale: "The eight aircraft were briefed to protect two U-boats and to undertake a rescue search. They failed to sight the U-boats and, as the weather was unfavourable, they were probably on their way back to base when . . . a DC 3 was sighted." The Ministry then states: "There is no evidence to suggest that the crews had orders to attack this particular aircraft. They would, however, undoubtedly consider it their duty to attack any allied aircraft encountered in the course of their normal operational flights. . . ." Back in England we cared little at that moment about why the plane had been shot down. All our thoughts and prayers were with the search planes which were sweeping across the gray, violent sea of the Bay of Biscay. Though we knew that if the passengers had launched their rafts the chance of staying afloat in the rough weather was a slim one, we still unreasonably waited for good news. The newspapers ferreted out any information they could and immediately let us know, but naturally security regulations made it difficult and we seemed helpless and cut off. It was worse for my brother, who was serving in the Navy in the Far East. We imagined his unhappiness, lonely and sweltering in an armed merchant cruiser in the Indian Ocean, not being able to get in touch with us, and waiting for news, surrounded by strangers.

And so the days passed and hope passed too. We realized that no miracle could be expected and that the plane was lost forever, but the heart always refuses at first to accept the rational conclusions of the mind. We still expected my father to come home each weekend, as he had since the war began, and subconsciously we continued to save things to tell him. We were surrounded by his possessions, and though his touch in life had been light, it was found to be everywhere. A curious thing, for his was a quiet and detached personality; he never demanded attention and often could be in the house for hours without anyone realizing he was there. Yet, when he wasn't there and now would never be there, we missed him in every part of our lives.

It is difficult to assess any personality; when that personality is one's father the image is clouded by many things: love, proximity, youthful impressions, and that splendid "taken for granted" attitude with which children eye their parents. Leslie Howard as the film and stage actor was frequently subjected to scrutiny by newspapermen and magazine writers; perhaps they saw him more clearly than his offspring ever could. They certainly could say things about him which reticence would not allow from us. Still, I feel that we, my brother and I, saw and understood more of what was really Leslie Howard than most of the interviewers. They dwelt at length on his pipe-smoking, tweedy, shy English exterior. They frequently printed the curious statements he made: "I hate acting"; "Film acting is a dreary life"; "Long runs in the theatre should be abolished"; "Acting is a woman's work." We read them with amusement but some skepticism. He said these things at home, too, occasionally when he was tired, but quite often simply for the entertainment value. We teased him a great deal when he produced them, which he always thoroughly enjoyed. Actually, there must have been a part of him which did hate acting, for I believe he was sincere when he said: "I am one of those unfortunate people to whom any kind of public appearance is an embarrassment, for whom to have to perform before my fellow men is a misery. I always sympathize with those wretched children who are made to exhibit their talents at parties. I, myself, never suffered thus as a child for the simple reason that I was utterly devoid of gifts of any sort; but from the moment when offered accidentally and accepted economically, I got my first job on the stage and sheepishly daubed my face with greasepaint, I had the inner conviction that this was the most embarrassing occupation in the world." He was essentially an unmelodramatic person. He was a technical actor —one who relied not on emotion but on technique to carry a part. I can never remember him "living" a role at home or for five seconds after he had stepped off the stage or away from a camera. This was most apparent during the shooting of Shaw's *Pygmalion,* which he co-directed with Anthony Asquith. So engrossed would he become with the direction of a scene, for which his brother Arthur was his stand-in and line reader, that he frequently gave the order, "All right, that's good, we'll shoot it—camera!" only to have it politely pointed out to him that he was in the scene. With some embarrassment he would then grab any props he was expected to have and hustle from behind the camera to his place in front of it.

We, his children, naturally agreed wholeheartedly that he did look a little ridiculous kissing girls and playing the juvenile because we did not feel that parents were supposed to do things like that, and he always roared with laughter and agreed that we were right: "I look like a silly old fool, not the respectable father I am." No matter how many people told me my father was a romantic figure, I still felt hot with embarrassment when I was taken to one of his films. I couldn't take this strange figure seriously. To me, he was the nightly storyteller, lying on my bed and sleepily inventing characters for my amusement: "Go on, Daddy!" "Oh . . . where was I?" "The little girl had just found the golden apple." "Ah yes, an apple . . . a beautiful, round . . . shiny . . . golden . . . zzz." And he would be asleep again. I never minded; I was inordinately proud of being called "his private soporific" and let him sleep happily every night on my bed until someone shook him and chased him off to the theater for the evening performance.

He was not a great party-lover, which also endeared him to his children, and most parties, when I was small, found him sneaking up to my room like a conspirator and again dozing off on my bed. He was usually found out; someone would miss him, and my poor mother then had to play the villain and come searching for him. Suddenly, her voice would be heard saying she hoped he was not in "that" child's room at "this" time of night. We would giggle with our heads under the blankets, and he would beg me to hide him. This was obviously terrible for discipline, but wonderful fun for me.

The desire to escape from people and relax was perhaps due in part to boredom with party conversation, but it also stemmed from an inner conviction that his physique could not stand becoming overtired. My father was infected with that incurable disease of many or most actors: hypochondria. He never moved without a perfect battery of pills and medicines. He was absolutely certain that he had heart trouble, despite the assurance from leading heart specialists in every part of the world that he did not. Our house always had the latest electrocardiogram somewhere about, and he insisted that each doctor in turn was a sham, a charlatan, and a quack. "They simply don't *know*," he would fume at my mother when she pointed out, quite reasonably, that no doctor had yet been able to discover any fault. In 1926, when only thirty-three, he was writing to my mother, "I seem to have a strange numbness in my left thumb; I do hope this doesn't mean some form of creeping paralysis"! I was often pressed into service to record his heartbeats, or, rather, the missing ones. He would lie flat on his back while I, armed with pencil and paper, would write down a series of figures. These idiotic numerals would then be shown proudly to the visiting doctor as irrefutable proof of an extra systole, the idea for which he had undoubtedly discovered in one of the many medical books he owned.

As an inheritor of his hypochondria, I can now sympathize with many of his feelings, not the least the panic, when away from home, that one is about to be mortally stricken and never see one's loved family again. In the 1920's my father went for a short holiday to Corsica with, I think, Noel Coward and a group of friends, leaving my mother, my brother, Winkie, and me in Cornwall. Immediately, he began to sicken, and his letters became more and more dismal. "Why did I ever leave my little family?" he moaned as soon as the Blue Train moved out of Paris (his compartment was over the wheels—it always was). By the time he boarded the ship for Corsica, visions of Byron and Rupert Brooke floated before his eyes and death in a strange land was imminent, in this case surrounded by Corsican brigands. "Last night on the ship," he wrote, "I had one of my 'attacks' and was quite prostrated to-day." Then, with a degree of pleasure: "I think I scared the others to death and they are now *very* worried about me."

This attack to which he refers with ill-disguised pride was a regular occurrence in our lives and was a rather terrifying ordeal for him and for us, as it took the form of a nightmare that sent him flying from his bed turning on lights and shouting in an effort to wake himself up. It had some connection with his war experiences and absolutely none with his heart, but no amount of evidence produced by doctors could convince him; for him everything pointed to the one terrible illness. The classic example of this took place one winter in Austria, where we had gone for a skiing holiday. My father met an old school friend and, encouraged by this, consumed three cocktails before dinner—a quite disastrous business, because he had no head for alcohol and seldom drank more than one drink in a whole evening. There was nothing unusual about his appearance, and we duly trooped in to dinner, where, after ordering what he wanted to eat with perfect clarity and some thought, he suddenly folded his table napkin into a small cushion, placed it under his head, and sank to the floor.

This naturally caused great consternation in a crowded dining room, and people clustered around his prostrate form while he groaned, "My heart, my heart . . . Ruth fetch a doctor . . . only three White Ladies with my old school friend . . . my heart." My mother was at first quite distressed, and I rushed from the room horrified by my father making what I considered a terrible spectacle of himself. When I returned a few moments later, he was sitting perfectly normally at the table, trying to pretend that nothing had happened. I gathered later that he had been nettled into getting to his feet by the man at the next table, who had assured my mother, "He's all right, madam, he's just had one over the eight." Father pretended to feel genuinely hurt that anyone could have mistaken a serious coronary attack for intoxication, but he laughed guiltily about it for years afterward.

The extraordinary thing was that this constant interest in his health never interfered with his enjoyment of life or the fun he had with us. This was partly because we never took him seriously—we were all hypochondriacs—but mainly it was his tremendous sense of the ridiculous which saved him at the last moment from anything pompous or self-important.

He was great fun as a father, and Winkie and I would never miss any opportunity to be with him. Being the younger and also at home all the time, I had more chance than my brother, and never had a child a more entertaining companion. He had a rare talent of being able to suit his humor and his interests to whatever age his children happened to be. Perhaps we unconsciously suited our age to his, but whatever the case, I cannot remember a time when he talked down to us or failed to get the same ridiculous glee out of little things. For at least the first twelve years of my life, I was his shadow, feeling no need for friends of my own, riding with him, learning to dance or draw or read with him, and always laughing with him.

He was often to be found accompanied by me and a camera.

A good many hours a day were spent in photography and, for obvious reasons, I appeared rather regularly in the finished product—there are literally hundreds of photographs of me at every age and stage of development. This is hardly a matter for general rejoicing, but it says a great deal for the blind and loving eye of a parent.

If I left quite a lot to be desired as a photographic model, the same could be said of my role as "Father's shadow." I was not an unassuming child; in fact, I was very bossy, and my poor father put up with a considerable amount of chivvying and organizing at my hands. As one interviewer reported: ". . . there is a managerial air about little Leslie." Strangely enough, though his discipline appeared nonexistent, it worked quite well. I always tried far harder to behave properly for him than for anyone else. I wanted him to think I was rather splendid. I can remember only one occasion on which he ever spanked me, and I still recall it with embarrassment because it was the only time I flagrantly overstepped the unwritten rules of good manners which were established between us. It is sufficient to say that I disturbed his favorite pastime, sunbathing, by dumping a quantity of very cold water on him. The first time would have been more than enough for most parents, but he politely asked me not to do it again. Here was where I made my mistake and received my well-deserved punishment.

It took a great deal of provocation to irritate my father. He had developed a remarkable defense mechanism. He simply did not see what he chose not to see. Once I remarked that some people connected with a particular film he was working on struck me as rather unpleasant. He looked at me thoughtfully for a moment and then said, "Yes, I suppose they are, but I don't really notice them." When I replied a little tartly that he was lucky, because I found them impossible, he answered, "It's not luck, Dood. You simply must learn to retreat inside yourself or you'll find life takes too much out of you—it's exhausting and a great waste of time to dislike people."

He had built up a reputation for shyness, which he took considerable trouble to maintain. He was excused from many parties because he was supposedly too frightened of large gatherings to appear. It really rather depended on the gathering. A huge group of painters at the Royal Academy dinner delighted him, but an invitation to a fashionable New York party brought the comment: "I did not go. . . . I don't like brokers, Long Island society, Italian princesses, etc., and I'm sure that's what I should get."

His vagueness, actual or imagined, was also a wonderful shield. For a man who was supposed to be unable to remember his own name, he was quite an able businessman. Though he always left to my mother the organization of all the nasty, dull things like tickets and passports and luggage, he made all the major family decisions himself; then, if the decision did not suit everyone, he could squeeze by on the basis that he was too vague to understand what he had done, knowing that my mother could readjust the details. It was a marvelous arrangement. He was helped in this by his nearsightedness; the picture of the vague professor was complete, myopia and all. He could not see without his glasses, and if he always seemed to be without them when someone he wished to avoid appeared, he got them on fast enough when a pretty girl went by. He wore them whenever he went out, particularly to opening nights or events where a fan might see him, which irritated my mother, who felt he earned his living from the public and should try to be attractive. The sight of him dodging along, his hat down on his nose, his hand over his mouth, and his glasses firmly planted, made her quite violent and she told him he looked as though he had come to rob the safe. He invariably asked her the same question: what did she expect him to do—drift down the aisle tossing back his wavy hair, with one hand on his hip, gurgling, "Here I am fans, come and get me"? This argument was always fruitless, and he continued to dart about like an espionage agent.

The design for living he evolved came slowly and sometimes with pain. As he always gave the impression of taking the line of least resistance, other people got the idea that he would do as they told him. Frightful battles broke over his head as a result, and, since he always ended up doing pretty much what he wanted, everybody was left unsatisfied and cross and yet not really able to be cross with him. He was a peaceful character to become such a storm center. Peaceful, and yet, when the need arose, capable of a biting sarcasm and a quite alarming temper. My mother never got used to the sudden violence of it and was almost as frightened when he lost his temper with someone else as when he was angry with her. It was the more shocking because it happened so seldom —rather like the trusted old family dog suddenly developing rabies. As children we were never subjected to his temper, but we certainly witnessed it, and I can remember admiring the quelling effect it had upon its victim. As we grew older, Winkie and I were sometimes the object of his sarcasm, but it was a very watered-down version, and even at our most infuriating ages I cannot recollect his anger being turned upon us. Possibly because his own father had been severe, he was determined to be understanding and easygoing and let us make our own decisions. We always got the impression that whatever we did was of great interest to him, and, no matter whom he might be working with, I always felt perfectly free to go into the room and was sure of a pat on the hand and a welcoming smile, even when he was deep in a script conference. I can never remember being told to "go along." Meals when he was at home were very nearly a three-ring circus— certainly two rings: my brother on one side of my father at the table reading with dramatic emphasis his latest piece of poetry, and I on the other side describing my morning ride and the actions of my horse in minutest detail, our poor parent trying, and really succeeding rather well, to listen to both of us. The third ring of the circus was periodically supplied by my mother from the far end of the table when she could no longer stand the monopoly of her offspring. It may seem extraordinary that someone whose life was as varied and interesting as his should not have wanted to hold the floor himself. He was, of course, a reticent man, but also a careful one. He sheltered his resources for the most important moments. His detachment was invaluable to him, and he knew it when the time came to work. Thus, he never tried to stem the flow of our rhetoric for a moment, but contentedly relaxed and drew some strength and pleasure from our unceasing chatter.

The picture of Sunday lunch in our dining room is still clear in my mind. The sunlight would be lying across the table reflecting the glasses on the shiny white of walls and ceiling; blue sky and blue curtains, the family all around the table, plus, perhaps, a friend or two; but the conversation comes from one end of the long, pale table, where my father sits leaning forward on his elbows, turning his head from side to side, occasionally nodding in agreement or tilting back to laugh. "Did he, Wink? I never realized Flecker wrote that. . . . Yes, out to grass . . . will do her legs good . . . she'll be fit for the cub-hunting then, Dood. . . . Yes, I like that line, Wink, it's very moving." So it would go, and all our ideas and plans and hopes rang so clearly off this sounding board.

It would be wrong to give the impression that he was only an echo for his children. His advice was always sought, but he gave it so easily and without any attempt to pontificate that we scarcely felt the parental hand. I am perfectly certain that he never read a book on child psychology, but his ideas of self-discipline would rival those of the most ardent proponents of free expression for small children today. Whether one agrees with his methodless method or not, he certainly made life enchanting for Winkie and me.

With the years, he changed—how could it be otherwise? The metamorphosis from a shy boy into a movie star is by no means unique; many famous men have started with far greater handicaps and by industry have overcome them. My father's growth is interesting partly because he never tried to overcome his weaknesses. He was in some ways quite lazy, and he found it delightfully easy to make use of his disadvantages: shyness and shortsightedness, vagueness and unpunctuality became his trademark, and he hid behind it shamelessly, sheltered from the outside world. But he seemed to have remarkable talents, and he was gentle and humorous and a splendid friend.

It is with interest and with new understanding that I have traced his career. Yet, I cannot help feeling that somehow I have missed the real point, or overstated it, and that he is laughing at me. I don't really mind—it was always the kindest laughter.

1 / Early Days and Amateur Dramatics

My father was born in London in 1893. "On April 3rd," he wrote, years later, "there appeared in a small house in Forest Hill, London, a very bald baby boy who was, at least at that time, a great pride to his newly married parents." His parents, Lilian and Frank Stainer, named him Leslie Howard, the latter a family name of his mother's.

They had little money, having eloped the year before against heavy opposition from Lilian's parents. Frank Stainer worked in London in a business office, and managed to increase his meager salary by accompanying on the piano the singing efforts of young ladies at their mothers' "At Home" parties. As all well-brought-up young women were expected to sing, there was a certain amount of work for an accompanist. Lilian was a typical product; aged eighteen, her water colors of Etna were much admired, she spoke French adequately, and her clear soprano was the highlight of her mother's tea parties. It was at such a party that Frank Stainer met her. Lilian was captivated by the young, artistic man. This was scarcely the case with her mother: one look convinced her that Frank Stainer was everything she least required in a son-in-law. Of medium height, and with a heavy black beard, he was hardly an Adonis, had no money, few prospects, and, worse than everything else in that day when English insularity was at its peak, he was a "foreigner." Though by then a British subject, he had been born a Hungarian. Lilian, previously dominated by her mother, showed in this situation the strength of character that was to stand her in such good stead throughout her life. She and Frank were married, cut off without a penny, and a year later produced the very bald baby boy, Leslie.

He was by no means a beautiful child, but his mother always possessed a lively imagination and a great sense of the dramatic, and one day while showing him proudly to her cousin said: "Isn't he a remarkable baby? He has the eyes of a genius."

To which her cousin, who was extremely practical, replied: "Nonsense, Lilie, he's simply going to be shortsighted," which he certainly was.

He was the first of a number of children. The family never had much money, but, in the way of similar families in those days, there was enough to travel a little and give the children an occasional music and dancing lesson. There was a maid or two to help around the house, and life was pleasant and easy in the last years of Queen Victoria's reign.

Soon after Leslie was born, the Stainers spent a few years in Vienna; then they returned and once more took a house in a suburb of London. Lilian's mother had decided that family relations should be reopened, and she found them a house next door to her own in Upper Norwood. It was a peaceful neighborhood of large, ugly red-brick Victorian houses mostly set back from the road, with short carriage drives and pleasant gardens. Jasper Road, where the family found themselves, looked over a green valley where trees hid similar houses, and circled a hill on whose summit stood the Crystal Palace. This glorious brain child of Prince Albert, with its glass walls and soaring towers, was a tremendous excitement for Leslie and his small sister, Dorice, and they were taken on their first visit to it by their grandmother. Granny Mary was an awe-inspiring object herself, to be treated only with one's best kid gloves. She swept her frightened grandchildren off without giving them a chance to say a word and then discovered to her humiliation that the only words they could speak were German.

Once having found their tongues, they rushed around excitedly pointing (which was never done) and crying: *"Was ist das, Grossmutter?"* at the tops of their voices. There were no more trips with Granny Mary until English had been successfully mastered. It was awkward not to speak English at a time when every Englishman had the comfortable belief that he was worth six foreigners. It was hard for a small boy to understand why, when he asked "Please, Uncle Vilfred, gif me something gut!" his English Uncle Wilfred would pop a piece of toast coated with mustard into his mouth because "he must learn not to talk like that, Lilie." He learned quite quickly with that sort of encouragement, swiftly forgetting every word of German.

In Upper Norwood the family settled down, and Frank Stainer traveled each day to the City. He worked hard, though never with great success, as a stockbroker. Young Leslie went to school, which he loathed and at which, owing to shyness and his afflicting nearsightedness, he never did very well. With his mother's encouragement, he wrote countless stories and short plays and dreamed of fame as a writer, an ambition that was to remain with him all his life. He wrote, years afterward: "As a boy the possibility of being an actor never even occurred to me. Nor could it have occurred to anybody who knew the shy and inarticulate youth that I was. I wanted to write. I felt I could express myself on paper; alone in a room I felt articulate and creative."

Though he had not thought of acting, it was at the theater that most of his writing was directed. His first play was written in Latin, with, it is suspected, a certain amount of "encouragement" from his schoolmaster. After that, for all his claims of inarticulate shyness, he blossomed out, and, with his two great friends Fred Buser and Fred Mitchell, he produced a number of musical comedies. He played the piano with great dash and verve, having a good ear, though much to the annoyance of his father, a serious musician who could neither understand nor bear the rattling ragtime that shook his house. Lilian could never believe that her family were not unique and she loved to share their talents with all her friends and relations. Large gatherings took place every few weeks to show off Leslie's latest production. Leslie and the two Freds would leap about the improvised stage, doing dances in the current music-hall style and singing such immortal lyrics as:

> Marriage is a great mistake.
> A simple life and free
> Is much the best you'll all agree
> For chaps like you and me.

> You'll have to mind the baby
> While mother talks to Cook.
> You're drawn from out your paper
> To fasten up a hook.

> But when you try to fasten
> A picture to the wall
> The whole affair comes sprawling down
> And causes you to fall.

All the writing was by the fourteen-year-old genius, with suitable music composed or plagiarized for the occasion. Leslie had certainly inherited his mother's imagination, and when musical comedies grew stale, everyone was invited to a band concert in the garden, where, on an impressive home-made bandstand, the trio played a number of musical instruments, all but the piano unknown before, and mostly drawn from the kitchen. Rain ended this affair, but everyone piled into the house greatly impressed with the afternoon's entertainment. Leslie's mother then decided that the time had come to place her son's work on a more professional and solid basis.

Though his father objected strenuously to such time-wasting activities, his mother connived and contrived and, serenely flying in the face of her husband's wrath, invented the Upper Norwood Dramatic Club, which blossomed under his nose and in his own drawing room. Lilian Stainer was, in her heart, a would-be actress, frustrated by the time in which she lived, a time when nice young ladies did not paint their faces and perform before "mixed company." What more perfect answer to her long-cherished dream than a son who wrote, in her opinion, delightfully entertaining one-act plays? If her husband's attitude appeared implacable, there were ways of circumventing it. Frank Stainer was scarcely more rigid in his feeling of right and wrong than any other middle-class father of that time. He had seen his own future as a brilliant musician sacrificed to the view that it was *déclassé* to entertain the public. He was persuaded, therefore, to allow the dramatic club to continue.

Amateur dramatics were "all the rage" and quite solidly respectable in 1910. The club soon outgrew the drawing room, and by 1912 it had moved into the more rarefied atmosphere of Stanley Hall, Upper Norwood. Here, bubbling with Christmas cheer, the club presented on December 26 a judiciously balanced brew of *The True Artist,* by Leslie Howard Stainer and *Ours,* starring Lilian and Leslie H. Stainer. To entertain the audience during scene changes, there was a spirited program of music including excerpts from *The Tales of Hoffman* and a two-step by a new American composer, Irving Berlin, entitled "Everybody's Doing It." The program also noted that "the club has a few vacancies for new members in forthcoming productions," and suggested communicating with the Hon. Secretary, L. H. Stainer, "Allandale," Jasper Road.

The communications to the Hon. Secretary found their way eventually to a small box room on the top floor of "Allandale," which Leslie had converted into a study. There he and Fred

Buser wrote their stories and plays together and there Leslie brought his mother to listen while he read aloud. To his great delight, one or two of his stories were accepted by *The Penny Magazine,* a pocket-sized publication crammed with thrillers and sensational advertisements guaranteeing cures for baldness, drinking, marital problems, and indigestion. In this periodical Leslie's "The Impersonation of Lord Dalton" appeared, with its subtitle, "A Story of the Diplomatic Service." How its author could have known much about the subject is hard to imagine. It was a gripping tale of a forger who is saved from the common jail to undertake for the British Foreign Office a mysterious mission in Vienna. The piece was liberally sprinkled with butlers, footmen, valets, and beautiful titled women. As could be expected, the forger is not really guilty, and in the end he is married to the beautiful titled woman "with the necessary secrecy by a Presbyterian minister at Baden," not before, however, she has looked at him "fearlessly" because "there was no unnatural shyness about her, no coquetry of any kind. She was a woman of the world. She knew men and this man was an open book to her."

From his eyrie on the third floor, Leslie remained enthralled with the glamourous and mysterious characters that he thought must inhabit the wonderful world of international society. They moved with statuesque glory through the pages of "The Story of the Green Pearls" and "The Lost Stiletto" and "The Magician's Mask," all, to his amazement, published by various magazines and obviously read with avidity by boys very like himself.

Lilian had always managed to take her children to the theater. When quite small, they had seen Gerald du Maurier as Captain Hook in the very first performances of *Peter Pan* by James Barrie, then one of the new twentieth-century playwrights.

Dramatic literature was undergoing a renaissance in those early years of the new century. A few fresh and brilliant writers now appeared to speak in terms completely new to the ears of audiences used to the cloak-and-dagger panache of nineteenth-century melodrama. Led by Pinero, Jones, and Oscar Wilde, whose plays were a success although the actor was distrusted and detested, the new playwrights spilled their works onto the London stage. Somerset Maugham had four plays running in one season. John Galsworthy's *Justice* was a brilliant success in 1910. The controversial George Bernard Shaw wrote the first "discussion" plays, which were produced generally at matinees on the outskirts of London and were attended by a completely new audience of solemn-faced young women who trooped to them with the air of converts to a prayer meeting, more to be lectured at than entertained, all anxious to prove they deserved the suffrage for which they had battled so determinedly.

Leslie had a wide choice for inspiration in the theater, with Beerbohm Tree at His Majesty's staging sumptuous Shakespeare; George Alexander at the St. James's encouraging English writers; and H. Granville Barker at the Court in Sloane Square with J. E. Vedrenne, producing plays by Euripides and Maeterlinck, Yeats and Galsworthy, in a partnership outstanding in British theatrical history. Later, Gerald du Maurier was at Wyndham's, and Leslie became much influenced by his work. Du Maurier was the "great exponent of natural acting and of the art that conceals art," and his light comedy became the ideal for the dramatic society in Upper Norwood.

Acting and writing might be all very well for a hobby, but in the eyes of his father, Leslie had seriously to consider earning a living. At nineteen, he seemed unsuited for everything his father wanted for him. Instead of concentrating on examination results, he had wasted his time writing trash, and now, instead of recognizing his previous folly, he was suggesting quite blithely that he should continue to write and his father should continue to support him. Such a proposal was so preposterous, so completely unthinkable, that it seemed an insult to a father who had done everything in his power to prepare a young man for the serious life ahead of him. Father and son had never been close enough to discuss their own private aspirations. They had so little in common that Leslie, from a young age, had hidden behind his mother and avoided his father. It was now too late to try to explain, if explanation had been possible. He was removed from Dulwich College, where he had been for some time, a position was found in Cox's Bank, and a life which he contemplated with utter disgust was set out before him, with, heaven help him, a pension at the end.

If Lilian was unable to save her son from bank serfdom, she could preserve the dramatic society as an outlet for his frustrated talents. So the 1913-1914 season was planned and presented. The plays given were revealing in their titles: *Deception,* by Leslie Howard and *The Perplexed Husband,* with his mother and sister Dorice. The audience was treated to the music from Bizet's *Carmen* and tapped their toes to a "Rag-Time Selection." The program requested that ladies and gentlemen occupying the front rows wear *"Evening Dress."* Even suburban theater-going was a great function in those days. Banking might be monotonous, but at the weekends there was tennis, and cutting a dashing figure on the court or in someone else's new motorcar, dressed in striped blazer and white flannels, was compensation at twenty for dull figures in a ledger.

Fortunately, Leslie found a person with his own interests at the bank—a Mr. Sellick, who, weighed down as he was by bundles of checks to be sorted, still found mental room for dreams of the drama. Leslie was in constant trouble with the ledgers and impossible arithmetical problems, for he was a hopeless mathematician, and he would take his worries to Mr. Sellick among the files and dust of the Upper Office. There, once the immediate difficulty had been sorted out, they would talk on matters closer to their hearts. During their lunch hour they would go out together to the land of the theater to gaze enraptured at the great men who emerged from stage doors. Leslie bothered little with lunch. His precious free time and extra shillings were spent wandering from bookshop to bookshop in the Charing Cross Road, where he sampled novels by H. G. Wells and plays by Shaw and Barrie and Ibsen. It was to be one of the few periods in his life when he had time to read as much as he liked.

The Stainers by 1914 had five children spanning sixteen years, from Leslie to the youngest, four-year-old Arthur. Dorice, who appeared so regularly with her author brother, was an aspiring student of dancing. She was petite and red-headed and constantly in love. Jimmy, seven years younger, was already the character of the family. There could never have been two brothers more different than Jimmy and Leslie. Jimmy was gregarious where Leslie was shy, independent where Leslie leaned on his mother. Jimmie was the wit and the despair of his family, the author of endless practical jokes, his gaiety undampened even by his father's disapproval. He kept the household between horror and laughter and brightened their days considerably. His younger sister, Irene, lived under his spell and, because she was rather a placid, easygoing child, she provided exactly the right foil for his humor and his pranks. The baby, Arthur, pursued his rather lonely course, ignored or bullied, seldom included in the life of his brothers and sisters.

The blazing summer of 1914 saw England at the end of nearly a century of prosperity and unparalleled world importance, with London the solidly beating heart of this affluence. Cox's Bank hummed with business, and Leslie had little time to dwell gloomily on his future prospects. That life would not go on as it had for the past one hundred years scarcely occurred to anyone, least of all to Leslie. He was depressingly convinced that an endless vista of dull repetition lay ahead; promotion was only a bare possibility, judging from his unremarkable aptitude to date. He faced fifty years as a bank clerk in an unchanging world.

As Leslie traveled to the City on the train one late June morning, contemplating where he would go for his summer holiday, a distorted Hapsburg took his morganatic wife to Sarajevo so she might receive the royal reception and honors in Bosnia that she was refused in Austria. By the time Leslie settled in his seat for the return journey, Archduke Franz Ferdinand and Countess Sophie Chotek had been shot to death by a Serbian nationalist and the world was moving relentlessly into the most horrible war it had ever known.

On July 28 Austria's declaration of war was delivered in Belgrade. Russia mobilized; Germany, backing Austria, declared war on Russia, and within days occupied Luxembourg and was at war with France. On the eleventh hour of August 4, when Great Britain's ultimatum to Germany expired and war was declared, the invasion of Belgium had already begun.

Mr. Herbert Asquith, the British Prime Minister, rose to face a tense House of Commons with the words: "If I am asked what we are fighting for, I can reply in two sentences. In the first place to fulfill a solemn international obligation . . . in the second to vindicate the principle that small nations are not to be crushed . . . by the arbitrary will of a strong, overmastering power." But to the young bank clerk and thousands like him, the war was more than a solemn international obligation; it was a release from all that was dreary and commonplace from nine to five at a desk. He and they visualized themselves in uniform, bringing tears of pride to their mothers' eyes and thrilling their girl friends. With the gay, marvelous optimism of youth, unable to know the cost, for they had never had to count it, the young men of Britain queued up at every recruiting station. Leslie and Fred Mitchell went together to the Inns of Court, which was an officer training company. There were two lines of men, one for the infantry and the other for the cavalry. Fred Mitchell prudently announced his intention of joining the infantry. "What? And walk?" Leslie asked. "When you could ride?" "But I can't" was the reply. "Well, nor can I, but I'm jolly well not going to walk," said Leslie, and joined the line in front of the cavalry recruiting officer.

Leslie's knowledge of riding was confined to small donkeys at the seaside in the summer, but this was not what he told the recruiting officer. Once in, he felt, they would probably have to keep him, a surmise in which he was absolutely correct. The next day, mounting an enormous charger, he was swiftly deposited in a sprawling heap on the ground and heard for the first time the classic cavalry sergeant's question: "Who ordered you to dismount?" His obvious incapacity to remount a now-delighted, self-important horse, drew the attention of the authorities to the fact that they had, to say the least, a novice on their hands. The next few months of cavalry training caused him to ponder many times, as he stood up to eat his meals, whether walking was not a great deal easier. Fortunately, he developed a hitherto dormant though natural aptitude, and emerged at the end of the course a second lieutenant and an excellent horseman. A chance decision had introduced him to a sport that he was to pursue all his life. More important at that moment, the bank was behind him, he trusted, forever.

2 / Cavalry Officer and Bridegroom

His first leave after receiving his commission was all that Leslie could have hoped for. Immaculate in boots and spurs, proudly bearing one "pip" on his sleeve to prove his elevated rank, he quite dazzled himself as well as his family. His mother sniffed a little but thought him marvelous, his brothers and sisters seemed overwhelmed with the romantic figure, and the girls he had known were enthralled.

London was a very exciting place to be in 1915. As he wrote in later years when broadcasting to America, "London was the showplace of the empire. It was a great holiday town. It appeared to exist solely for pleasure and that was a strange paradox. The morning papers would come out with the most appalling casualty list and at night against the unseen background of tragedy and heartbreak the place assumed an atmosphere of gaiety, enjoyment and lighthearted revelry which it had probably never equalled before and certainly never has since.

"One recalls the great throngs of people moving about in the streets at all hours, the enormous numbers of men in uniform, the interminable singing of 'Tipperary,' the Australian soldiers in the Strand, the packed theatres, music halls, restaurants, bars and dance-halls, the jam of midnight traffic in Piccadilly Circus, the ear-splitting whistles of commissionaires calling for taxis and, above all, the bright lights. Those were the days when 'Princes' was the smartest restaurant in London and the old Café Royal the most interesting, when the Monico and the Trocadero were great meeting places, when, though we were engaged in a deadly war, people dressed to go to the theatres and the opera. Covent Garden was at its peak and brought fame and fortune to many great singers. Those were the days when every theatre in town was open and packed to capacity, especially the farces, the musical comedies, the great spectacles and the music-halls. Those were the days when George Robey held forth at the Alhambra in "The Bing Boys," when "Chu-Chin-Chow" was at His Majesty's, great ballets like "Sumurun" at the Coliseum, "A Little Bit of Fluff" at the Criterion, all running interminably and making fortunes, and when the old Empire music-hall in Leicester Square still had its naughty Edwardian promenade and was shockingly like the Moulin Rouge in Paris. Those were the days when you could go a long way for twelve cents in a taxi—when whisky was about a dollar and a quarter a bottle and beer, glorious beer, four cents a pint. Those, in brief, were the days when London was the richest city on earth; when the most extravagant era in English history was drawing to its close— only nobody knew it."

But leave there for Leslie was, though memorable, all too short. As he boarded the train amid a flutter of handkerchiefs and damp-eyed womenfolk, he felt he was going to the front bravely and tight-lipped. Instead, he was only going to Colchester, a green and beautiful town, where a battalion of the Northamptonshire Yeomanry was training. Colchester was famous for its historic castle and its oysters. And for it, another second lieutenant was as unremarkable as the pebbles on the local beach.

Leslie found life as the most junior of junior officers in the regiment dull rather than glorious. But there were compensations. The cavalry had not yet had their horses replaced by tanks and armored cars, so they could ride every day through the fields and lanes, or down the river bank to the sea. The battalion was still many months from going to France, and the pace was easy and relaxed. The junior officers always found time after the morning parade to wander into Colchester and have their coffee in the local coffee shop. Leslie invariably drank milk and ate a square of sponge cake, obeying a last instruction of his mother's to "keep up his strength."

Every day the same young group sat at the window table, and every day at the next table sat four young women enjoying their midmorning break from a local war job. After some days, they began to exchange greetings. Leslie, though ruminating fondly about his new fiancée, could not help noticing one of the four girls particularly. She had large gray eyes under a fringe of brown hair, and lovely features. She appeared to view him with some amusement, occasioned, though he did not know it, by his milk-drinking habits. She had firmly dubbed him "a mother's boy" and had disdainfully pointed out to her friends his pink-and-white skin, fair wavy hair, and the silver bangle he wore on his wrist.

But somehow, for all her scorn, the two tables joined one morning and Leslie found himself gazing into the large gray eyes and talking as he had never talked to anyone before. He drew breath long enough to discover that her name was Ruth Martin, that she was twenty-one, and worked in the recruiting office. What more was there to know? She seemed to understand when he talked about himself and his hopes and his future as a writer. He asked her to tea on Sunday at the Red Lion. She said "no" and then "yes." He told her about his family and about his fiancée, who was the eldest of three sisters and called "Buzz." (Ruth privately nicknamed the other two "Fizz" and "Pop.")

Tea on Sunday with Ruth became a standing arrangement. Leslie would show her his letters to Buzz, and she would add a note saying she was taking care of him. (Women were apparently most trusting in 1916!) They met privately in the coffee shop, they walked in Castle Park. Once he took her to the Theatre Royal and she had to pay for the tickets.

She was teased about her boy friend by her friends and questioned by her father, who was a regular soldier and not impressed with untrained, jumped-up, wartime officers, particularly one who wore a bangle. Ruth answered truthfully that he was just a friend, that he was engaged to someone else.

The idyllic triangle might have continued for several more months had Ruth not suddenly become bored with being a footnote to another girl's letter. Leslie got a weekend leave and left to visit Buzz. Ruth, slightly piqued, went to lunch at the Red Lion with another subaltern. The hotel seemed perhaps a little dull without the earnest young man, but with a glass of sherry and a charming companion, one should be able to forget. . . . Leslie would be halfway to London by now . . . Buzz would be waiting. . . . Ruth's glass paused on its way to her lips. A familiar figure was coming up the steps of the Red Lion. Leslie was not on his way to London.

The respectable gloom and tranquillity of the lounge was shattered by the scene that followed. Many and various phrases from nineteenth-century drama were bandied to and fro, with Ruth delighted though ruffled, the subaltern confused and pink-faced, and Leslie injured, betrayed, and haughty. Amateur dramatics were a very useful background. His exit was as impressive as his entrance: "I would not have believed that you could behave in this wanton manner." The dust settled again, the air became calm, the ferns and African grass relaxed. The day was thoroughly ruined.

At 7:30 next morning a small khaki figure approached the Martin house—Leslie's batman, carrying a note: "I shall be at the coffee house at eleven. Yours, if you want me. Leslie."

Ruth was at the coffee house at eleven. She was destined to be anywhere he wanted her for the next twenty-seven remarkable years. She might have guessed as much when they met that morning, but there was little time to discuss the future. There was no time left for a gentle courtship. Leslie's regiment was leaving for France. Only lovers in wartime will ever know the real meaning of counting the hours and even the minutes together—so often it is all the time left in a lifetime.

On an early spring morning with a gentle sun slanting through the windows of St. Mary's-in-the-Wall, Ruth and Leslie were married. No parental consent; a special license and a bunch of violets. The bride in her best brown suit, the groom in uniform. No ring, because Leslie, true to form, had forgotten to buy one. No witnesses, either, until the caretaker and the charwoman came forward to watch the quiet, lonely little service. "In sickness and in health till death us do part."

Then they were outside, blinking in the sun—hand in hand, not fully aware of what they had done. Parents had to be faced as a first problem. Ruth managed to avoid her father, but Leslie found his waiting when he returned to the barracks. Word had reached Upper Norwood that all was not well between Buzz and her soldier. Father wanted to be quite sure that Leslie was not falling into the hands of an unscrupulous woman. His marriage to Buzz would not only be suitable, it would be economically sound; she would be able to bring to it a considerable dowry. For the first time in his life, Leslie could listen to his father with detachment. Though his father argued, propounded, tried to dominate, as he always had, Leslie knew that at last he was free. He waited until the storm had worn itself out. Then he quietly said, "I'm sorry, Father, but you're too late. I was married this morning." It was a marvelous feeling not to be afraid any more, to know that his future was his own—his and Ruth's. His father was too late altogether.

Never had a newly married couple a more unusual first day.

Frank Stainer stayed for lunch which, though it afforded him a chance to meet Ruth, was neither very comfortable nor very romantic. At the end of an afternoon of extreme stickiness he was put on a train back to London, and Ruth and Leslie returned to the Lion, where Leslie had booked a room for a few days, until they could decide what to do with their strange new life. There was a message waiting—a reminder that he was duty officer that night! Another little matter he had overlooked when making his extensive plans for matrimony. Ruth could scarcely be blamed for beginning to organize this vague young man. Arrangements clearly could not be left to him.

Then the regiment moved, not immediately to France, but to Mayfield, a sweet, gentle Sussex village—a lovely place for Leslie and Ruth to get to know each other in an English spring.

By 1916 the British army in France had sustained a half-million casualties. Extensive plans had been laid for a great summer offensive. This was to be the final blow, the breakthrough that would get the "troops out of the trenches by Christmas." This was to be the Battle of the Somme. The British General Staff had decided to place every possible division in France, and General Douglas Haig received nineteen divisions before the summer. Leslie went with one of them. Until then, he had been incredibly lucky; two years of war, with none of the misery and a lot of the fun. Now it was goodby to Ruth—this time not romantic or easy; this time he really was leaving his heart right there.

Next came France, then the front; the guns heard for the first time, "the slow rolling rumble from the eastern horizon." Leslie's regiment was not in action immediately. Cavalry had limited use in the mud and misery of trench warfare where the infantry of both sides served as compressed cannon fodder for artillery consumption. For a week or two behind the lines, Leslie watched the reserve battalions marching up, keen and gay, a whistle floating on the air behind them. "Oh! ho! ho! I *am* surprised at you"—that miracle of humor and humanity that is the British soldier.

July the first, a day of fiery heat; a day in which British casualties numbered 60,000, battalion after battalion in futile waste. Waste that continued for many weeks. Waste that brought lists greater than even the worst battles earlier. For Ruth, now living in London with Leslie's parents, it was an agonizing time, which she shared with every other family in the British Isles; 400,000 casualties and still the lists lengthened.

Then, suddenly, leave. A tired, mud-covered khaki figure at the end of the street. "I think that soldier called to you, Ruth dear." "Called to me? I don't know who—Mother, it's Leslie!" Ruth started running down the street into the soldier's waiting arms. "Oh darling! Never mind my suit—thank God you're home!"

Leslie went back to France; back to the grueling, tragic existence of attack and counterattack. In April the United States declared war. The tired spirits and hearts in the trenches and at home were lifted. Help was coming. It was sorely needed. The German submarine blockade of Britain was now at its worst and with it the danger of collapse through starvation. France was plagued with depression and defeatism. The British and French General Staffs could not agree on joint strategy. The British accused the French of "squatting and doing nothing," and the French called British plans for attack "futile, fantastic and dangerous." The losers in the *"entente discordiale"* were the Allied troops. Against French advice, the British launched another offensive, which, after three dreadful months, foundered in the swamps of Passchendaele.

It was then that Leslie's part in the war came to an end. His nervous, highly strung temperament let him down. He was returned to England—a case of severe shell shock.

Though Ruth had a job in the War Office, her salary was hardly enough for two. It was possible, while Leslie convalesced, to scrape by with army pay, living with his family. But all too soon the army, which had saved him from his problem, released him to face it once more—how to earn a living, and, now, how to keep a wife.

The family sat in consultation. His father, naturally, insisted on Cox's once again. But Father was no longer omnipotent; Father was ignored. His mother suggested the theater, where his thoughts had already turned. She felt he had a remarkable talent and should go to see an agent.

So, full of enthusiasm, he went to see an agent, but somehow the agent was not as convinced of Leslie's talent as his mother. He went to see another and another and another. Every day the dreary ride on the district railway, the depressing round of office after office. Every day, "come back next week, sorry, nothing at the moment."

3/ Just an Actor

One morning Leslie Howard pushed open a door marked "Ackerman May, Theatrical Agent" and found an agent who paused in the middle of saying "nothing at the moment" to notice that Leslie's voice seemed unusually attractive. Mr. Ackerman May suggested that Leslie might do for a new road company of *Peg o' My Heart*.

Peg o' My Heart, by J. Hartley Manners, was playing to capacity houses in London, with the playwright's wife, brilliant, volatile Laurette Taylor, as Peg. There was quite a large fraternity of *Peg* actors all over the world that year; the touring company of which Ackerman May spoke was the fifth to be formed. It was suggested that Leslie go to see the London production, which had A. E. Matthews in the male lead. Leslie went to see the play not once, but every night. He and Ruth traveled to London each evening to spend their few remaining shillings so that he could master and learn every word, mannerism, pause, and inflection. When the day for the audition arrived, Leslie was ready—nervous but letter perfect. He read for the part; the producer was enchanted, convinced he had found another A. E. Matthews. What he actually had was the performance of a well-trained monkey; it was pure imitation, but it was a beginning, and Leslie got the job and with it

£4.4.0 a week. The producer was so captivated that he gave Ruth a job as the understudy for two lesser females in the company. The family income increased by another £2.2.0 a week.

There was great celebration that night in Upper Norwood. Even Father seemed moderately pleased. He, after all, had visualized supporting his son and daughter-in-law for a much longer time and had kept meticulous account of their cost to him. He hoped, if the £6.6.0 continued, he would see some return.

Leslie's feet now began to grow cold and he was quite sure that he would never be acceptable during the rehearsals, let alone worth four guineas a week on the tour. He longed to have a talk with A. E. Matthews, whose work he had so usefully plagiarized, and get some advice from this clever and experienced actor, but he felt he had to have a suitable excuse for going to see him. It would not be a good idea to rush in and beg for help—it might look as though he had never acted before. After mature consideration, Leslie struck upon a solution to his problem. He was delighted with his brilliant idea, but he must have surprised A. E. Matthews, who recorded the interview with amusement: "Leslie Howard came round to my dressing room to see me. He asked me who had made the riding gaiters I wore—he had been watching the play . . . and had seen every performance for a couple of weeks being full of admiration for my gaiters rather than for my acting." From gaiters they progressed to horses, and, to Leslie's delight, Matthews asked him to come over and ride at his house at Bushey. It was hardly what Leslie had gone to see the star about, and Ruth was a little puzzled when she asked him, on his return, what he had learned and was told that A. E. Matthews had a polo pony.

So Leslie was without advice or guidance when the rehearsals began, and his lack of experience seemed crippling. Professional theater was very different from the easy camaraderie of the dramatic society and altogether confusing and agonizing. Leslie wondered if he would ever learn to enjoy this public display of inner emotions.

The company left London to open in a staid seaside resort, out of season. The depressing effect of empty piers and wet beach huts, torn awnings blowing in a biting east wind and dreary digs with actors from other touring companies removed some of the excitement and most of the romance. Acting was hard work and there was a great deal to learn. By opening night, Leslie had still not encountered grease paint. He required a lesson at the last moment and appeared, vastly over made up, more pink and white and gold than ever.

Touring companies in 1917 had to be incredibly bad to fail; people longed for an hour or two of peace and laughter—of forgetfulness. The army camps needed entertainment, and they were springing up everywhere, covering the landscape. Leslie was pleased to be playing in these camps, even though he knew it was a small contribution and even though he was made to feel quite uncomfortable time after time when he was pointedly asked for his discharge papers. Despite everything, Ruth and Leslie had fun. It was their first time alone together since Colchester, and they loved it.

After the tour ended and the Howards (the Stainer name had been dropped) had returned to the family fold, visits to theatrical agents started again. Finally, a part in another touring company was produced. More out-of-season towns in the rain, more depressing boardinghouses with indigestible food. Then a sharp, horrid glimpse of a world almost as dull and dreadful as the bank. Leslie wrote: "My second engagement on the stage was in an ancient farce, 'Charley's Aunt' which had been touring the provinces regularly for over twenty years. One member of this company had played the same part for nine years. Another for fourteen years! They were horrors, poor fellows, they were terrifying. They seemed to be not quite human any more. They existed in dismal rooms, from one dismal town to the next, and lived only for beer, roast beef, and that ghastly rigmarole they went through at every performance." Though the posters for *Charley's Aunt* bore a grinning cat and proudly announced, "Enough to make a cat laugh," it left Leslie deeply depressed.

It was clearly of first importance, if one wanted to be an actor and enjoy it, to ignore touring companies and tilt only at London windmills—an easy and sophisticated thing to say but unbelievably hard to achieve.

After *Charley's Aunt* closed, Leslie's father took up book-keeping again. When a tour in a frightful farce called *The Glad Eye* presented itself, the debit balance made it impossible even to consider holding out for a West End play. Ruth wangled a job in this stellar production, and for the first time had a "speaking" part as the French maid; the fact that Fifi had only one line, "Good evening, Monsieur," did not prevent Ruth from giving it her all. After a few weeks, *The Glad Eye* closed and was forgotten.

Though Leslie was now determined to succeed in a London production, it was, ironically, his stage-struck wife who got there first. H. B. Irving, the well-known son of the brilliant and famous Henry Irving, was reviving, at the Savoy, his father's first great success, *The Bells,* with *Hamlet* as its running mate. Ruth, unaided by her husband, came home with a walk-on job in both productions for £1.1.0 a week.

Leslie went back to the round of agents. There seemed to be nothing available, not even a tour of *Charley's Aunt*. He tried writing, but no one wanted this either. Every day he carefully studied the advertisements in the *Times,* and one morning he read, "Mr. Matheson Lang requires a young gentleman as secretary who must also be able to understudy a role in his present production. Applicants apply to the Strand Theatre."

He rushed to apply, and was interviewed by the magnificent Mr. Lang himself.

Leslie had few qualifications as a secretary, but his acting apparently suited the great man. This was a strange thing, for no two people could have been more different. Matheson Lang was a tall, exceedingly handsome man with a strong, resonant voice; his style of acting was physical and emotional; he was an awe-inspiring figure at the very top of the theatrical profession. He had played with Lily Langtry and Ellen Terry; he had traveled all over the world. Leslie, by contrast, looked thin and unprepossessing and was beginning to develop the restrained, highly technical acting on which his career was to be based. Still, Lang saw something in him and he got the job. He understudied the juvenile lead in Lang's production *Under Cover*. The actor he was understudying had, apparently, remarkable health, and London did not see Leslie this time either. Then, by good fortune, Lang took the company on the road and Leslie was given the juvenile lead—not London, but a first-run company, and things began to look better.

It was at this point that Ruth, who had unselfishly given up her important work in *Hamlet* and *The Bells* to accompany Leslie's tour, found she was displaying certain rather trying symptoms. Leslie was not exactly practical, but even he felt that a touring company was no place for Ruth and her symptoms. He immediately wrote to his grandmother, the redoubtable Granny Mary, asking her if she would take charge of his pregnant wife while he was away.

If Ruth did not always live in harmony with her mother-in-law, both being far too interested in one man, she found Granny Mary remarkably easy once she overcame the somewhat imperious exterior. Moving into her house, still a part of an age that had gone away forever outside its windows, Ruth learned to live with an old woman and to love the sort of life that she preserved. Circumstances might make it necessary to have an occasional paying guest, but Granny Mary insisted on her standards being maintained. Brothwell, the maid who had been with her for half a century, managed to behave as though the paying guests had simply been invited for the weekend, and everyone else adjusted themselves to this pattern. Even trips to the cellar during air raids had a certain decorum, and protocol was observed.

The year 1918 came in without celebration. The news from France was threatening. The German army, freed in the east after the Bolshevists grabbed power in Russia, began pouring onto the Western front. The British and French armies were below strength and tired from constant and abortive offensive action. By the end of January, Germany outnumbered the Allies in France, and the scene was set for tragedy. On March 20, through a swirling gray mist, preceded by a gigantic barrage and accompanied by the stealthy patter of gas shells, the German attack was launched on the British positions. Wraithlike figures emerged from the mist, overran the forward positions, and moved on. Within two days the British troops were ordered to retire to a prepared line, but communications were poor, control had lapsed, and 80,000 British soldiers were prisoners in German hands.

Into a world that looked perilously close to ruin, into a land facing a grim defeat, Ruth's and Leslie's son was born on April 7, 1918, in the front bedroom of their first house, rented a month before. The total cost to his parents for this remarkable bundle was four guineas. It was difficult for Ruth to believe that the future could be all misery and ruin when her first-born snuffled and wriggled in his brand-new cot by her side. When this miracle happens, for a few hours everything else seems remarkably unimportant; it is a joy unexplainable, short-lived, but never forgotten, fair recompense for any suffering before or after.

These were grim days for everyone, days that seemed full of retreat and withdrawal, of heartbreaking casualty lists again. Those at home, feeling useless, never forgetting the agony of the troops in the trenches. And yet in France, out of the holocaust, slowly and painfully, the impossible was happening.

The Allied line dug in and miraculously held. Thus checked, the German attack lost momentum, and the Allied positions were able to be reinforced and strengthened during the next weeks. By midsummer, twenty-seven American divisions had arrived, and the Allies began the historic attacks that were to culminate on a marvelous November morning.

That summer, work for Leslie was scarce and money somewhat scarcer. He had finally opened in London, in February 1918, in *The Freaks* by Arthur Pinero, but it was a short-lived triumph. It seemed at any moment that he and Ruth might have to forgo the delight of a house of their own and return to the family. Leslie spent his unwarranted, unwanted leisure writing in the thin ribbon of a garden, while his son shook his pram and waved his legs nearby. Ruth, watching them, knew her good fortune. There might be little money, but few women in England in 1918 could see from the window both husband and son together in the bright summer day. She was lucky and grateful.

The war, which on a June afternoon could seem an impossible midnight fear, came to London in the haphazard air raids of a dispirited, vicious enemy. This enraged Leslie more than it frightened him and he wrote:

"When the bombardment started, my wife shoved my very new son and heir, cradle and all under the dining room table upon which she piled a number of mattresses. I remember gazing with fury upon this spectacle. It seemed to me so undignified and so utterly ridiculous. This was no way for the offspring of a great and powerful people to be ushered into the world."

Late in the summer, Leslie's impotent, unemployed anger was assuaged by a part in his second London play, *The Title* by Arnold Bennett. It starred Aubrey Smith, Eva Moore, and Nigel Playfair, and was an immediate success. Leslie and Joyce Carey were said to "represent youth of to-day with convincing naturalness." His convincing vagueness was apparent during the run of the play, too, there being one of those lines that inevitably prove fatal even to attentive actors. At one moment in the second act Aubrey Smith had to go to the window and say, "I see him coming now," meaning Leslie, who at that moment was reclining in his dressing room. Smith began to ad-lib valiantly: "At least I think I see him . . . yes, there he comes . . . through the trees and . . . across . . . the . . . garden." Then the sound of feet running up a metal staircase could be heard all over the theater, and as Aubrey Smith repeated hopefully, *"Here* he comes now," Leslie darted onto the other side of the stage looking very hot and disheveled. This was the first of a number of close calls.

September, with its gentle rain and yellow leaves sifting into the garden, also brought victorious news. As the month opened, the Allied commander in chief sent this message to all his senior officers:

"Everyone is to attack as soon as they can, as strong as they can for as long as they can."

By the end of September the much-vaunted Hindenburg Line had been breached, the Allies were moving forward everywhere, and the German alliance had started to crumble.

The slow, grinding agony of the past four years left people somehow unprepared for the final speed of the breakup of German resistance in October. On November 8, Marshal Foch received a delegation from the enemy and accepted the surrender of the German forces. The ordeal was over. Leslie wrote, many years later: "At eleven o'clock of the eleventh day of the eleventh month we all went mad with joy—the bells of victory were rung in London and New York and Montreal and Paris and in every other home of freedom—and the world was saved for democracy.

"Our generation will never forget that day, will it? For we were the youngsters of that time—it was we who fought through those four grim years—it was our generation which was decimated in its prime—which lost many of its choicest spirits—its Wilfred Owens and Rupert Brookes and emerged from the conflict a skeleton of a generation, haunted by the ghosts of its brothers.

"So those of us who were amongst that remnant will not easily forget the day of victory. We were young and the bitterness was soon drowned in the triumph. We had a righteous cause and believed in it. We were determined to build a better world—a world which should be the inheritance of the weak and the meek as well as the strong and the ruthless. The American President himself had propounded the noblest structure of international security to which the political mind of man had ever dared to aspire. We, who were on the threshold of life when the mess was over commenced our civil careers with a feeling of wonderful security; we were sure at least that never again in our times would our peace be shattered. After we had nursed our wounds all we wanted to do was to live and work and create."

The sudden release from the misery of years of bloody conflict was overwhelming and wonderful. Christmas was to be a time of true celebration and thanksgiving. People believed that the babies held up to see their first Christmas tree with its candles burning would never have to know what their fathers had known. The shops, released from a long bondage, advertised "wide selections" for "your first Christmas at home."

Leslie and Ruth and their new son, christened Ronald, for Leslie's part in *The Freaks*, but for no particular reason called Winkie, celebrated in their small unfashionable house with a happiness that would never be quite the same again. Peace and even prosperity quite unimagined before were theirs.

The Stainers had moved closer to the center of London. The family house in West Kensington was large, and when once again, soon after Christmas, Leslie was looking for a part, it seemed prudent to move Ruth and Winkie to the top floor and give up their own small house. This meant buying furniture, and it was soon obvious that their taste and their finances were not mutually agreeable. They were not unduly disturbed by this, for they discovered the glories of a wonderful system called "hire purchase." Neither Ruth nor Leslie had much idea about money, and the never-never plan appealed to them enormously. You had what you wanted today and worried tomorrow. With this first small purchase they set a pattern that became hard to change—a pattern that through good and bad times, they followed somewhat helplessly and, to their own sorrow, transmitted to their offspring. There was a hard lesson to be learned, but no Howard has ever really learned it—that a pound note or a dollar bill can only be spent once. So it was that Leslie, having convinced himself how much he was saving by moving into his parents' house, then gaily spent the savings on furniture, quite oblivious of the fact that the money was in his mind and not in his pocket.

It was necessary to spend something each week going to the theater if he was to know what was happening and to learn more about his profession. This, Leslie thought, was a justifiable business expense, never mind about next month's hire-purchase payments. Ruth and Leslie sampled all there was on the London stage, though the pickings were a little lean.

The postwar theater in London had to find a new level and a new importance after four years in which it had been required to produce only fun and forgetfulness. In 1918 Sir George Alexander died, and a vital era in theatrical life closed. George Alexander had been the last of the great actor-managers; the last of a tradition which Irving and Tree, Forbes-Robertson, Charles Wyndham, and John Hare had established, and through which they had molded and controlled public taste for half a century.

In 1919 management by large variety chains had taken over, and these commercial managers were being vilified for lowering standards. A special meeting was called in Hamp-

stead at which Bernard Shaw spoke eloquently on "the predicament of the theatre." There were those who disagreed,
and James Agate, the acerbic drama critic, wrote, "Go to
Hampstead and you will find a lot of moping owls complaining in whispers and horn-rimmed spectacles of the Decay of
the Drama."

The commercial managers, criticized though they were,
brought many remarkable productions to the London stage
in the early years after the war. The great Eleanora Duse
came; there was a Sacha Guitry season; *Hassan,* by the poet
Elroy Flecker, was staged; and Gay's *The Beggar's Opera*
was revived. If simpering, slightly nauseating comedies produced an imbalance on the West End stage, it was the public's
fault.

In one of these contrived plays Leslie got his next part, as
the somewhat unlikely Lord Bagley in *Our Mr. Hepplewhite,*
by Gladys Unger, which was produced by Wyndham's widow,
the beautiful and clever actress Mary Moore. The play opened
in April 1919 at the Criterion, and Leslie's entire family turned
out to see it, even Arthur, in his best gray flannel suit. All were
agreed that Leslie was simply marvelous. The critics, less
partisan, called it "a pleasant little artificial comedy," and
committed themselves on Leslie to the extent of again saying
he was "very natural."

It was certainly not a play that would satisfy the earnest,
bespectacled Hampstead coterie, who were far too avant-garde
to be caught doing anything as outmoded as laughing. Still,
the public enjoyed it, and to the critics it was a blessed relief
from the improving plays which the Revivers of British Drama
forced on them at endless Sunday matinees. The number of
new theater groups, all working fervently to nourish the English drama, was astonishing, and though they reviled the commercial manager for "comfortably squatting with all his
weight of hoggish greed on our nearly lifeless English drama,"
they came perilously close themselves to killing the patient

with their stark, depressing, antiseptic sickroom, their diet of parboiled gloom and grit. The paradoxical state of the theater in 1919 was only a reflection of the state of the nation and was a natural outgrowth in a time when a way of life had died and a new pattern was fighting to take its place.

There was unrest throughout the world and the beginning of disillusionment at home as two millon servicemen started streaming back into the industries, trades, and professions. Unemployment became a bogy, terrifying every young man. Leslie's play was still running, but the theater suffered generally from the unsettled situation, and at the end of the year one drama critic commented: "The season 1919 to 1920 will live in the history of the finance of the drama as a time of terrible portent—a time in which the hideous murk of misunderstanding was rent only by the dying shrieks of expiring musical comedies and revues, in which straight comedies, strong dramas and sword and cloak productions were alike flung indiscriminately one after the other into Limbo. Almost more terribly inexplicable than the failures of that dreadful time will seem its successes. For, unscorched by the lightning, unshaken by the earthquakes, 'Chu Chin Chow' and the 'Maid of the Mountains' each ran for a fourth year."

Fortunately, Leslie had established himself with one or two of the remaining actor-managers, and, in the autumn, when his play closed, Dion Boucicault offered him a part in A. A. Milne's *Mr. Pim Passes By,* which Boucicault and his wife, Irene Vanbrugh, were to present at the New Theatre in January 1920. When it opened, *Mr. Pim* was called a "tissue paper comedy," but it was said, ". . . its faults are easily pardoned, especially as there is a refreshing boy impersonated by Mr. Leslie Howard and an exquisite picture of fumbling senility provided by Mr. Dion Boucicault." It was clearly set for a long run, and in February moved from the New Theatre to the Garrick.

Nineteen twenty was a great year for revivals: Sir John Martin-Harvey was again portraying Sidney Carton at Covent Garden in *The Only Way,* a dramatization of Dickens' *A Tale of Two Cities.* He had played this part on and off since 1899 and was to do so on tour until the end of the 1920's. Martin-Harvey believed that the purpose of the drama was to teach moral lessons, and this was a last attempt to counter the modern trend to naturalism and sharp wit with the historic art of elocution and bravura.

If *Mr. Pim* provided Leslie with a growing reputation in the theater, it also provided £12.12 a week, a fortune before unknown. The wealth and comfort, which showed every sign of continuing, produced a leisured and relaxed atmosphere in his life for almost the first time since he had taken up the precarious career of an actor. For the moment, the problem of feeding his wife and child was resolved and he could turn his attention to something else. The first thing he wanted to investigate was the new "talking" pictures, which were being experimented with earlier in England than in the United States, and which he still rather pedantically called the "kinema."

London heard its first real "talkie" in 1920, and some senior members of the stage fraternity began to see a possible future of importance for this admittedly rather peculiar form of artistic expression. Leslie's uncle Wilfred Noy was directing films at a small studio at Bushey, very near where Ruth and Leslie had lived. Leslie went there often to watch and learn and to talk to, and get to know, the people concerned. There he met Adrian Brunel. This remarkable young man, after war service in the Ministry of Information (first under John Buchan and later with Lord Beaverbrook) as liaison officer for the film department, was now scenario editor for the company operating at Bushey. Leslie was immediately attracted by this sensitive and thoughtful man and would drop in to see him quite casually at odd moments. Adrian would go on working and Leslie would talk or, as Adrian has described it, would go "roaming around sucking his pipe and fidgeting with books and papers and, whenever he caught my eye, smiling and giving a characteristic little laugh." Finally, in the course of his wanderings one day, he stopped in front of Adrian and announced that they must form a film company—Leslie would be the managing director and Adrian the producer. It would seem today a monumental undertaking for a young man of twenty-six, and though in 1920 films were much simpler, it was still a sizable plan for someone earning twelve guineas a week.

Leslie was able to persuade Adrian Brunel to join him and then to excite Aubrey Smith and A. A. Milne. The well-known actor and the well-known author were both greatly interested in films. Leslie and Adrian discussed it with them during many Sundays spent at Aubrey Smith's country house, and it was decided to waste no more time. Britain's answer to the American industry was born in Minerva Films Ltd. A. A. Milne immediately set to work to write suitable stories for Aubrey Smith and Leslie to perform. Another director of the company was Nigel Playfair, and Leslie could feel satisfied that he had gathered a distinguished group together.

The directors immediately invested in a rather splendid sepia pamphlet setting forth their plans, which they said were "offered as a first attempt to get away from the comic picture-postcard type of film which at present appropriates the trade name, comedy." They required a little capital, and set their objective at £10,000. When half had been subscribed, they went ahead, for their expenses would not be heavy— one simply needed a camera, which was quite small and stood on a rather wiggly tripod, and one or two lights; the actual shooting could take place anywhere and could be fitted in whenever some of the directors were not engaged in earning their living. The company, which was held together entirely by Adrian Brunel, took space at Bushey Studios for two weeks, and there Brunel directed the scripts that he had prepared, cast, dressed, and set-designed. He rushed from tiny set to tiny set, and in this way three one-act extravaganzas were produced; they were called *Bookworms, Five Pounds Reward,* and *The Bump.* As the finances were rather slight, the two actors in the company had to be fairly versatile, but with the assistance of crepe hair and inches of grease paint, they bravely tackled every characterization. In addition, Leslie took up his pen to urge the public to "cultivate the Kinema Mind." He warned them that they had better "be on the side of the big guns," and assured them "the kinema is here to stay." He lamented that more than one "intelligent" man of his acquaintance had characterized the films as "an incoherent jumble," and blamed this on lack of experience in the viewer and also the "unnecessarily intense darkness maintained in many picture theatres . . . and the continued breaking up of the story by the insertion of sub-titles." Brushing aside these minor imperfections, he called on his "high-brow friends" to persevere, and encouraged them by saying that one out of every four films was worth seeing and they must learn to take the chaff with the oats. He also reminded them, rather mysteriously, that they would find "a complete disregard of the Unities," but they must not be disconcerted because, whether they believed it or not, this was "actually the greatest privilege possessed by the screen"!

In the spring Leslie took part, for the first time, in one of the Sunday matinee performances of a theater group. This was not, fortunately, one of profound and depressing validity—simply a gay gambol called *The Young Person in Pink,* by G. E. Jennings. This was a success, and shortly afterward opened in the West End. Leslie was unable to be in it because *Mr. Pim* was still drawing full houses, but to be sought after was a new and beautiful experience.

Suddenly, Ruth and Leslie found themselves invited to rather exciting fashionable parties. It was at these parties that Ruth first encountered the loneliness of being "the wife of that charming young actor." She watched with mounting fury her shy husband being flattered and flapped at by a host of women. Ruth knew, somehow, that she was far shyer than Leslie, but it would have been a waste of time to say so, for with her quick humor and rather quicker temper she always seemed highly self-confident. An outsider would not have guessed that this self-confidence was an act to hide her painful nervousness and to cover up the inferiority she felt when faced by a roomful of expensively dressed women who all seemed, to her not-very-experienced eye, to be frantically sophisticated. Frantic they certainly were, and Ruth must be forgiven for thinking them sophisticated—they were under the same misapprehension themselves. They were emancipated womanhood anxiously trying to prove their equality with men—equally hard-boiled and unshockable, able to drink an equal amount of whisky and conduct their amorous pursuits with an equal disregard for propriety. They were busy proclaiming their disgust with everything their mothers had held to be important. Family life was to be ridiculed, a baby was a "mistake," and a husband was rather like a stamp collection, to be traded with your friends. There was a wild irresponsibility in the search for pleasure that found outlet equally in cocaine, the Schneider Cup races, Suzanne Lenglen's triumphs at Wimbledon, short skirts, and midnight bathing parties in Trafalgar Square.

The serious-minded young woman who had gloried in the discussion play at the turn of the century was to be succeeded by the addlepated flapper who gloried in nothing more highbrow than Tallulah Bankhead in her underwear. Although this was a delightful sight, there were those who considered it a curious result of the emancipation of womanhood. It was scarcely for this that the militant suffragettes had chained themselves to railings. But the freedom for which they had fought went to the heads of their younger sisters along with the new cocktail. They cared only to pursue amusement, sweeping their disillusioned men behind them.

With the arrival of summer, Ruth was able to escape from London and take her son to the seaside to stay with his grandparents. Leslie stayed behind because he was rehearsing for a new play in which he had his most important part so far. It was a strange drama by Samuel Shipman and John B. Hymer about the Chinese community in San Francisco, called with slim originality, *East Is West*. Leslie was to play a fine upstanding young man who rescued an innocent Chinese girl from the fate that invariably awaits innocence, and the Chinese girl turned out to be a kidnaped American, and they lived happily ever after. There was nothing particularly remarkable about this Oriental thriller, but it was to have a profound effect upon Leslie's life and his future as an actor, for in it he came to the attention of an American theatrical producer, Gilbert Miller.

The son of the famous actor-manager Henry Miller, Gilbert was anxious to bring English actors and plays to America. His father had opened his own theater in New York four years before, and in the autumn of 1920 was to present *Just Suppose,* by A. E. Thomas, the story of a prince who falls in love with an American girl. There was little doubt which prince this was intended to represent. In that year there was only one in everybody's mind, the darling of the English-speaking world, Edward Albert Christian George Andrew Patrick David, eldest son of King George V of England. The whole world thought of him as a magical sort of Prince Charming, and the American people could be counted on to love the idea of a local girl becoming his bride.

Leslie had a letter from Gilbert Miller asking him to consider a part in *Just Suppose,* and he rushed down to Rottingdean, where Ruth sat on the sand with Winkie, to tell her the good news. It was a tremendous thrill for Leslie to be offered a part, and a good one, on Broadway. It could mean he would have an international reputation, that he might become really well known. Ruth was excited, but with typically feminine lack of logic she was also a little sad because he must go without her, there not being enough money for her passage. Leslie spent several hours explaining to Ruth why he would be foolish to miss this wonderful opportunity, and by the time he had finished he had convinced himself that he should not go. Then there was hardly time to catch the train back to London for the evening performance, and they had to hire a taxi, a great expense. After a most terrifying ride to the station, both clutching the sides of the heaving and smoking motorcar, Leslie just caught the train, and neither he nor Ruth had a chance to find out from the other what decision should be made. The next morning Leslie was faced with the appalling problem of making up his mind all alone. For him it was rather like being asked to take out his own appendix—it almost could not be done. Ruth was not near a telephone but, the British telephone system being what it was in 1920, it was probably just as well. He was cut off, isolated in the agony of indecision. He walked around London trying to think. Up St. James's Street, with a long pause on the corner of Piccadilly, down St. James's Street, gazing vaguely around him as though he had never seen the place before. Then he marched into his manager's office and announced rather dramatically that he would go. His manager replied equally dramatically that he would cable New York immediately and informed Leslie that he should sail on Wednesday on the *Majestic*. Once the irrevocable step had been taken, Leslie became a jellyfish of misery and regret.

Ruth came up to London to pack his clothes and see him off looking like a sad, homesick child going back to school after the holidays. As each piece of clothing went into the suitcases, he would reiterate that "after all it won't be for long," and he kept promising that he would send Ruth the money for her passage immediately. He was still repeating this as they embraced on the station platform.

Leslie found his first ocean voyage most confusing and

tiring. He discovered that he was sharing a cabin, and thus frightened out of his only sanctuary, he hid in the writing room, pouring out his feelings to Ruth.

"I am undergoing my Transatlantic Graduation which, I gather, everyone must go through on their first trip. This consists of wonderful instruction in ocean travel by every other soul on the ship. I appear to be the only passenger making a first crossing. I gather that nobody ever makes a second. At least not openly. They make their first and then are never heard of again until they are suddenly seen on their twenty-third voyage!"

Leslie had his initial glimpse of Americans en masse on this crossing. Since 1920 was the first real opportunity in seven years for a European holiday, the ship was full of tourists returning home after the summer.

When the ship arrived off Sandy Hook, the bar was closed "in obedience to the principles of democratic liberty," for the United States had, the previous year, adopted Prohibition, and the habitués strolled up on deck to instruct the newcomer and point out the landmarks. As they entered New York Harbor, Leslie prepared himself for the moment he had been told about all the way over, his first sight of the Statue of Liberty and the New York sky line, but at that moment all first-class passengers were hustled below for immigration check. Other than a frustrated glimpse of the Lackawanna Ferry, which amazed him, Leslie saw nothing more until, wrapped in his heavy winter overcoat and carrying two others, he walked down the gangway. New York was enjoying an Indian summer, and he was immediately overcome by the heat. His new American friends assured him it was a lovely cool day, but he could remember no English July as hot, and this was October. He had a sharp tussle with the customs inspectors, during which, in order to get their attention, he loudly insisted that he favored freedom for Ireland, and found that this worked like magic. The officials immediately cleared his suitcases and even told him the story about what Mayor John F. Hylan said to the Queen of the Belgians. Then he was standing outside the dock, surrounded by baggage, waiting for a taxi.

He suddenly found himself face to face with New York and the American Continent. He thought of St. James's Street, his family, Waterloo Station, the telegraph boy at Southampton . . . he felt distinctly lonely.

4 / New York and the Intrepid Twenties

The first taxicab Leslie took in America broke down. As he sat immobilized on Twenty-third Street, he wondered if it was an omen. New York City in 1920 was not, perhaps, the friendliest place for an Englishman. Americans, always ready to champion anything that looked like an underdog, were vociferous in their support of Irish home rule, and New York had a large Irish population, well represented where they were readily heard—in the police force and the taxi companies. Eamon de Valera, the Irish leader, had spent a considerable amount of time in America the previous year, raising money to help the fight for an Irish republic.

Coupled with this was the chronic mistrust of the British, who were considered artists at the understatement and the underhand. American troops had just returned from France, and the U.S. government, conscious of their contribution to the victory, smarted under European jibes of "too little and too late." If that was the gratitude of their late allies, then American boys would never again be sent to die in foreign lands. Though the League of Nations had been envisaged and brought forth by an American president, his country could not be persuaded to nourish and support it. Fearful of becoming involved in the machinations and evil pursuits of

European diplomats, the United States withdrew from the League and, pulling the Monroe Doctrine over its head, concentrated on its own personal indigestion.

The nation was at that moment suffering from a severe attack of hiccoughs induced by a diet of water and bathtub gin. The year-old Prohibition was scarcely having the effect anticipated by its supporters. Instead of deterring the drunkard, it appeared to bring on, in even the mildest of sherry tipplers, a passionate desire for alcohol, and a great many people wasted a great many hours tracking it down.

Leslie, whose interest in drinking was negligible, had the names and telephone numbers of four bootleggers thrust into his hand in his first four hours in New York. Within eight hours he found himself, in company with Geoffrey Kerr, who was playing the lead in *Just Suppose,* sampling the hospitality of a hip-pocket club. There, to their amazement, they discovered "gentlemen busily engaged in violating the Constitution of the United States" by transporting flasks of liquor to the club in their hip pockets, as far as could be ascertained, "simply for the satisfaction of having committed High Treason." It seemed that drinking safely at home would have been too law-abiding and boring for words. Since English suits were constructed without hip pockets and since neither Leslie nor his companion had a flask, they could only watch the proceedings with interest until a member took pity on them and insisted that they should consider themselves at home in his hip pocket. They gratefully availed themselves of this kindness.

Leslie found his first rehearsal at an American theater surprising. He was introduced by the stage doorman, who rushed onto the stage announcing loudly, "Mr. Howard of England is here." Feeling heavy with imperial responsibility, he walked on stage only to discover that several other gentlemen of England were there also. Five, out of a cast of eight, were from England, and one other was an Irishman. The two lonely Americans who were present hardly spoke to anyone else, being constantly engaged in battle: one was a violent anti-prohibitionist and the other a Quaker from Philadelphia. Realizing that little could be learned about New York from this pair, Leslie investigated the mysteries of the city for himself. He had already tasted the joys of a bathroom all his own, and he jubilantly wrote to Ruth:

"My hotel contains two thousand rooms and two thousand baths—my first experience of the Great American Bath System and I must say I find it very delightful. It is great to think that while one wallows in one's bath, 1,999 other people are, have been or will be wallowing in 1,999 other baths in the same building. It gives a wonderful atmosphere of cleanliness easily attained. In England there would be one bath for twenty people and this delightful modern habit would not be encouraged by the fact that nineteen people were fiercely waiting to attack the bathroom in which the twentieth was temporarily enjoying himself."

Baths he approved, but his first American salad terrified him.

"Having conjured up visions of a little simple lettuce, I observed strange pieces of fruit surmounted by a large canned pear, the whole being covered with a mixture of mayonnaise, sauce, nuts, vinegar and olive oil."

From one salad, he immediately and clairvoyantly deduced that Americans as a nation did not like things too simple, "whether they be people, food or any of the commodities necessary to civilization."

One thing about New York that seemed distressingly similar to London was the low standard of theatrical production. As one wit put it: "Broadway is awash with bilge from the sinking ship Thespis." But, whereas London suffered more from a plethora of small theatrical groups, New York's problem was the opposite—the war had killed most of them. Such bright lights as the Neighborhood Playhouse and the Washington Square Players had been extinguished. This meant, in the main, that there was nowhere for an untried playwright to get his work performed. The commercial managers were not prepared to risk their money on anything but a known success.

Yet this time of dramatic famine was an age of giants in dramatic criticism. In the daily field there were, among others, Heywood Broun of the *Tribune,* Alexander Woollcott of the *Times,* and Percy Hammond, also of the *Tribune,* known, from the size of their waistlines, as "the Three Fat Fates of Broadway"; and writing for the magazines were such people as Dorothy Parker, Robert Benchley, and George Jean Nathan.

Leslie found the atmosphere stimulating, and he throughly enjoyed the company of *Just Suppose.* He had feared that the much-advertised American efficiency would make rehearsals streamlined and grim, in violent contrast to the pleasant, easygoing ways of London. He was relieved to find that the stage and the acting profession were much the same the world over.

"I need not have worried. American efficiency may control the Box-Office (fortunately) but, thank Heavens, it has generally speaking gained no admittance at the Stage Door." This he wrote in an unpublished essay called "The Experiences of an English Actor in America."

His first rehearsal seemed so like any other he had ever attended that he felt at home right away.

"Nobody quite knew where our rehearsal was to take place, who was to direct it when it did take place or who was to play an important part as yet unfilled. In addition, though the play was to be presented to the public a fortnight hence, another important character had only just sailed from England and could not be with us for a week or so. Just like old times.

"After some delay it was announced that the rehearsal would take place in the smoking room, the stage being occupied. (In London in similar circumstances one always repairs to the Stalls Bar.) There we commenced work under the auspices of the Stage Manager. But as no self-respecting actors or actresses would permit themselves to be directed by a common or garden stage-manager nothing very exciting happened, barring the mumbling-through of our respective parts until the arrival of the actor-manager just about lunch time. And as the poor man was himself acting nightly in Philadelphia and had to catch the three o'clock train to that city, only a very short rehearsal was possible under his guidance and that at the heroic sacrifice of lunch on the part of the company. The actor-manager was undoubtedly an inspired director whose presence would have been invaluable under normal conditions but his time was so short that this rehearsal did not effect any very lasting results. We flitted violently from scene to scene in a most hectic and feverish manner, the actor-manager with one eye on his watch dashing forward now and then to enact personally a passage which seemed beyond the power of one or another of the players. I had only received my part that morning and at this stage I wasn't at all sure whether it was supposed to be a funny one (reading it gave me no clue either way) so I tried being comic and tragic by turns, the latter producing quite a lot of mirth from the company and a sad smile from the actor-manager. Suddenly, however, the latter shot through the door and the rehearsal was over. That was all we had to do for that day."

The next two weeks were full of rehearsal, and Leslie was not able to continue his exploration of the fascinating and frightening city. He did find in Geoffrey Kerr a fellow horseman, and they managed to sneak an odd hour now and then to ride in Central Park. Geoffrey Kerr was great fun, and Leslie thoroughly enjoyed his first weeks in America. New York was most receptive to two young Englishmen without any apparent female connections and, though Leslie's letters to Ruth were dutifully lonely, he found it undeniably amusing to sample life as a carefree bachelor.

He also found time to write to Adrian Brunel about Minerva. The three films had been shown in London and received excellent notices. Leslie was working hard at selling them in America, and he told Adrian: "I have seen Lesley Mason who takes a keen personal interest in the films and is convinced they would appeal to American buyers. . . . I must, of course, have copies before anything can be done—then Mason will himself take one round to likely people . . . it means a small outlay but I think it worth taking the risk."

After this big-business discussion, Leslie thanked Adrian for being "a brick" about letting him have his typewriter and assured him that he would forward "some dollars at the earliest possible moment." Rather a comedown for the film mogul!

His only worry was with his part, which, from the first, he had found difficult to understand. The director wanted it "played for the laughs," and Leslie did his very best. But three years' experience had not prepared him for the sophisticated extreme of light comedy; he wrestled violently and manfully with the part, and was unfortunately still doing so on opening night.

"Leslie Howard as the Prince's chum was a trifle too exuberant in his comic anxieties," wrote one of the *Tribune's* critics. "But he too was applauded." It was fortunate that the audience still had simple comedy tastes and could applaud his frantic romp, but one critic, the *enfant terrible* of Broadway, who, not for nothing, had earned his soubriquet "The First Grave Digger," wrote with relish:

"There should be a word too for the amusing and engaging Leslie Howard as the Prince's pal who, however, indulges in the most extraordinary clowning, expressing mild surprise by almost falling down and the slightest embarrassment by something strongly resembling convulsions."

This was Leslie's first experience with the sharp pen of Mr. Alexander Woollcott. No one ever wrote like this in London; if an actor was bad he was ignored, not exposed to the contempt of the world. Poor Leslie, even the kinder critics called him "obstreperously comic," and he was very downhearted. Americans were surely hard to understand, for were they not the inventors of slapstick humor? And did not the custard pie in the patron's eye still set them rolling in their seats?

The play was a great success; the public enjoyed every moment—laughed with the Prince's boisterous equerry and sniffled sadly when His Royal Highness put duty to his country before love and left his American sweetheart. A prophetic piece, though no one in 1920 could foresee how the Prince would rewrite the script.

Now there was time for Leslie to taste the pleasures and amusements that surrounded him. He was admitted, through kind friends, to various clubs. He went to a number of rather stylish parties, one at Henry Miller's and others at Condé Nast's and Laurette Taylor's, where he met and began to know members of his own profession in the United States. The women were outstanding, and with their long limbs and flat figures seemed far better suited to the strange clothes that women had then adopted than their rather plumper English sisters. The fashion in interior decoration had changed too, among the more advanced thinkers, from the comfortable frills of 1910 to the starkly modern, or what people hopefully called the Russian school. Borzoi dogs were much in favor, and women affected rather odd-looking trousers. Leslie found himself quite often in one of these modern apartments, frequently sitting on a black velvet cushion breathing warm bathtub gin over an exotic young woman so loaded with beads and bracelets that she seemed hardly able to move off the skin of whatever animal she happened to be lying upon. It all seemed very daring, and Leslie could not help wondering a little nervously what Ruth would think when she arrived. He wrote encouragingly about America but kept remarks about Borzois and beads to himself. Ruth's imagination was vivid enough, heaven only knew, without his help.

Ruth was, in fact, indulging her imagination as she sat in the family house in London. What was Leslie doing? When would she be able to join him? Every letter she wrote asked this question. When could she escape from his family to him? Not that she mentioned her difficulties—well, not more than a hint here and there. She was a young woman who for many years had ruled her father's house, and organizing was both her strength and her weakness. Lilian, her mother-in-law, was gentle and rare and charming but used, in her own quiet manner, to having her own way too. Their ways were often divergent. Both loving their sons, the older woman accustomed to receiving the devotion of her family, the younger still sampling this new experience, it was natural that jealousy should rise up and make Ruth feel she was competing for affection. Her memories of her own mother were few, and she had not had time to learn from her the boundless infinity of love before she had had to take her place. When in the course of time Ruth's father married again, the young girl had felt put aside, and she seemed to become afraid that love and dependence might always be taken away from her. She was an outgoing, generous person, but this chimera of her girlhood made her often inclined to pull her loved ones too close, as though there was not room for others. Thus, the decision to leave her son with his grandmother was a hard one. But she made it because nothing meant what being with Leslie meant, and certainly Winkie would have a wonderful time.

In December, Leslie scraped together some money, and Ruth bought her ticket to America, first class on the *Olympic*. Such extravagance shocked Leslie's family. Ruth, nevertheless, decided to start as she expected to continue, and bidding a tearful farewell to Winkie, so small and beautiful with his blond curls and blue eyes, she set out resolutely to see what her other boy was up to.

As the boat nosed into the pier in New York, Ruth hung over the rail, searching the crowd for the familiar figure. New York looked awfully big and forbidding. The person next to her on the rail sighted her family and began shouting loudly. Ruth felt more panicky by the minute. Where was Leslie? It was difficult to pick anyone out from the hundreds of upturned faces. And then she glanced up at the roof of the building on the pier, where a few less exuberant people were standing, and right at the end, comfortably removed from the fuss and bustle, she saw what she was looking for—a figure not unlike the one she had left behind, fair head uncovered, a scarf wrapped around his neck, waving politely.

"Leslie!" she shrieked.

"Hello, darling, hello. I'm up here—hello—here dear, up here." He waved again. "Hello, Ruth darling. Yes, yes, I can see you." With this, he turned around and disappeared.

The gangways went down, Ruth went down, but there was no sign of Leslie. She was waiting, huddled miserably on her pile of luggage under the letter H, when she saw him again, walking toward her with a customs official with whom he seemed to be on the friendliest terms.

"Leslie darling!" She flung her arms around him and was rewarded with a self-conscious peck on the cheek, as though it were parents' day at school.

"Hello, dear. This is Mr. Murphy, Ruth, who will look at your luggage." He added, "Mr. Murphy's grandmother is a respected member of the Sinn Fein."

Mr. Murphy beamed at this sally and made a few chalk marks on the suitcases, and, after a further jocular exchange, bowing and smiling, the Howards were swept off the pier and into a taxi run by a Mr. O'Toole. Leslie seemed very friendly with all these expatriate Irishmen, and Ruth listened in amazement to the virtues of Mr. de Valera, the glories of the Irish Republic, and the perfidy of all Englishmen. "No offense meant, you know."

Leslie appeared somehow much more at home in New York than she remembered him to be in London. The taxi pulled up in front of a large and imposing-looking hotel, the Woodstock, and Ruth imagined it must be the biggest in New York. Leslie pointed out the theater right opposite, and she felt it was an amazing coincidence that the best hotel should be across the road. (Leslie did not attempt to disabuse her about the hotel; he was afraid she would find out soon enough.) New York was more splendid than anything she could have imagined. Decked out as it was for Christmas, glowing and sparkling with colored lights and tinsel, the whole place looked like a gigantic Christmas tree. The shop windows full of dresses and furs made her almost ill with suppressed desire.

Just Suppose, playing to a packed house of festive people, was another thrill for her. Needless to say, she did not agree with Mr. Woollcott and wrote immediately to her mother-in-law: "The play is very funny and Leslie is frightfully good. He has made a great personal success."

After the performance Ruth met Geoffrey Kerr, who most solemnly assured her that Leslie had been pining away from loneliness, and then proceeded to charm her by initiating her into the cult of the Great American Ice-Cream Sundae. If Leslie had been worrying about Ruth's first reaction to New York, this stroke of genius by his friend removed his worries. No hip-pocket clubs for Ruth—nothing more heady than a banana split. When her eye would be caught by a shapely, silk-clad leg and a whisk of fox fur, the two young men would insist that American women were too thin, too hard, no charm whatsoever—that is, the ones they saw in the street, they really had not met any others! How much Ruth believed of this was never recorded, nor was it a subject about which she would write to her mother-in-law. It was, at any rate, not yet more than the faintest shadow of worry and, though there were to be times when the agony of jealousy over beautiful women, real and imagined, would fill her days, Christmas in New York in 1920 was without care.

Ruth took to New York immediately and began to enjoy the parties and the speakeasies far more than her husband had expected, and rather more than he did. Leslie had made a number of friends, and Ruth felt at home with most of them. The more glamorous women still alarmed her, and there was a perfect galaxy in New York that winter. Leslie reported in another letter to Adrian Brunel that he had had "the signal honour of dancing with H.M. Dorothy Gish last Sunday and also at various times with Norma Talmadge, Alice Joyce, Mae Murray and Mabel Normand, the latter insisting in loud voice that I should at once go with her to California to play in Goldwyn films. I explained this was quite impossible at the moment but that as soon as I were a free man I should at once turn my steps towards the City of the Angels." At the same party, Leslie and Ruth met Charlie Chaplin and found, in common with all film fans, that it was really rather amusing meeting these people: "one feels one knows them beforehand."

There were several interesting productions in New York that winter which they saw together. John Barrymore was playing in *Richard III,* and they were much excited by his performance, Leslie noting it so carefully that he was able to reproduce it exactly a year or two later when he was asked to do an excerpt from *Richard* at a charity performance. From the sublime to *The Blue Flame,* with Miss Theda Bara, there was quite a lot to see, but Leslie privately commented that *Just Suppose* was "almost the best acted piece on Broadway, (tho' it's me that says it)."

The Howards pursued their gay life, rising late and going to bed even later. "I should be ashamed to admit to you my average hour of retirement," Leslie wrote to England.

He was interested in doing some film work, and he had many discussions with Mrs. Sydney Drew, whose earlier films, with her husband, had inspired Leslie in Minerva. She wanted to produce some five-reel comedies early in 1921 and sought Leslie for some of them. It was strange that, with his enthusiasm for moving pictures, circumstances should contrive to keep him away from them for another nine years. But in February, when Mrs. Drew needed him, his play was on tour. He also had to turn down his old part in *Mr. Pim* because of the tour, but his salary, which was small for America, still seemed incredible to him and made up in a way for the disappointment. He was making $250 a week, in those days about £62, and intended to ask $400 for future engagements. With profits like this, he felt he could not afford to return to London, though he was already suffering those pangs of homesickness which were to send him scuttling back and forth across the Atlantic for twenty years, finally not able to be sure where he wanted to live. In 1921 he was still very much the young Englishman abroad, and his letters were peppered with Anglicisms like "brick" and "jolly," "rotten" and "cheerio." An amusing beginning for a man who, before many years, was to be known in London as "that American actor."

Geoffrey Kerr and Leslie seemed the prototypes of Englishmen to the American public in 1921, and they created great amusement at a party at Laurette Taylor's when, with their recently acquired ukuleles, they sang a parody on Gallagher and Shean:

> Oh, Mr. Howard; oh, Mr. Howard
> By a fear I have been lately much oppressed.
> That we've been here now so long

And our accents are so strong
That they'll think we're a couple of rubes
from the Middle West.

On tour, Geoffrey and the Howards were inseparable. Ruth
often calmed irate hotel managers after complaints about their
ukulele practice. The two young men generally managed to
find a horse to ride, even in Atlantic City, where Geoffrey
Kerr took a photograph of Leslie riding on the sand, with
the boardwalk and a number of large hotels in the background. Underneath it he wrote, somewhat prophetically, "Les.
Howard the well-known cinema star and polo player. In the
background may be seen 'Les Cottage,' the new Howard
home."

The tour took them to Toronto in Canada, where Ruth sat
freezing in an unlined winter coat and a large white woolly
hat pulled down to her eyebrows while the boys skated elegantly in their immaculate plus fours. Toronto filled the English company with patriotic fervor because of its British background. When the strains of "God Save the King" could be
heard floating through from the front of the theater, Kerr and
Howard would be seen in their underpants, half made up,
standing rigidly at attention in the passage outside their dressing room.

Finally, in March, *Just Suppose* arrived in Chicago and
settled down for a six-week stay. Ruth and Leslie lived in the
Parkway Hotel on the lake, and there Leslie started to write
again. He ambitiously began a play and had "another in mind,
for myself, of course," he told Adrian Brunel when he wrote to
ask about Minerva. The news about the film company was
sad. Minerva had died of starvation, although Adrian had
worked hard himself to raise the needed capital to keep her
active, and for a moment he came close to success. He later
wrote about the company: "Minerva was never saved. H. G.

Wells was one of our biggest shareholders and he lost £250 but I don't suppose he noticed it. A few people lost small sums that they couldn't afford but nobody was ruined. It was not a spectacular crash but it might easily have been a spectacular success. Minerva was a great loss."

Leslie had not heard any of this, and he wrote just before the end of the *Just Suppose* tour to Adrian Brunel in a cheerful frame of mind: "Just a line to let you know that we are sailing for England on the 7th of May by the 'Lapland' so I hope to see you about the 16th. I am quite out of touch with Minerva's plans but hope you and I will be able to do a film together again when I get back. I don't know quite what I am going to do or even whether I am going to stay in England for the Autumn. Lynn Fontanne wants me to return to New York and play with her. But I don't know yet. It depends on what sort of offers I get in London. I plan to take Winkie for a holiday when I get back but I should not mind doing a film first."

Lynn Fontanne was playing in Chicago in *Dulcy,* by George S. Kaufman and Marc Connelly, while Leslie and Ruth were there, and they had seen quite a lot of one another. Leslie was utterly charmed by her and very tempted to join her in a play. About this time he also heard of a part in a play called *The Wren* by Booth Tarkington. It was to star Helen Hayes, who was a young, new, and very clever actress. It was to be produced by George Tyler in New York. Leslie made no decision before he left, because he hoped a play would turn up in London, and it was there that he saw himself acting permanently. The most important and only definite plan was his holiday with his son, Winkie.

Ruth and Leslie sailed in May and experienced, for the first time, the excitement of all seafaring Britons when the long, rough coast of Cornwall first slips into view on the port bow. Then, home on the train through the green loveliness of England in the spring, to Winkie at the station in London, rather like a little crocus himself, much taller and more golden than they had remembered.

The summer passed happily and uneventfully. Minerva was moribund, so there was no film work for Leslie. The family went back to Rottingdean and spent the months happily splashing in the sea and running on the beach.

It was a disappointment for Leslie to discover that his American success had gone entirely unrecorded in London; in fact, his seven months' absence had created an unfortunate effect: the producers had forgotten about him, and no work was forthcoming. London was full of good young actors, in direct contrast with New York, and competition was very brisk. Leslie, reluctantly and a little sadly, made up his mind that a reasonable living for his family must be provided in America. It was not that he disliked it there, but once he went again he knew that his hopes of returning to work in his own country for some years were slight. It was thus a solemn little trio who leaned over the rail of the *Adriatic* as the tugs nosed her away from the familiar English dock and pushed her downstream to turn her bow toward the Atlantic.

Leslie had agreed to do *The Wren* with Helen Hayes, and she was on board with them. She was a pretty, round-faced little slip of a thing, looking more like a schoolgirl, in her sailor hat and long brightly striped scarf, than New York's most talented young actress. Her charm and intelligence delighted both Leslie and Ruth. This, coupled with small Winkie's excitement over the big boat, helped them to overcome their initial loneliness. By the time they landed in New York their spirits had risen. Leslie took photographs of the famous skyline and marveled at how knowledgeable he had become, being able to point out the various buildings to other English visitors with the air of a resident.

Back they went to the dear, familiar old Woodstock Hotel, with the friendly elevated rattling along outside, back again to their friends and to rehearsals, with a modest little bit of publicity for Leslie.

The Wren tried out in Boston and received only fair notices. It was with small hope that the company opened in New York at the Gaiety Theater. It certainly did not overwhelm the critics: "Such a diminutive comedy, it might better be called 'The Hummingbird,'" and, of Booth Tarkington: "A good writer into a bad playwright." But Helen Hayes had superlative personal notices, and Alexander Woollcott unbent on Leslie to say: "Whatever there is, is charming and charmingly played . . . by Leslie Howard, a singularly engaging English actor who will be remembered by playgoers who went to 'Just Suppose.'"

A great friend of Woollcott, Marc Connelly, the playwright, first saw Leslie in *The Wren* and disagreed sharply with Woollcott's review. Connelly was later to become a close friend of Leslie and godfather for one of his children, but his first exposure to the Howard charm left him unexcited—"one of the worst young actors I have ever seen." He felt no urge to write a play for him.

It was a blessing for the Howard family that his view was not universal, though it was probably accurate, for when *The Wren* closed after a month, Christmas would have been lean indeed if another play had not come to take its place. Leslie went into *Danger,* by Cosmo Hamilton, starring H. B. Warner. Rehearsals began at the 39th Street Theatre, where the play was to open on December 22. Undoubtedly Leslie was in New York at exactly the right moment, a moment in the history of the American stage that was to be remarkable and golden. The 1920's may have produced a plethora of second-rate plays, but they also produced a few playwrights of a high standard not seen before in New York. If the actors came up to this standard, they never tried to tower over their plays with performances of dramatic virtuosity and bravura. Second-rate plays were no longer made famous by a single glittering and incredible tour de force. Nothing was overstated any more, nothing larger than life.

The most widely acclaimed of the new writers was Eugene O'Neill, whose plays *Beyond the Horizon* and *Emperor Jones* had startled New York in 1920. With O'Neill arrived other names soon to shine out over Broadway for fifteen years: Sidney Howard, Elmer Rice, Maxwell Anderson, and Robert Emmet Sherwood, who one day wrote a play that fitted Leslie almost as well as Leslie fitted the play. Into this bright dawn of the playwright's era, Leslie seemed somehow to have been led by more than the tireless search for a dollar. His personality suited the plays that were being written, and these plays provided the training ground from which his style was to develop.

Ruth was dispatched at this time to look for a suitable inexpensive apartment where Winkie could have more freedom and Leslie could find space to write. Ruth was born under whatever star it is that grants the ability to turn up needles in haystacks, catch trains that have pulled out, find lost passports, and provide comfort for her family almost anywhere. So it was not surprising that within a few days, though hampered by a three-year-old, she had installed her boys in a tiny furnished apartment on Claremont Avenue, just off Riverside Drive. It was not exactly a place of great charm and had only four rooms (three if you did not count the curtain that could be pulled across the sitting room), but it was their own, and blessed privacy after a hotel.

Leslie set himself to writing, and Ruth, with equal zeal, to finding someone to help her with Winkie, for she was completely tied to him and weary of bus rides and trips to the zoo. She put an advertisement in the paper and awaited results. Her lucky star never helped her more than at that moment. On Long Island one morning, a fellow countrywoman picked up the paper and read: "English family want mother's help. Small apartment, one child." Florence Gospel read it again and thought about it. She liked it in America, but if she was to stay she must find a job. Her family lived in Newcastle-on-Tyne, in the north of England, and they wanted her to come home. She called a friend and discussed the advertisement. To work for an English family would be rather nice, less lonely. And so, still undecided, she wrote to the box number given in the paper. Ruth answered at once. They met for an interview. Did they sense, when they sat opposite each other on Claremont Avenue, that theirs was to be a lifetime association? Probably not, but Ruth immediately liked the slim, dark woman with glasses and an easy, gentle manner. She knew she would be just right with Winkie. But afraid of what might turn up in a strange city, she asked her to come back and see Leslie.

"My husband is rather hard to please," she temporized.

The next evening, Florence Gospel and her friend, Mrs. Tennant, were sitting waiting in the lobby of the apartment building to see this difficult person, when the door opened and a thin, fair young man came hurrying past. As he walked away from them, he suddenly gave a little skip and, using his walking stick for support, leaped neatly into the elevator and shut the door.

Mrs. Tennant turned to Miss Gospel and whispered: "That was Mr. Howard."

"How do you know?" asked Florence Gospel.

"I feel it—that's the sort of person you ought to work for—come along, we can go up now."

When they rang the apartment bell, the door was opened by the same young man. He and Florence Gospel only spoke half a dozen words to each other before he said: "Will you come to us?"

And she answered without thought: "Yes, I would like to."

That way the Howards acquired "Miss Goss," for so she was to be called, and, though Ruth invented Gargy as easier for Winkie, he never used the diminutive. Miss Goss became the confidante, the helper, the companion, and at many lean times the general factotum for the Howards. She also became their closest friend and their dearest. Her quiet, gentle good sense and loyalty were to be a great stay in their lives, and she was the perfect foil for Ruth's more volatile nature. Miss Goss gave them the feeling of such immediate confidence that Ruth decided to go to Buffalo with Leslie for the opening of *Danger,* and the new arrival found herself almost at once alone with Winkie. She scarcely returned their confidence, and spent the next few days wondering what sort of people would go and leave their baby with a totally strange woman. In this she underrated both her own worth and her employers' perception. For though you may know someone a lifetime and never feel able to trust him, you will meet another person and know at once that you can trust him with your life. Miss Goss was one of these.

It was a little crowded in the apartment at 195 Claremont Avenue. Winkie had to be settled for the night on a sofa bed, and the kitchen would not allow two people to operate at one time. Leslie managed, somehow, to find a small space and a little privacy in which to work on his plays. By this time he had two or three under way. His favorite, and the one for which he had rather high hopes, was a comedy in three acts called "Willie" (or "The Black Knight"). The title was the name of the principal character, The Hon. William Marquand, who was described in the play as "the silly ass Englishman par excellence." Of course—but this was a jealously guarded secret—he was also the Black Knight, a glamorous highwayman of the twentieth century, who held up rich Americans on Long Island.

The other play was called "Diana's Second Marriage" (or "The Impossible Marriage" or "The Impossible Age" or "The Gulf"), and it took place in London. Nevertheless, the same butler was found gliding through its scenes, speaking, as only a good stage butler should, in an obsequious whisper. The male lead was described as "outwardly a rather serious and quiet young man of twenty-eight with a reserved and slightly embarrassed manner. He possesses, however, a good sense of humour which accounts for his success as an author."

It was a very bad play, but Leslie undoubtedly read it with avidity to any of his friends who would sit still, and a few years later was proposing it to Ethel Barrymore as a possibility. He was a prolific writer, and dialogue flowed from him in ceaseless torrent. His plays were not serious social documents. Every one was "a comedy in three acts." His characters were all immensely rich and worldly-wise. Whether this was because he was rather poor and shy or because he felt it was the right background for comedies in three acts is not known. He had support for his views in no less a person than John Mason Brown, the critic on the *Evening Post,* who wrote later that a play of this sort must contain "well dressed people who belong to that world of comfortable means which has always been—and must ever be—the background of high comedy." At any rate the drawing-room comedy flourished in the 1920's, and without money it was difficult to have much of a drawing room.

Danger closed early in the new year, and Leslie immediately went into rehearsal for *The Truth about Blayds,* with O. P. Heggie and Frieda Inescort. It was another play by his old friend and co-director A. A. Milne. In it Leslie played, as usual, the young lead in his easy, good-natured style, and no one objected or raved.

"Leslie Howard is particularly good as the grandson" was his longest notice.

The play opened on March 14, 1922, and ran happily along into the hot weather. Leslie suddenly wanted to see the countryside in the spring, as the old urge for England that had quietly slept through the winter began to move restlessly in his subconscious. Since every American they knew had a motorcar, why not the Howards? They invested a substantial

sum in the smallest car they could find, a 1922 Dart. It was
an excellent object, a two-seater with room for four in front!
Every Sunday they bowled along the roads of Long Island,
Leslie and Ruth and Miss Goss with Winkie on her knee,
gazing enviously at the impressive gates of the rich country
dwellers. The sight of green fields precipitated a family decision; they must leave New York City and find a suitable
small house where Leslie could write and Winkie could have
more room to maneuver. This desire for more space for the
same activities was to pursue them relentlessly for twenty
years.

June was a boiling month in New York, and Ruth was
absolutely unprepared for the stifling wet blanket of heat that
wrapped itself around the apartment on Claremont Avenue.
It had not seemed too small or airless when there was a bright
crisp layer of snow on the roof and when Leslie and Winkie
had dashed out, muffled to the ears, to toboggan on Riverside
Drive. Then it had been warm and cozy, a snug little nest.
Now it was a snug little boiler room in which tempers and
temperatures were steadily going up. Everyone fretted, no
one could sleep, and Winkie began to look pale and dark-
shadowed. Ruth reached such a pitch of despair that she had
her waist-length hair cut into the new shingle, and then was
afraid to face her husband. The big city was a nightmare to
the surprised English family, and Leslie helplessly turned to
his American friends for advice. By luck he was told of a
small cottage on Deer Isle in Maine. It sounded highly primitive, but it was surrounded by miles of cold water, the very
thought of which would have been enough.

Leslie could not take them up there because his play was,
fortunately, showing no signs of closing. Ruth and Miss Goss
made the long journey with Winkie on the train and then by
boat from Boston, for Deer Isle is well off the coast. They
were immediately delighted with what they found—a green

and pretty island set on the edge of the Atlantic, with only a few farms settled by quiet, friendly people.

Winkie had a wonderful time when his father arrived, for out they would go in a little rowboat on the bright blue water and fish for dabs. Ruth had no passionate interest in such pursuits, but she was never allowed to stay at home, a fact that might have flattered her very much had she not been fully aware of her importance to the fishermen. Neither Leslie nor his son would take a fish off a hook, and as they were hauled in, the dabs would be thrown in Ruth's lap to be taken off and more bait put on. Muttering furiously about the inadequacy of lily-livered men, she nonetheless sat out in the boiling sun, which she always hated, and patiently unhooked fish.

Leslie had no work lined up for the autumn, but he was feeling carefree and fairly optimistic. So long as the shortage of young actors continued, something would appear. In fact, while he lazily sunned himself on the sand or rowed Winkie around the bay, plans were forming in New York that were to involve and employ him for several months. John Golden, one of the most astute and amusing New York producers, had been offered a play by Arthur Richman called *A Serpent's Tooth*. It was a play about English people, and Golden thought it a good play, but it had a very difficult, exacting part for a leading lady. He had agreed to produce it if a great actress could be found to do the part, had suggested Marie Tempest to the author, and forgotten about it. Marie Tempest was in South Africa, but when Robert Milton and Arthur Richman got in touch with her she agreed, amazingly enough, to play the part of Alice Middleton. It was thus that John Golden found himself casting the play in the summer of 1922. Quite how and why he chose Leslie for Jerry Middleton, the spoiled wastrel son who, for sheer nastiness, is finally rejected, even by his devoted mother, is not easy to understand. Leslie had never played anything except polite comedy juveniles. But it is the ability to see the scope of an actor that makes a great producer.

Leslie was, as usual, out on the water with Winkie when the telegram came from Golden. Ruth screamed and waved, and the two blobs in the boat waved back. "Come in," she yelled. "Can't—we're busy," the reply floated back to her. "It's a play," she shrieked. "Later" came the voice from the boat. Ruth nearly expired from frustration for the next two hours while she watched the blond heads just out of earshot happily engaged in some important work that could not be left. Ruth was a direct, impulsive, and well-organized person. When something happened, she wanted to hear about it, decide about it, argue about it, but not ignore it. To Leslie, nothing was so vital that it must crowd out what he was doing. Anything could be left for a few hours or even days. Haste was ridiculous.

He should have been delighted with the offer, but he had just begun to enjoy his holiday—and New York in August was going to be unspeakable. If it had not been for Ruth's prodding, he probably never would have made the journey to the city to start rehearsals, but she packed his clothes, sent his answering telegram, and pushed him onto the boat. He was also instructed to find a house for the family when they came back to New York: on Long Island, somewhere with "room"!

Leslie trundled back to stay at the Lotos Club, where he was now a member, and began to earn his living once more. It was a slightly awsome experience working with an actress of the caliber of Marie Tempest, but her technique and the warmth and gaiety she brought to a part improved his own performance and he found it really quite exciting. The play was not so good as it had seemed, but Miss Tempest added a wonderful vivacity and sardonic humor, a beautiful timing and ease that created an effect of brilliance in rehearsal, and the company went forward to the opening night with great hopes.

Leslie missed Ruth's comments on his performance, caustic or otherwise, and he felt rather dejected that she would not be there for the first night.

On August 24 the play opened, and both the excitement and the heat were overwhelming. The theater was packed, for it was a great occasion to see Marie Tempest on the American stage again, and the audience was as notable as the cast. Nothing, however, could be done to match the quality of the play with the cast, and Alexander Woollcott quipped, "A Tempest in a tea-pot." The Tempest naturally got the notices that her fellow actors had known she would: "as adroit, as gleaming, as delightful as ever." But there was a personal triumph for another member of the cast, too. Leslie had at last found a part in which he could be more than himself, more than "convincingly natural." Woollcott wrote: "There is, by the way, a young upstart on the same stage with her [Miss Tempest] in this present enterprise who is not to be sneezed at as an actor. That is the engaging Leslie Howard, who plays the son admirably, quite sharing the honors with her. . . ."

This was praise indeed from one who had not been a great supporter in the past. Another notice, in *Theatre Magazine,* was to come a few days later: "A notable performance and quite the best thus far this season is given by Leslie Howard as Jerry. This young actor steps into a position of enormous importance with his work in the Richman play. O'Neill or perhaps Richman himself will before long provide this youngster with a part in which he will stand the town on its ears. There is truth in his playing, sincerity, intelligence, no exhibitionism, no trick technique. His performance is the most significant thing about 'A Serpent's Tooth.' "

What more could he ask than that? Anyway, he had more important things to think about: he was house-hunting. He started his search around Great Neck, Long Island, for this small town had become a center for country-dwelling actors and writers and theatrical people generally. There he found on Maple Drive (they were nearly all Drives in Great Neck; it was the air of respectability one paid for), a three-story red brick house with an elegant glassed-in veranda and, joy of all joys, a garden. The home seemed huge and so did the rent, but the leaves were falling fast and Ruth and Winkie and Goss would soon be freezing on their island in Maine. He took it.

Ruth and the family arrived at once and were suitably overwhelmed with the magnificence. Here the Howards began a life that was not to change (except in houses) for over four years. It was the first settled life they had ever known. They made friends in Great Neck, many friends. Leslie commuted to New York by train, and often Ruth went in to collect him after the theater. He also spent a lot of time with Winkie. A stage actor has the opportunity to be a better father than a man in almost any other profession. He can be at home with his children for all the hours of the day (matinees excepted) that they are awake. And if he is a good father he can leave a memory with his children that is far clearer and closer and more fun than the average parent can who comes home from the office at dusk with the evening paper.

Leslie, in Great Neck, tried to establish a routine: breakfast in bed (a boiled egg, toast, and tea), late because of his nocturnal occupation, followed by a walk with Winkie before lunch. Then he settled down, in a small study, to write his plays or short stories or to follow whatever literary pursuit he had in mind. At such pleasant work he could remain relatively undisturbed until teatime. Of course, there were days when a recalcitrant Winkie would be brought before him for punishment. Leslie, in his heart, invariably agreed with his son, but, prodded on by Ruth, he would weakly try to be severe. The two men would look at each other, and in order to preserve the conventions, they would play the parts as written by their wife and mother until she left the room. Then frightful subterranean whispers and wicked giggles would be heard. Ruth despaired. How could one bring up a small boy with another small boy for a father? The two miscreants found time on Leslie's rare evenings at home to sneak off together for a bedtime story. Winkie often wondered whose bedtime it was, for Leslie was usually put to sleep by the figments of his own imagination. During these sessions a couple of lads were invented—a couple of lads, indeed, who, but for Ruth's vigilant eye, could have been Leslie and Winkie. They were called Pim and Peter. The adventures of these intrepid fellows were always "continued in our next," as Leslie dozed off at a critical moment and then was forced to confess that Pim and Peter were in such awful circumstances that he was licked for the time being.

As a result of this, Hairpin was born. Hairpin was a "situation saver," a miracle worker, who by his remarkable thinness and elasticity could worm his way under doors and through keyholes. The whole adventure series, which was to last for years, was liberally sprinkled with private and rather grubby schoolboy jokes over which the fair heads bent together in paroxysms of mirth. No one else was ever invited to share these glories, and although later a new tale was developed for the next Howard, "Pim and Peter" was their personal story and no mere girl was ever admitted to it.

A Serpent's Tooth was not doing much business, and John Golden reluctantly put up the closing notice. The play had done Leslie a great deal of good, given him a chance to prove he had become an actor of some ability, and released him from the slavery of type casting. He searched around for something else. *The Romantic Age* by A. A. Milne was light and frivolous, but Leslie enjoyed any Milne. When he was offered a part in it opposite Margalo Gilmore, he sighed with relief. He seemed constantly drawn to plays by Milne; in fact, Alexander Woollcott had commented after *The Truth about Blayds:* "Leslie Howard should be immediately placed under contract to play nothing but Milne plays as long as they both shall live."

After the fiasco of Minerva, Leslie was unable to face the

reproach he felt in Milne's eyes and had been rather glad to
escape to America. But he was greatly entertained by their continued association. "Poor Milne undoubtedly thought he was
rid of me. Nothing of the kind. I am three thousand miles
from Mr. Milne. But fate knows no boundaries. Distance means
nothing to Destiny."

The Romantic Age opened in November 1922 and closed in
November, but it added a new friend to Leslie's life: Margalo
Gilmore, one of the brightest and most sought-after young
actresses in New York. She knew great numbers of the more
entertaining people. She was one of the few women allowed to
join the "Algonquin Set," a group of bloodletting, word-eating
tigers who met regularly at the Algonquin Hotel to discuss,
classify, condemn, and occasionally praise the world of literature and the arts in New York. She was quick, intelligent, and
amusing. Leslie had met her before, but, with his innate terror
of smart and clever women, he had not known her well. Now
she came down to Great Neck to spend gay and foolish Sundays with the young group who often assembled at Maple
Drive. Ruth and Leslie found themselves more and more a
part of the extraordinary and fascinating life that was New
York in the 1920's. Although Leslie was never a member of
the Algonquin Set—he was still too reserved and shy for such
brilliant badinage—he often dined at the Algonquin and quite
often joined the circle at the "round table." There, on almost
any night, he would find Alexander Woollcott, Harold Ross,
soon to start the *New Yorker,* Bob Benchley, writing for *Life,*
F. P. Adams and Heywood Broun, the critics of the New York
World, Marc Connelly, Robert Sherwood, and "Les Girls,"
the brilliant, satirical Dorothy Parker, Elsie Janis, Edna Fer-
ber, and Margalo Gilmore—altogether an awe-inspiring group.
"They appraised, debated, rejected and finally placed the seal
of their august approval upon a favoured few."

The sophisticates, as they were called, were pleasantly aware
of their sophistication, and most of their more pungent re-

marks were delivered in voices loud enough to reach the outer populace. Their reputations were enormous; they were admired, loathed, or envied, but they certainly could not be ignored. Half the wisecracks of the next ten years were attributed to them. They became great drawing cards for the hotel, and Frank Case, the owner, finally gave them a special poker room, where they would often sit down on Saturday night and play until Sunday afternoon. The London salons of the Regency period produced a clique of mannered and brilliant conversationalists whose epigrams were quoted avidly in less gilded surroundings and whose every foible and fashion were lapped up by the unadmitted. The sophisticates recreated this atmosphere but in a style quite their own. Theirs was not the elegant rhetoric of the idle rich; their vocabulary was fluent, fresh, and very tough. They were the unshockable shockers. The inspiration for the round table undoubtedly came from Alexander Woollcott, the "Pepys of the Algonquin," who called himself "a great writer with nothing to say." He kept the circle together by the constant stirring he gave to the stewpot. He was rather like a bad fairy fomenting discord and then reveling in the confusion.

Leslie was never one for epigrams. His humor was much more gentle and, in a way, subtle. He was immensely entertained by the group, but they exhausted, amazed, and rather terrified him. Not for him the whip-crack wit of Dorothy Parker, called by Woollcott "a combination of Little Eva and Lady Macbeth"; not for him the all-night poker sessions, the endless dramas. He had a country retreat and he knew he was safe and protected there. Ruth would take charge of him, for, irked though he might be sometimes at her slightly dictatorial manner, he liked it; it comforted him. Perhaps his friends complained that Ruth would not let him out to do what he wanted, but he had created her, he had formed her in that way for his own purposes. When he was young and inexperienced and totally unorganized, when they had first met, she had taken the lead, but since then, intentionally and a little unfairly, he had traded upon her strong character and made her the bulwark between himself and anything unpleasant in his world. She was always left to guard the portals, to decide, What does this man or, more important, this woman want of Leslie?

Marc Connelly understood the situation well when he said that "Leslie is always afraid Ruth will go out in the morning before he's awake and forget to put the manacles on." Ruth was by no means a little country girl at heart. She dearly loved sitting up until the early light if the party was fun, and she found the sharp wit of New York very much to her taste. Her humor was exuberant and, once she had become used to the strange surroundings, she could hold her audience with the best. Her clothes, which had been tweeds and sensible shoes the year before, became much more chic, if that is what the 1920 fashions can be called. She was given her first evening dress by a famous actress, Constance Collier, and in it, covered with pink beads and trailing lengths of stuff from the shoulder to the floor, she made her first triumphant appearance at the "60" Club, a monthly dance at the Ritz-Carlton to which the theater world belonged. The dress made her feel almost as fetching as the beautiful Constance Bennett, whose entrance into the club ballroom was always awaited with delight by the men and a certain amount of envy by the women. Her graceful progress down the steps, trailing a fishtail train and wrapped casually in pale fox, was one of the events of each dance. When anything as delightful as this came in, Leslie's neck always seemed to grow a little longer, and a finger went to the edge of his eye to pull it sideways and achieve a better focus. It was an old familiar signal to Ruth, and her "Yes, dear?" was sharp and to the point.

"Oh! What, dear?" he would reply, looking a little guilty.

"I only said 'yes, dear?'" remarked Ruth.

"Oh—er—I just—thought—er—her dress was very pretty tonight."

"Yes, darling, *very* pretty."

Ruth did not really object to Leslie admiring anyone as breath-taking as Constance Bennett, but she was quite annoyed when his head would turn and stretch up as an overdressed, made-up siren went slinking past. It seemed unjust that his taste should be for the obvious vamp when he would never allow her to put on much make-up and agreed to only very simple clothes. Ruth tried eye shadow, only to have Leslie peer into her face with a look of disgust and ask what "all that blue stuff" was. When she retorted that he had admired it on a girl the night before, he looked most surprised. "Certainly dear, but not on my wife."

Men, how could you ever understand them? And there was none more complex in his quiet way than her Leslie.

There was certainly none more lucky in finding work, though perhaps unlucky in that the work was seldom long-lived. After *The Romantic Age* departed, Leslie found himself in a small part in *Lady Cristilinda* with Fay Bainter. It was a delicate, sensitive, humorous play, written with imagination and a distaste for the banal, by Monckton Hoffe, but it lasted only a short time. Monckton Hoffe was an Englishman, and perhaps his humor was too dry and too English for the American public. The stage lost him to Hollywood a few years later but Ruth and Leslie kept him always as a devoted friend.

Leslie had now appeared in six plays in a year, so many that one critic remarked, "Leslie Howard seems to be in every first night I have attended." His seventh effort, *Anything Might Happen* by Edgar Selwyn, opened on February 20, and was turned down by the critics: "There is nothing in the piece to raise it from utter mediocrity."

Fortunately, there was a bright and charming report of Leslie in *Theatre Arts*. "The more I see of Howard the more

established I am in my original view that he is one of the
very best young actors in America. There is nothing the lad
cannot do, from tragedy to farce and do superbly well."

The lad certainly had a friend in this critic. He was also
about to celebrate his thirtieth birthday, but his blond curls
and blue eyes obviously accounted for the impression of extreme youth that he gave. The curls, or "kinks," to him, were
his greatest annoyance. He hated them with a passion. He had
not yet discovered the value of the curling iron for straighten-
ing, something he came to rely upon a few years later. Every
sketch and caricature showed him with a mass of wavy lines
all over his head, which, for some extraordinary reason, seemed
to attract the women of New York very much indeed.

Second Lieutenant Leslie Howard Stainer
of the World War I British Cavalry

Ruth Martin Howard (1935) married to Leslie in 1916

Leslie and son, Ronald ("Winkie"), born April 7, 1918

Leslie and daughter, Leslie Ruth ("Doodie"), born October 18, 1924

"Winkie" looking like a pocket-sized edition of Leslie

Two family scenes at Bramley, Surrey, England. Above, Leslie, kitten, "Doodie," and doll; below, the four Howards in the walled garden

Leslie wanted the children to ride. "Doodie," once planked on a horse, stayed there, and became the rider of the family

Father and daughter reading together on the terrace of their New York apartment, 1935

Leslie, "Winkie," and "Doodie" enjoying the beach while visiti
William Beebe in Bermu

"Doodie" enjoyed playing tennis with her father

Stowe Maries, the Howards' house in Surrey, restored to its early beauty after much travail by Ruth and much expenditure of money by Leslie

Another view of Stowe Maries, with Lesl
mounted on one of his polo poni

*Spring 1938 at Stowe Maries
—father and daughter with
polo ponies*

*The swimming pool of
Lily Pons' house in Hollywood*

A garden scene at one of the Hollywood houses

The Howards with the Robert Montgomerys at a Hollywood première

Leslie and "Doodie" taking delivery of a new Bentley

Leslie and "Doodie" rehearsing James M. Barrie's "Dear Brutus," a short scene of which was produced on Rudy Vallee's radio show May 16, 1935

Leslie, Leslie's sister, Dorice, Ruth, and "Doodie" skiing
Kitzbühel, Austria, in the midst of shooting "Pygmalio

Leslie and "Winkie," the look-alikes, studying play parts

*Compton, Ruth Howard, "Winkie," and Leslie
Leslie's brother's wedding in London*

A familiar portrait of Leslie at the height of his Hollywood ca

England, 1938, and the Munich crisis. Leslie and "Doodie" standing in the air-raid shelter constructed at Stowe Maries

One of the last peacetime pictures the "inseparables" had taken

1941, Denham Studios, the last picture of the three

"Doodie's" wedding to her Canadian soldier, Robert Dale-Harris

5/ Long Island: Suburban Retreat

The snow left the ground, and the crisp clear air of Long Island was warmed by an April sun. The English family searched anxiously for signs of their first bulbs, put in with care and excitement in the autumn. They were quite alarmed at first when nothing came up, used as they were to the long, early spring in their own country. Winkie watched his little bed of crocuses, covering them every night and rushing out to lift off the leaves when the sun lay across the garden.

Leslie and Winkie celebrated their birthdays at the beginning of April—thirty years and five. A shining red wagon took the place of the toboggan and hop-scotch the place of skating. It was splendid to be a country family with a garden and a fruit tree.

Nothing much was happening to *Anything Might Happen,* and it died quietly at the end of April. Leslie had been discussing for some time a part in Frederick Lonsdale's new play, *Aren't We All?,* which had been playing in London. Charles B. Dillingham, one of New York's most versatile managers, had contracted to stage it after it closed in England. Owing to a surprisingly short run there and because Charles Dillingham had suffered a very poor season in New York, *Aren't We All?* found itself in rehearsal early in May. Cyril Maude played the

leading part of Lord Grenham, Mabel Terry Lewis, a niece of
Ellen Terry, played Lady Frinton, and Leslie played the Hon.
Willie Tatham. It was altogether an excellent cast, but no one
felt entirely happy about starting the production in May, particularly because the play had managed only 110 performances
in London. The heat of a New York summer had a deflating
effect on even the biggest hit, and, much though the company
enjoyed *Aren't We All?,* they were not expecting to see it go on
in July and August.

Aren't We All? opened on May 23, 1923, to rounds of applause. The critics, though recognizing how slight it was,
praised its charm and frivolity. New Yorkers adored Lonsdale.
He seemed better understood in New York than in London.
Leslie's notices were excellent and his part a delight. It was not
going to enhance his reputation as a serious tragic actor, but
never mind that, he had at last found a play that would run—
for eight months, through heat and cold; *"Aren't We All*
lucky," the company felt. Leslie was going to have the unbelievable experience of leaving a play before it folded around
him; for in December he was to start rehearsal in an occult
piece called *Outward Bound,* by Sutton Vane. But the spring
and summer and autumn of 1923 were settled and successful.

There was more time for writing and for Winkie. Occasionally, the small boy would be taken to the theater to see his
father deftly handling "The Hon. Willie Tatham." In the quiet
dark of a theater time stood suspended; was this 1923 or 1953?
Was this Leslie or Winkie? In 1923 it was Leslie; in 1953 the
son stood where his father had stood, deftly handling the lines
of "The Hon. Willie Tatham" when *Aren't We All?* was revived in London. In the darkness of the theater even Ruth
would be unsure who was on the stage, the two heads were so
alike.

Long Island proved to be a very attractive place in the summer. Various, and wealthier, friends, who did not live on
"drives," invited Leslie and Ruth, and often Winkie, to swim

and play tennis at their homes. Oscar Hammerstein, the young musical-comedy librettist, had a lovely spot on the edge of the Sound, and there the Howards used to swim. The Herbert Bayard Swopes also lived on Long Island, were renowned as hosts, and every weekend kept virtually open house for their friends. Sunday-night supper at their house was a standing engagement. Herbert Swope was editor of the *World,* with a long and brilliant career as a reporter and city editor (the best in New York) behind him. At his house, Leslie met Frank Crowninshield, who edited *Vanity Fair.* Quite a few humorous Howard essays found their way into that magazine because of this meeting.

The very tempo of New York at this time attracted a vast number of intriguing and unusual people, and their fusion resulted in an exciting atmosphere. Nearly every night someone appeared in Leslie's dressing room after the show, and he was persuaded to go out with him. No one had the least desire to go to bed, certainly none of the theatrical people. There were innumerable supper parties given by Laurette Taylor and her husband, Hartley Manners. At many of these Leslie would find Jack Buchanan and Gertrude Lawrence, Freddie Lonsdale, Ethel Barrymore, and A. E. Matthews. If Ruth did not come in to New York, he would sometimes end up in Hartley Manners' bed at 5 A.M.

Conversation seems to have been as varied and odd as the cocktails. Leslie remarked after one session that it had "ranged from abortions to Queen Anne chairs," and that at another Laurette Taylor had informed the gathering that "Christ was a modern, a European, had written the Bible and the Ten Commandments and other interesting and previously unknown facts!" The pace set by those who were young in the 1920's cannot fail to shock the slightly solemn generation of their children. Thus the pendulum swings, from the frivolous excesses of the late eighteenth century to the sedate conformation of the late nineteenth century; from the giddy, thoughtless

1920's, when everyone tried to be different and some degenerate, to the serious difficult years of the 1940's and 50's, where the young wanted, and still want, only to be the same as everyone else, to shun the eccentric, to bring up large families and sit at home watching television. What a pity it is that seemingly no compromise can be arranged between these points of view—these overexaggerated opposites.

The early 1920's undoubtedly produced an excess of social activity in Leslie's life, such as he had never undertaken before and most assuredly was never to repeat. He must always have seemed somewhat removed from the hilarity, and probably his friends decided he was not quite aware of what went on and not quite able to keep up. Nothing could have been farther from the truth. Private comments in his diary are sharply perceptive; after one party, he wrote: "greatly entertained by drunks, perverts and bores." He was beginning to lose the ingenuous approach and to become impatient with the slightly pretentious "naughtiness" of the age. He weathered it well but it left him with a strong distaste for large parties, night clubs, and going to bed after midnight.

By Christmas 1923, there had been two major changes in the Howard program. Leslie had left *Aren't We All?* and was rehearsing a new play, and the family had left Maple Drive in favor of a larger house on Magnolia Drive. The excuse, as ever, was "more room." Leslie's uncle Wilfred Noy was coming over from London to do a play in New York with Richard Bennett called *The Dancers,* by Gerald du Maurier. Wilfred was bringing one of his daughters with him, and Ruth and Leslie were to put them up until they found an apartment.

Christmas was hectic that year because Leslie's play was to open out of town. New Year's Day found him in Washington, D. C., still in frantic rehearsal. *Outward Bound* had been imported from England, where it was still running successfully. William Harris had collected a strong cast for its American debut. With Leslie were Margalo Gilmore, Alfred Lunt,

Charlotte Granville, and Eugene Powers. Leslie had two friends who were also in the company, Lyonel Watts and J. M. Kerrigan. Every day a tremendous rehash of the play would take place, and, finally, "various authors, wives and retinues" arrived and "great fun was had by all altering everything."

"Which version do we play tonight? Do we know we're dead or don't we?" was Leslie's comment to Ruth in Great Neck.

Outward Bound told the story of eight people who found themselves on board a small liner about to put out from land. How or why they came on board none of them is quite sure. One by one they realize that this is a ship of the dead and they must all meet the Great Examiner before they can land. Leslie and Margalo were two young lovers, victims of a suicide pact; Alfred Lunt a sodden university graduate ashamed to admit that his mother is the charwoman, played by Charlotte Granville. It was a chilling and intriguing piece of theater, lauded in the Playbill by Arthur Conan Doyle as "the most daring, original and arresting play that has been seen in my time," and by Arnold Bennett as "far more gripping and exciting than any crook play I ever saw."

The cast traveled back to New York for the opening, and Leslie was at home for the first time in five weeks. The family had left the Christmas decorations for him to see and he had brought Winkie's Christmas present with him: an electric train, which had to be tested immediately.

On January 7, 1924, *Outward Bound* opened at the Ritz Theatre. Leslie was an hour late for the rehearsal, which he considered utterly futile, and then, after trying to calm his nerves at the Lotos Club for a few hours, he had dinner with Alfred Lunt and went on with "much heart-pounding and jumping of nerves." The audience was "reduced to a jelly" and most enthusiastic. Leslie was still on his feet at the end and reported going out with Ruth and some friends after the show "to low haunts—whisky followed by gin at Great Neck."

The play caught the public fancy and every performance was packed with terrified but hypnotized individuals. The theme of *Outward Bound* was argued at dinner parties all over New York. It was an assured success. Leslie had spent weeks wondering how it would go, but when it exceeded his most optimistic hopes, he decided he should leave it. "Feeling particularly depressed. Part seems hopeless and ineffectual—does me very little good—another packed house." To understand the contradiction of this, one has first to understand the young man. He was capable of great industry, and while he was working hard he could not think too seriously about himself. Then—and Ruth learned to expect this every time—the play would settle into a routine; Leslie would relax and begin to ponder why he was doing it, how bad his health was, and how ghastly it was anyway to work in the theater at all. Ruth had a difficult job keeping him on the path between joy and despair, the common road of the majority of the world's population.

The most significant change that took place in Leslie's personality as he grew older was the gentle submission to this comfortable grayness, the careful avoidance of the too-strong black, the too-glaring white. Whether from laziness, exhaustion, or plain common sense, he became a strong advocate of compromise and the middle-road policy. It may have seemed to his associates that this was always his maxim. Only his wife knew better, for only with her could he afford to be temperamental. He would never make a public exhibition of his feelings.

On his thirty-first birthday he wrote: "It seems a long, long time to have been in the world and not so very much to show for it. A little knowledge, a little happiness and a good deal of waste."

He must have been at a very low ebb when he produced that pathetic little comment. One is tempted to wonder if he wrote it because he liked the idea, it sounded rather splendid and worldly. He could not honestly believe that at thirty-one he had had such a sad and fruitless life. Nevertheless, the next five years were going to see an incredible rise in the family fortunes and, incidentally, an increase in the family numbers.

Leslie had recorded in his diary on February 1, 1924: "Ruth full of apprehension for twelfth time this last twelve months."

Well may she have been apprehensive, for shortly she learned that another Howard production would take place in the autumn. A costly production it was going to be, with expensive upkeep. Fortunately, this was still hidden from the parents, and after the initial distress they looked forward to the new baby with a form of pleasure.

The impending birth engendered in Ruth an immediate desire for nesting, and they were off to find a house where they could have their own furniture (they had none, but that did not matter). Sundays were now spent driving around Long Island with real-estate agents. Driving had become very much more comfortable, in fact, sublime, for Leslie suddenly bought a Cadillac. Elegant automobiles had a great attraction for him. The car looked a little incongruous in the garage of the house they finally found, for it was an old shack converted to modern use. The house, however, was charming, with fields on three sides, a picket fence around it, and a garden full of flowering bushes and large trees. There was an uninterrupted view of the landscape, with small copses, rolling grassland, and soft green valleys full of wild violets; at last it seemed like living in the country. The house, though not beautiful, made of roughcast and brick, was happy and friendly and, for them, quite large— drawing room, dining room, sun room, all decked in gay colored curtains run up by Miss Goss on the sewing machine.

Leslie took a deep interest in furnishing this, his first unfurnished house. He bought a bargain line of furniture in a wholesale shop, and Ruth took one look and sent it all back. After that, Leslie confined himself to buying books and occasionally a carpet or two.

The extra expense must have been bothersome at this time, for Leslie had taken a salary cut of fifty dollars a week because *Outward Bound* was doing less business. For all his gloom at being in the play, it had done him quite a lot of good, and the company was enormous fun. On one occasion, they had put on a performance at Sing Sing state prison, "to the dear convicts, for the good of their souls," Leslie wrote. "We were met by an Ambassadorial gent looking like Sherlock Holmes or Lord Grey who turns out to be a forger doing second term. Performance rather agonizing in brown paper scenery. Dinner was pork, potatoes and salt-petre."

In April it was obvious that *Outward Bound* could not last much longer, and Leslie looked around for something to take its place. He saw George McLellan about a part in Gladys Unger's play *Spanish Nights*. The rehearsals for this play started two weeks before the close of *Outward Bound,* and Leslie's only comment was, "very Spanish and very nocturnal." After four days of rehearsing all day and playing at night, he was tired and disgruntled.

"Rehearse. Exasperating. Leading woman being bad actress and congenital idiot combined. Horribly fatigued." During rehearsals the title was changed to *The Werewolf* in the hope of attracting some sort of audience, though what sort is hard to imagine. Then it was decided that the play should not open in New York before the summer but go first to Chicago. Leslie was most annoyed.

The play was tried out in Stamford, Connecticut, and Ruth attended. It went surprisingly well. Ruth Chatterton and Basil Sydney were, "among others," reported to be very enthusiastic first-nighters. Then the company was off to Buffalo and Chicago. Ruth stayed behind, and Leslie said "sad farewell to my Ruthie at Grand Central Station amid confusion and babel of traffic. It is always so hard to leave the ones one loves."

Ruth was much occupied for the next five weeks moving to the new house and working with her usual inexhaustible en-

ergy and strength to have it finished when Leslie came back.
Cleaning houses was really Ruth's hobby. She had the most
passionate interest in scrubbing anything, particularly dirty
things, and she was entirely contented brandishing pails and
scrub brushes. She took on the heaviest manual labor with
apparent joy and kept working until she was nearly dead on
her feet. Poor Miss Goss remonstrated with her, begging her to
remember the unborn baby, but without success. Ruth clung
to high ladders washing ceilings, lugged heavy furniture
around the house, washed windows, and scrubbed miles of
floors. She was never still from early morning until late at
night. The baby was apparently as tenacious as its mother, for
nothing hastened its birth; in fact, it remained contentedly for
an extra month at the end to prove how much it enjoyed these
capers.

Leslie, meanwhile, worked and worried in Chicago. The
play went badly—"house not so good, disappointing." Then it
picked up: "Business a bit better . . . Begin to feel confident
about play after all. . . . Business fine." Then it went down
again. Finally, after five weeks the closing notice went up and
everyone packed and went home.

Leslie had really enjoyed himself, playing tennis every day
and swimming in the arctic waters of Lake Michigan. He was
very pleased to get home, nonetheless, even though he was
lured to dinner in New York before catching the train to Great
Neck. Ruth, just a little miffed by this pause en route, took his
diary and wrote in it, rather crossly, "dinner with lady in New
York," heavily underlining the word "lady" just in case Leslie
might think she had believed his story about a business meeting. He knew he would be found out because he was incapable
of subterfuge, but instead of being contrite he invariably got
the giggles if he ever did anything he should not. It was difficult for him to refuse some rather enchanting female when she
chased him. Few men can reject a beautiful woman, and Leslie
was hardly a strong-minded man. He always imagined that

Ruth would understand his predicament—he could not be rude. If Ruth had understood, she would have been strange indeed. No wife wants her husband pursued by designing women, and Leslie was relentlessly pursued. They wanted to mother him, they longed to baby him, and quite a number were anxious to marry him. He really was not very interested most of the time, for he loved his wife and his house and his son. He was essentially a family man, and was only occasionally what he would have called a "victim of circumstance." Though he might pretend to dislike being victimized, it can not have been unpleasant.

It was Ruth who minded; she could have been far happier in some ways with a husband who came home at the same time every evening and who did not work with fascinating actresses every day. It was quite hard for her to appreciate that most actresses bored Leslie—rather like working in a candy store and being sick of the smell of chocolate. Ruth felt it was flattering, in a sense, that so many other women shared her taste in husbands; but a taste was one thing and a four-course dinner quite another. There were often times at parties when the hostess would sweep up to Leslie, fling her arms around his neck, make endearing little sounds, and bear him off to another part of the room without indicating that she had noticed Ruth at all. The better known Leslie became, the more this happened. Ruth finally had a black list of parties and people, and did everything she could to avoid going near them.

The Werewolf was to open in New York on August 25, which gave Leslie a period of idleness after Chicago. He worked at revisions on his play "Higginbottom," which he had actually finished in February. He conceived new ideas for new plays every day. His black leather loose-leaf notebook became full of lists of titles and outlines: "The Wanton" (the story of plain Jane), "The Speak-Easy" (remittance man), "Rip Van Winkle" (up to date), "Old Grey Squirrel," "The Prince and the Millionaire," "Boredom" or "They Were Just Bored,"

"Polygamous Paul," "The Iceberg" or "Possession" or "Mine" or "The Curse."

There were pages of outlines and characters—plays about parlormaids, Spanish *señoritas,* and bored debutantes, plays about old actresses, young artists, marriage, and murder.

There was one play, on which he worked from time to time, that had a number of titles: it was called "Tweedie" and "Elizabeth Sleeps Out" and, later, *Murray Hill,* when it finally reached production in New York. Leslie worked hard trying to get someone interested in this play. He sent copies all over the place. A. E. Matthews in London had a copy and so did Oscar Hammerstein in New York. Gilbert Miller had been given one, and Marc Connelly and George Tyler and George Cukor. Perhaps if enough seed was scattered, somewhere a tree would grow, as, indeed, it did.

F. Scott Fitzgerald, already a novelist of exceptional success, was Leslie's most faithful reader. He read all Leslie's plays, which in itself was an act of unselfish friendship, and, more than this, he commented and criticized and advised. When Leslie lived on Magnolia Drive in Great Neck, the Fitzgeraldses' garden backed on his, and there they had got to know each other.

Leslie's move did not disrupt this friendship. Scott Fitzgerald dropped in at odd moments, and on Sundays they always walked together over the golf links, their pace curtailed by Winkie's short legs but their conversation ranging over diversified and fascinating subjects.

The Fitzgeralds gave a lot of impromptu parties, and Ruth was not always enthusiastic about them. Leslie noted one day: "Scott Fitzgerald calls up at midnight asking me to go over to their party. Ruth threatens separation if I go so decide it isn't worth it!"

Going out at midnight was obviously too much for Ruth's English background, though she was a splendid impromptu hostess herself. Clearly, she must have felt that Leslie would come to no good in the middle of the night at the Fitzgeralds'.

July and most of August passed without work. Leslie lamented his unemployment, money being scarce. He began to work again on *The Werewolf* before its New York opening in August, but still no salary was coming in, because the hours of rehearsal time were unpaid. He could feel the expenses mounting all around him: the house, the furniture, the new baby. It was all "very worrying." There had also been some mistake in dates, and no one seemed to know whether the baby would appear in August or September. Fortunately, it held off in August, and Ruth was able to attend the first night of the play. The notices were awful, but business seemed to jog along, and by the end of the first week everyone felt it might run.

Ruth still went dashing in to New York practically every day to have dinner with Leslie and bring him home, and, owing to the problem about dates, there was "much anxiety that the latest Howard may be given birth to on Broadway or other inconvenient spot." The nervous strain of living so far from the hospital began to have its effect on everyone, and Leslie complained bitterly: "Endless discussion concerning impending confinement. It grows very wearing. I might be having the baby myself."

So it was not surprising that at the first suggestion of a pain, Ruth was rushed to New York and planted firmly in the hospital. There, poor girl, she languished from September 28 to October 18; Leslie took her to dinner and to the movies, but she was too afraid to go home, and he certainly did not encourage her.

It was a boring time for all concerned. Winkie and Miss Goss had to be ferried occasionally in to New York to see Ruth; Ruth and a nurse periodically ferried to Long Island to see Winkie.

The play was doing less and less well, everyone was taking

salary cuts, and Leslie protested feebly to Lee Shubert on the iniquity of it all. The play was under Shubert management, but Leslie's letter produced no results at all. There was a strong rumor going about that the Shuberts' conversation was confined to the celestial and no mere mortal was spoken to at all. According to current opinion, this could have been because few earthly bodies were still speaking to the Shuberts. So Leslie went on accepting his reduced weekly pay checks and grumbling bitterly to Ruth. He was so tired and depressed by dashing about being mother and father and chauffeur and general organizer that he had no strength left to write a word in his diary each night.

So it was that when at 7 A.M. on October 18, 1924, Ruth finally produced a daughter, Leslie recorded nothing. Ruth later wrote rather archly in his diary: "To-day I presented my husband with a beautiful daughter, eleven pounds and eleven ounces; maybe sometime he will write on the subject."

But he did not; rather as if the blow had been too much for him, he never wrote in that diary or any other again. Perhaps his daughter kept him too fully occupied. Certainly he was greatly excited. He had wanted a girl, and he expressed himself as absolutely delighted. Ruth was not quite so pleased with what she saw. On first being shown her child, she told the nurse firmly that a horrible mistake had been made: "That black-haired creature that looks like an all-in wrestler is not mine—I am fair, my husband is fair, my little boy is as golden as a flower—that baby looks Italian and I did not produce it." Little Winkie looked at his sister and only prayed gently for the spots on her nose to disappear.

The production of such an enormous baby left Ruth far from well, and, although her natural energy and good spirits carried her along, the next year was a difficult one for her. The baby came home with a trained nurse so that Ruth should not be overtired, but the family finances were so overtired that they could not afford to keep the nurse. Anyway, Miss Goss, professing to know nothing about small babies, was really itching to get her hands on this corpulent object, and within a few weeks the baby was moved to her room, where she was to stay for seventeen years.

Leslie proved himself once more an excellent father; unlike most men, to whom small babies are at best a slight bore and at worst a damp depressing chore, Leslie adored the baby. He spent hours carrying it around, wheeling it around, dancing with it, talking to it in a rather scholarly way. Admittedly, he never did anything practical for it, but then anything too practical made him feel a little queasy.

The appearance of a new baby was not allowed to put his son in the background, for the two boys continued their long and learned conversations. Leslie had hated the moment when Winkie had gone to school that year.

"First day at SCHOOL. What a terrible word. Instinctively he recoils from it at the last moment with a nameless dread which I can so well understand having never got over it myself. Thus must the young bird feel on the first day its parent tells it it must fly for the first time. Hated letting him go. Society has laid its first grasp upon him and *it* will never let him go."

In those few words Leslie expressed the overwhelming feeling of protection that he had toward his children. He suffered their agonies at each strange step they took. Indeed, he suffered far more than they, and shielded them sometimes far more than he should. When Winkie was bitterly teased for taking his Teddy Bear to school, it struck at Leslie's heart and he wrote: "Pathetic little incident with the Teddy Bear. The world is fastening its grip on my little Wink. He must not let the world think he is sentimental. He must be hard and manly, reserving the soft things for the privacy of home. Please little Wink, don't lose your sweetness."

On December 7, 1924, at a fairly large family gathering, the baby was christened Leslie Ruth. Because she was named for both her father and her mother, she was called by neither name. Within a year, after an attempt to say "Daddy," she was nicknamed "Doodie."

Marc Connelly and Margalo Gilmore were two godparents, and Mrs. Tennant, who had come with Miss Goss for that first interview, was the third. Leslie recorded in an elegant leather-bound book given by "Uncle Marc" every event in the first months of his daughter's life. Each waggle of her foot or turning of her head was meticulously noted. Ruth took over the job of official historian when, in the middle of December, Leslie started once more to rehearse. This time he was in two plays: *Isabel,* adapted by Arthur Richman from the German of Kurt Goetz, and a curtain raiser called *Shall We Join the Ladies?* by J. M. Barrie. It must have been one of the last times that a double bill of this kind found its way onto the professional stage. Used greatly in the nineteenth century to whet the appetite of the audience, the curtain raiser was the last relic of the days when a full evening's entertainment included several plays, and late-comers were admitted for a reduced price. With Leslie in *Shall We Join the Ladies?* was Ilka Chase, and both Ruth and Leslie found a friend in this witty and charming girl. They also became devoted admirers of her mother, who was the editor of *Vogue.*

Christmas was again disjointed for the Howards, because the plays were undergoing tryouts and opened in Buffalo two nights before the New Year. Leslie loathed this constant traveling; he never did well on hotel food, always complaining that it was too rich; he could not sleep on trains, and, if he had a nightmare, he terrorized all the other passengers by crashing around in the aisle shouting and banging. Ruth tried to laugh him out of his more dramatic complaints, but, though he was able to laugh at many things about himself, his health and welfare on tour were not funny and he thought her simply heartless. Nothing could have been less true, for Ruth concentrated on Leslie, worried about him and babied him to the exclusion of every other interest in her life. She hated his being out of reach, where she could not watch over him, but it would have been worse than useless to take him seriously.

It was a lonely New Year's Eve for both of them, although they spoke to each other on the telephone. Ruth was certainly not left alone. Her friends came to cheer her, and one or two attractive bachelors provided the "first foot" with coal and evergreen at midnight. Still, the family was small and close-knit, and separations were hard. Luckily, Leslie was back for the New York opening early in January, and, as usual, Christmas was celebrated on his return.

The plays were put on at the Empire Theatre on January 13, 1925, without any particular enthusiasm. Edna May Oliver appeared in *Isabel* and was well received, but to poor Leslie there was a faintly familiar ring to the remarks of the drama critic in the *World*.

"Leslie Howard plays well as the husband but there are scenes in which he does too much. Evidently there has been a feeling that since the play itself is so very slight a certain number of mugs and grimaces must be supplied by somebody—this duty seems to have been fastened on Mr. Howard."

One more unsuccessful play and another uninteresting part. Before long, Leslie was looking around again for something to do. Though he felt *Isabel* to have been an entirely fruitless experience, this was not quite true. It marked a return to Gilbert Miller's management, which, with a few exceptions, was to continue for some years and become a most successful partnership.

Gilbert Miller had no play for Leslie after *Isabel* though, and he endured some weeks of interviews and discussions trying to find another part. It was always the most difficult and embarrassing time for Leslie. He was by nature absolutely unable to sell himself to any producer; if they wanted him he was there, but he loathed the necessity that forced him to press his services on the rather hard-boiled impresarios. He spent a certain amount of time hopefully trying to peddle his own plays, sending them to be read by managers and by leading actors and actresses, but nothing came of this at all. Then one day Leslie recorded:

"A great American impresario sent for me and said, 'Sweetheart' (although this salutation must not be regarded literally). 'Sweetheart'—I am going to give you the greatest part you ever had in your life.'

" 'That,' I observed lugubriously, 'would not be difficult.'

" 'I am producing,' continued the impresario, ' "The Green Hat" by Michael Arlen which he has adapted from his great best-selling novel of the same name.'

" 'I don't care who wrote it,' I replied rather rudely, 'so long as it runs.'

" 'It will run,' said the producer bringing out a contract. And it did."

The Green Hat was directed by Guthrie McClintic and starred his young wife, Katharine Cornell, as Iris March. When Leslie first got the play to read, he was excited by it. Arlen had captured much of the brilliant, subtle insinuation and craft of his book, but, after a few days spent trying to learn the lines of Napier Harpenden, Leslie suddenly recognized that the whole play bordered on the burlesque. How could he possibly say the things that Napier was expected to say? The rehearsals made even the cast laugh. No one could quite get through to the end without finding some wildly dramatic moment slightly ridiculous. Nearly everyone knew the story, for there were few homes in America that year that did not have at least one copy of the book, and someone had quipped: "Probably more upstairs work was left undone when *The Green Hat* came out than at any time since the big second maids strike in 1913." Well known were the trials of Miss Iris March driving her yellow Hispano-Suiza at an extreme speed to the elegant resorts of Europe with her green hat pulled over her beautiful, wanton face. Reckless she was, and frustrated; jilted by Napier Harpenden, the one man she loved, she raced about trying to satisfy her passion for him in wild amours with innumerable other gentlemen. At last, fate gave Napier back to her but, suddenly finding a most unlikely conscience, she returned him to his wife and dashed herself and her Hispano-Suiza into an old trysting tree. It was a difficult assignment for Leslie to play the piece of flimsy romantic baggage who gets traded back and forth between these two young women, charmingly though they were played by Miss Cornell and Ann Harding. He had to keep his tongue in his cheek all the time, "fighting against the realization that never in my life could I talk the way I talk on the stage."

It had been decided to open the play in Detroit and then hope for a long run in Chicago in April. The New York date was set for September. It was the usual old merry-go-round, and Leslie once more left his family and settled down for a long stay in the Middle West. He found a small apartment in Chicago full of plush sofas and pseudo-Jacobean furniture, with a piano and a large desk and his own kitchen. It delighted him so much that he photographed all three rooms from every angle and sent the pictures to Ruth. Then she could see how he spent his spare moments. The piano was littered with music, and the tune on the music stand was "All Alone," in case she had any comments. His favorite photographs of Winkie and Doodie gazed happily from his chest of drawers. It was all very homey.

Once opening night was over, the cast spent most of their time golfing, and, though Leslie never played golf, he followed the players around taking photographs. Paul Guilfoyle and Gordon Ash, who were in the play, were, with Leslie, enthusiastic outdoor types. Ruth received roll upon roll of photographs taken on the tennis court, on the beach, and in swimming pools. She also was sent the notices from Chicago and heard the news on all sides that *The Green Hat* was a hit. It was the kind of play that people talked about even if they thought it terrible, and the very strength of their feelings sent other people to see it. So it gathered momentum and the trumpets of victory heralded its appearance in New York.

In the few weeks of July and August before the play's eastern opening, Leslie went to England to see his family. He had been away for four years and was worried about his mother's health, for she was not strong. Ruth stayed behind because they could not afford her fare, but it was one of the hardest things she ever had to endure.

"Don't cry, Ruthie darling—we'll all go next year—I promise you." Leslie said it and meant it, but next year was a long way away.

As usual, he photographed everything he saw, everywhere he went: the dock, with Ruth's sad face and helplessly waving hand almost lost in the crowd; the boat; the first sight of England and the family waiting for him; the little cottage with its thatched roof where they spent their summers. They were all thrilled to see him and terribly proud of him. Soon he was on his way back, and Ruth dressed Winkie in his best coat to meet his father. It was a splendid reunion.

The Green Hat reopened in Atlantic City. The cast was the same except that Margalo Gilmore had replaced Ann Harding. Miss Goss and Winkie went down to look after Leslie for a week, and father and son went for long walks together on the boardwalk, which Leslie knew almost as well as Piccadilly by now, and made up for the many weeks that they had been separated.

Opening nights in New York were always a strain no matter how long one had played a part. There had been so much advance publicity for *The Green Hat,* such a chorus of superlatives and cheers from out of town, that the company was necessarily a little anxious.

Leslie woke up on the morning of September 15 to the gentle music of birds and the leaves of trees. Life seemed so simple. Then someone brought him the morning paper with his breakfast. All his feelings that day are recorded in an article he wrote a month later for the *New Yorker*. He began to eat his boiled egg and glanced at the paper.

"10.00 A.M. Observe it is opening night of 'Green Hat.' 10.05 A.M. Realize I am in it. Not interested in breakfast."

Then, after trying to summon enough strength to get out of bed, he went on:

"10.45 A.M. The day commences. Immediately on appearance am informed by various members of household that 'Green Hat' opens tonight. Reply coolly that I have noted fact in morning paper. Am asked if I am nervous. Refuse to reply. Dress—sketchily."

He spent a typical vague Leslie day. He went to New York and wandered around. At 1:05 P.M. he remembered he was lunching with someone and walked about rather quickly trying to think who it could have been. By 2:00 P.M. he had recollected (quite wrongly) and decided he was too late. He dropped into the Coffee House Club for lunch, where he found Frank Crowninshield, Gilbert Miller, Roland Young, and various others. They remarked about the *Green Hat* opening, but quite impersonally. Leslie thought they probably did not know he was in it.

He was unable to account for his afternoon but found himself at the Lotos Club for dinner carrying a parcel of collars, which made him think he might have been shopping. He decided not to have his dinner there because eleven members reminded him about *The Green Hat* and nine asked if he were nervous. By some miracle, at 8:30 P.M. he was in the theater, dressed and ready. Over his mirror were various telegrams, wishing him well—the one in the place of honor being from Winkie and Doodie. There was a most tremendous din coming from the street, where motorcars piled up in a huge traffic jam as they deposited the all-important audience. It had been extraordinarily difficult to get a seat for opening night, and huge prices had been paid by many people. Leslie was made even more nervous by all this and recorded his feelings thus:

"8.45 P.M. Bell outside dressing-room rings violently indicating curtain up and slaughter on. Small dose of spirits of ammonia. 8.47 P.M. In the wings. Am so early that words from stage sound entirely unfamiliar thereby strengthening suspicion that I am in wrong theatre. 8.50 P.M. Fears allayed by inspiring spectacle of fellow players feverishly offering one another felicitations. ??? P.M. Time stands still as cue reverberates on ear drum. Wonder dimly how fast heart can beat before it collapses. Dash on stage boldly."

To Leslie, it seemed about 118 years later that the applause from the vast audience signaled the end of the first act. "Unable to ascertain name of play but there are three more acts."

Between Acts I and II he found he had forgotten his dress studs. Fortunately, his dresser, Arthur, who had coped with him for some years and had learned to be dismayed by nothing, produced wooden laundry studs, and on Leslie went for round two.

"Fight pretty even so far. Imagine we are holding our own."

At 11:25 P.M. it was all over, and everyone told everyone else that they were a hit.

"Author gives whole credit to cast. Cast hands entire kudos to author—and observe later, 'Well, anyway, if they don't like the play they must appreciate the acting.' 6.45 A.M. September 16th. Never read notices but must see if Gordon Ash was well treated. He does deserve it, poor fellow. 7.00 A.M. He is. Note further that Leslie Howard is also in the cast. He is likened, wittily, to everything from an undertaker to the leaning tower of Pisa. Well, what of it? Doesn't everyone know that dramatic critics are, ipso facto, illiterate dolts who have no right to criticize? Not that anyone ever reads what they write —least of all the people they write about."

The notices were varied. Every New York critic made it plain from the very beginning that he was not to be taken in, as confreres in other cities might be, by pseudo-brilliance and emotional rubbish. George Jean Nathan called it "mostly flapdoodle." It was dubbed "tosh" by one and "old-fashioned" by another. A fourth wrote resignedly that "one who raises his head and croaks solemn protestations about taste and reality stands only a night-toad's chance under the wheels of the Arlen furor. Yet the play he has made of his 'The Green Hat' is an extract merely of the maudlin, fattier portions of the book sometimes fearfully and incontestably effective, sometimes . . . steaming up into thin caterwaul."

For all their careful protestations about the lack of truth in the play, every critic knew it was a public success. To a man, they crowned Katharine Cornell the most outstanding young actress on Broadway. She was called "brilliant," "vibrant," and "a living flame." The other members of the cast fared well or badly depending on how much space and patience was left after the play had been dissected and Miss Cornell applauded.

Some critics thought Leslie quite good. "He manages admirably the mixture of gallantry and indecision in love"; "Leslie Howard gave exactly the right value to his curious part; he is indisputably the right man for Napier."

But there were those who said he looked unhappy in his role and, at times, more than a little ashamed of it, and that he went about "like a young undertaker made somewhat uncomfortable by a sense of humor that he once possessed." John Anderson in the *Evening Post* remarked that he seemed little like the Napier of the book but "tricked though he is out of his character, [he] might at least imitate something occasionally besides the Leaning Tower of Pisa or whatever he thinks he is when he teeters around all out of plumb."

Leslie obviously agreed with his least enthusiastic critics, for he came out strongly against the play and against his own part in an interview in the *Herald Tribune* the very next Sunday. "It's the hardest part I ever had to play because I know that under the given circumstances nobody in the world would say the things I have to say in the show." He went further and told the interviewer that the play did not merit the superlatives that had been pinned to it by one critic. When asked if Miss Cornell felt as he did, he replied, "No, but she is a colorful actress with a vivid personality that rather shines in this sort of thing, while I am a drab sort of person who can fit in only when the play is an exact picture of life."

It is doubtful that these frank utterances can have been greeted with any pleasure by the management. To have Broadway's most successful play cried down by a member of its cast must have been as refreshing as falling into a lake in November, and the reaction of Michael Arlen can only have bordered on the choleric. But it did not seem to worry Leslie at all. He went on nodding and smiling sweetly at everybody, apparently blissfully unaware that he was *persona non grata* with his employers. This was the first statement to the press he had ever made, and he must have considered it successful, for he made similar remarks with commendable honesty but doubtful tact for the rest of his life. He got great pleasure out of potting at idols. This, as was to be expected, had a shocking effect on the idols, for he was the last person they suspected of such infamy.

Still, it made little difference what Leslie thought or said; *The Green Hat* was a smash hit. No matter how it embarrassed him every night and twice on Wednesdays and Saturdays, he held Katharine Cornell in his arms and told her that she was "a woman with magic eyes and a soft, white body that beats at my mind like a whip" and the public loved it. His popularity increased every day. The women who sat beyond the footlights, half faint with pleasure, imagined themselves clasped by this glorious expounder of purple prose and heard him tell them: "You are my dark angel and my tower of delight in the twilight of the world."

Ruth could hardly contain an ironic smile as she pushed her way through the stage-door crowds each night, knowing how all the women envied her this fascinating lover. She loved him, naturally, but he could never have been called demonstrative. A devoted husband and wonderfully affectionate, but scarcely impassioned.

On and on went *The Green Hat,* while the leaves on the big trees in the garden at Great Neck changed to red and then slipped down to be raked and burned by Winkie and Leslie in large delicious bundles. Snow fell quietly over the country-side, and Doodie took her first uncertain steps, clutching her father's hand. Each day, muffled in rugs and an enormous white angora bonnet, she sat on a sled like a pudgy little queen and was devotedly pulled about the roads and fields by Leslie. Winkie went off to school every morning and left his new sister in command. Propped up in her father's bed, she watched him shave and dress, and he watched every small change and gradual growth in her with fascination. The family finances became quite sturdy as the weeks of full salary continued. Leslie bought a piano, which was always a most important part of his life, and the happy weekend parties rocked and sang. Doodie was carried around on Leslie's shoulder while he sang her favorites, "Who?" "Sleepy Time Girl," and "Show Me the Way to Go Home."

Christmas was a wonderful surprise. The family was united for the first time since 1921, and Doodie sat at the table and ate her turkey for the first time. It was a typical suburban Christmas, but everyone enjoyed himself, even Leslie, who always expressed a horror of domesticated suburbia.

Two very close friends of the Howards shared their Christmas—Mignon and Tom Nesbitt. They were both in the theater and lived in Great Neck. Migs and Tom had been on hand during many of the small crises that had befallen Ruth and Leslie. It was they who had gone with Leslie when he rushed Ruth to the hospital for the baby's birth. Now both Tom and Leslie heard of a play they could do together in London during the next summer. It was called *The Way You Look at It.*

It was a heaven-sent answer to the question of a holiday in England. Leslie had promised Ruth a trip home in 1926 and, impractical though he still was about money, he had been vaguely wondering how he was going to move five people three thousand miles. Now he had only to move four people— his fare would be paid. That made little financial difference but it provided an excuse. It was all this family ever needed. Show them the smallest reason for spending more money than they had and they could rationalize the whole endeavor into necessity.

Ruth began to plan at once. They would rent the house, and, of course, that would practically pay for the entire holiday. Now, tickets, passports, new trunks, somewhere to live in England. She was in her element planning and organizing.

Another piece of fortune materialized at almost the same time: Gilbert Miller was casting a play called *The Cardboard Lover,* a French play by Jacques Deval. The part of the cardboard lover was a magnificent one. Every suitable actor in New York wanted it, and one or two thought they had it. One was a friend of the Howards, and he had waited in great excitement after his agent told him the chances were good, only to be called later to hear it had been cast with someone else. Heavy with depression, he went out to Great Neck to tell his sad story to Ruth and Leslie. Ruth met him at the door in high excitement.

"Come in, dear, come in. Leslie has just been offered the most wonderful part, and he's reading the play to us now."

The poor man sat dejectedly through the next hour, never able to tell his story, for the play that Leslie was reading was, naturally, *The Cardboard Lover.* The contracts were signed, and rehearsals were set for late August.

By June, everything was settled—the house rented and the trunks sent to the boat. Ruth, with her usual passion for cleanliness, had worked interminably to leave the house as clean as a clinic for the new tenants. As a result, she was quite exhausted and, though she did not complain, in very bad health by the time they were ready to sail.

Leslie was not helpful on journeys—he did carry the heavy baby, but that was his contribution. Ruth and Miss Goss were left to bring up the rear, pay for the taxis, go through customs and immigration, and always keep an eye on Leslie, Doodie, and Winkie in case they drifted off and could not be found. Once on board, life was a great deal easier, because Leslie could be counted on to look after the children for hours.

As soon as the gong rang the "all ashore that's going ashore," Leslie went up to the sun deck to show his children the New York sky line, though he had to keep a rather tight hold on Doodie, who was more interested in investigating the swimming. Thus they sailed, full of anticipation and delight at the thought of seeing England, for they were indeed a very English family.

6 / London Is a Fine Town

To most Englishmen who have lived abroad for some time, to come back to London is to come home, no matter where they were born. This was even truer of Leslie, for he was a Londoner from the beginning. He loved the quiet contentment of the huge city. It was such a blessed relief after the glaring frenzy of New York. Nowhere in the world could he feel as energetic, ambitious, and capable as in New York, and nowhere as comfortable as in London. Even the sun was gentle and hazy as it was reflected off the lakes in the parks or brightened the long beds of tenderly cared flowers and moist green bushes. Leslie felt one with all the millions of Londoners who had gone and those who were still to come as he wandered down Piccadilly from Hyde Park to Green Park, from St. James's Street to Regent Street. It was enough just to walk about drawing into himself the sight and smell and comfort of the place.

There was an extra family feeling among Londoners that summer. They had all worked together in the crisis of the General Strike early in May, when they had been left without food and transport, and angry strikers had roamed the streets. Undaunted, the residents had run the buses (in plus fours), directed traffic (in Homburg hats), and proudly pulled out their old army uniforms to wear as they did service as mounted policemen. Undergraduates had manned the docks to unload food, and businessmen from the City had organized food depots in Hyde Park. Supported by the Horse Guards, picketed in Rotten Row in full marching order, the citizens had showed what they thought of any strike that tried to paralyze a nation. Within a few days, the strike was over, a monument to the ingenuity and hard work of the average citizen.

There was a lot of fun to be had that summer. Everyone danced ecstatically to "Valentina," the current hit of the *Piccadilly Revels*. The great Charles Cochran had a revue playing, with his beautiful "Young Ladies" and the sly wit of Hermione Baddeley. Ivor Novello, looking sixteen, was appearing in his own play, *Down Hill,* acting the role of a public-school boy who sets up house with an actress and becomes a wastrel, a wicked and daring theme that set the debutantes chattering like little birds. Yvonne Printemps was in London in Sacha Guitry's production of *Mozart,* looking delicious in white tights and a powdered wig. Diaghilev and the Russian Ballet were at His Majesty's, delighting the senses of their followers, and a few hardy balletomanes trailed out to Sadlers' Wells, where a little English company was trying to prove that not only the Russians could dance.

Sport flourished, as ever—the races at Goodwood, the rowing at Henley, and the holy game of cricket at Lords, the Englishman's shrine.

Leslie established his family in a quiet hotel on the northern fringe of Hyde Park, and took to a little sport himself. He could never bear to be long away from horses, and he began riding each day in Rotten Row. Winkie was not keen to follow his father in this pursuit, because he had had quite a bad fall a year or two before. As Leslie was desperately anxious that one of his children should ride, he took his still rather unsteady and fat eighteen-month-old daughter, plunked her on a horse, and, to his delight, she stayed there, crowing with pleasure. He had a minute pair of jodhpurs made by his tailor, because nothing small enough could be found, and Doodie was introduced to a life of pleasure and expense that must have caused Leslie to regret the introduction on more than one occasion.

Riding was interrupted a little by rehearsals, but Leslie took Winkie and Doodie down Oxford Street every morning on the top of a bus when he went to the theater, and he watched them set off again tugging at the hands of the much-bullied Miss Goss. Ruth did not take part in any of these jaunts; she was feeling less and less well. Leslie worked and worried and finally insisted on bringing a doctor to see her. As a result of the visit, she was sent to a nursing home in London, where none of the doctors could agree about her illness. The children were packed off to the seaside to stay with their grandparents, and Leslie went on rehearsing.

Horribly worried though he was about Ruth, Leslie got a lot of amusement out of *The Way You Look at It*. Written by a young English peer, Edward William Bootle-Wilbraham, third Earl of Lathom, it was well and expensively cast: Edna Best, Martita Hunt, and Isabel Jeans were the women most concerned with the young man played by Leslie. It was a silly story but well suited to the silliness of the age. Leslie, as Bobby, lives a delectable life of sin, being kept by an older woman. Naturally, he falls for the sweet freshness of a bright young thing, played by Edna Best, and ends up jilted by the lot.

The author, Lord Lathom, was an amusing person, an attractive, dark-mustached, urbane young man, fascinated by the theater, who wrote very bright dialogue of the period. The lines of *The Way You Look at It* were never going to be immortal, and, in fact, were not even mortal for more than a few weeks. They were thought by the critics to be pretty shallow, and the critics, oddly enough, would seem in retrospect to have been right. Not much can be made out of: "She was my worst friend and she married my dearest enemy" or "She means well but oh! so little."

After the play opened to lukewarm notices, Leslie drove Ruth down to Lancing, where the children were disporting themselves, in the fond hope that a little sea air would improve her. The English have remarkable faith in the efficacious quality of salt water. He whisked her there in his beautiful rented Sunbeam, a charming object with two seats inside and one rather dashing one over the left back wheel. It was a sturdy little car, too, often accommodating four or five members of the family inside and, invariably, Leslie's father seated precariously over the wheel. The whole Stainer family had forgathered at Lancing for the holidays—Irene, plump and pretty and starting to cast hopeful glances at the stage; Dorice, taking a rest from her growing dancing school; Arthur, taking a permanent rest from school, and even Granny Mary, enjoying the company of her great-grandchildren. Lilie Stainer ran the house in that charming, vague way that made her so lovable, but Leslie was not always entirely happy surrounded by so many people, and by this time the house was absolutely bulging and every sofa and chair was being used for a bed.

He and Ruth had just begun to think of moving their brood to another spot, when the blow fell. In the middle of one night, Ruth was carried out of the house on a stretcher in frightful pain. There was no time for London specialists; she had to be operated upon within hours. Leslie canceled his performance and for two days waited like a frightened little boy, praying that Ruth should live. He had never fully known what she meant to him, never realized the strength that had flowed from her to support him. Now he knew, now he realized. After a nightmare of waiting, she came around slowly and began the long climb back to normal. Her stoicism in pain and unhappiness moved Leslie almost to tears. He was always sentimental, and his regard for Ruth's courage and endurance was expressed in a tiny gold medal made, perhaps a little pre-sumptuously, in the shape of the Maltese cross and bearing the words "For Valour" in his handwriting across its face. He put it around her neck on a long gold chain, and she held it clenched between her fingers on the morning he came to say good-by before leaving for New York. All their lovely plans for a holiday in England had been ruined, and now she was hardly well enough to lift up her head to kiss him as he went away. The tears, which she had promised herself would not appear, slipped helplessly down her cheeks and soaked into her hair on the pillow.

"My darling, you shall come out just as soon as you're well enough," he promised her. "Don't cry, my dearest."

Leslie did his utmost to cheer her and to leave her with happy thoughts, and he was a master at the job. He propped her pillows and straightened her blankets and made her com-fortable in mind as well as body. By the time he left, Ruth was more cheerful and prepared to look forward to the day when they would be reunited. Off went Leslie to drive up to London with his mother to catch the boat train. He had "a good but nervy trip" by car and was "feeling very depressed" by the time he arrived for dinner at the Ivy Restaurant, where he sent off a short letter to Ruth. This was the first of a long series of wails that he wrote every day and which must have been cheerful reading for a patient.

He sailed on the *Majestic* and wrote immediately.

"Here I am on this beastly ship crossing the Channel which is quite rough and I don't feel any too well—what with the excitement, etc. I'm sick of the sea already!

"I was so sad at leaving you, my darling, and my babies and everybody else. There are some children on board with their parents and I'm so envious of them—one little girl rather like Doodie and it makes me terribly homesick. You and they are all I have in life and it's terrible to be separated. I'm getting too old to be rushing about by myself and I want to settle down quickly in England with my little family." Later, he wrote:

"Darling, I read your sweet little note last night in bed and wept over it, of course. . . . It comforted me a lot. I shall never forget how brave and good you've been, darling, and I shall try to make it up to you when you're better for all the terrible ordeals you've been through.

"I pray you may get well quickly, my darling, and come out to me very soon. . . .

"Mary and Doug [Fairbanks] are here and all the Pickford family. Also Constance Talmadge and husband, Philip Moeller and Theresa Helburn, as per last year. It is strange, I went exactly the same voyage last year only you were all at the other end waiting for me."

Once he was off the ship and into New York life, he perked up and began to enjoy the people he knew. He was delighted to find Gilbert Miller waiting for him on the dock. "A most unexpected attention and he had been waiting quite a long time. So far as I am concerned everything is O.K. He is very enthusiastic about my being with him and has a wonderful play by Molnar which he wants to do after this. Also he has *promised* to let me do "The Cardboard Lover" in London and I told him I would only sign a contract with him on the basis of equal appearances in London as well as N.Y.

"I am off to Easthampton to-day [to stay with Laurette Taylor and Hartley Manners]. We are supposed to rehearse on Monday. Laurette and Gilbert are not hitting it off at all well. He said to me: 'All I want is for you to walk away with the show.' He has got the French author here and the woman who adapted it and Laurette is holding up rehearsals because of her contract. To-day I shall hear Laurette's version. As usual I am the confidant of both sides—my mission in life."

Leslie felt helpless without Ruth to pack for him and get the tickets, but somehow he traveled out to East Hampton to stay with the Manners'.

"The Hardly-any-Manners atmosphere being very prominent. Laurette *means* well, of course, but you know being a guest in that household is not so amusing as it sounds. One just fits in somewhere. I slept in an attic with a very nice fellow named Meredith who *snored* violently all night. It was quite terrifying and I didn't sleep much. I kept getting up to look at him in amazement. He seemed likely to asphyxiate any moment."

The weekend was otherwise highly successful. Leslie went swimming and played tennis. Geoffrey Kerr and his new wife, June Walker, were staying with the Mannerses, and Leslie drove back to New York with them and was taken on to a party at Gloria Swanson's apartment where he saw a movie, *The Grand Duchess and the Waiter,* with Adolphe Menjou and Florence Vidor. He thought it "very good indeed. She [Vidor] is too lovely! What is the matter with King Vidor? The fool! I quite fell for her, only darling my heart is very much in England just now.

"Gloria Swanson is very attractive and has great charm and her Marquis is a delightful chap. The apartment is miraculous. High up on a roof—very early Metro-Goldwyn style. Soft lights and Russian orchestra which never ceased playing! How tiring."

The rehearsals for *The Cardboard Lover* began at once, though still under strained relations and complicated conditions. The French author, Deval, and the adapter, Valerie Wyngate, with Gilbert Miller, producer, and George Cukor, director, and a few other people were all trying to co-ordinate the production. Leslie found the company rather dull, with the exception of Harry Kendall, who had come from London and was waiting to leave again at any moment because the author thought him twenty years too young. Miss Taylor was still very angry with the management, and Leslie described it all as the extreme of dreariness. "Two or three very fat old ladies, a couple of rather dirty Frenchmen and Laurette looking more acid than vitriol."

By the time Ruth got the letter with these remarks, she had recovered enough to leave the nursing home and, steadfastly refusing to rejoin her in-laws, had rented an apartment in a charming row of Regency houses in Brighton. There she was joined by Miss Goss and the children.

Leslie hurried to the Lotos Club every day to see if there were letters from his family. He wrote nearly every day himself. He spent most weekends at East Hampton, in spite of his complaints about the comfort, and was devoted to his leading lady. "Laurette is very charming and we get on excellently so far. She is a very sincere woman."

Rehearsals took place at the Henry Miller Theatre, reminding Leslie of his loneliness six years before. The play was booked to open on September 23 in Great Neck—more reason for nostalgia. "It's awful to think of nobody being there—I can't help thinking of it as home. But, of course, it's people that make a home—the *place* means nothing."

Rehearsing was in earnest now, and even on the weekends Leslie worked with Laurette in the country. He felt the play might be all right because Laurette Taylor was very good, though he found the intimate scenes with her a little difficult. Jacques Deval was "a comic little creature and completely unintelligible in his excitable moments." Fortunately for Leslie, Harry Kendall had been kept in the company, but the whole play was so French that Leslie remarked: "Harry and I are getting more like Alphonse and Gaston by the day, which gives us something to laugh at."

There were a lot of good plays on in New York, and Howard and Kendall saw most of them. Leslie wrote to Ruth:

"We went to see 'The Ghost Train.' It was quite thrilling but ruined slightly by having been turned into an American play and then acted by an all British company. We went round after and saw John Williams and Eric Blore and Isobel Elsom whom I haven't seen since 'The Freaks'—and that's a tidy while ago. Eric Blore is an excellent comedian. Last night I saw 'Cradle Snatchers.' Very amusing in spots. I think Mary Boland could have been good but is pretty terrible now. She kept spitting and exploding like a fiery tomcat. I could hardly sit still. Edna May Oliver was quite the reverse. Beautifully restrained. She spotted me in the third row and made a face at me. I went around to see her and tell her about 'The Man from Crumbles.' She is tied up all this season, however."

"The Man from Crumbles" was yet another title for *Murray Hill,* and Leslie nurtured great hopes for it. No matter how hard he worked as an actor, he never lost sight of his dream: to be able to give up all the ghastly embarrassing mumbo jumbo in front of the footlights and to sit behind them watching other poor fools reading his lines. He sent "Crumbles" off to Brock Pemberton in the hope that he might produce it.

Another play that he enjoyed was *Sour Grapes,* by Vincent Lawrence, with Alice Brady and John Halliday. He was taken to this by Lois Wilson, and found one of the theater party to be the beautiful Florence Vidor. He hastened to set Ruth's mind at rest about Mrs. Vidor. "I was so interested to meet her—and what a charming well-bred woman. You would like her. Fancy a lady in the movies!"

After the play they spent an hour at a night club called the Lido, he reported, and then went on to a party at the house of some theater people. Leslie was furious with them. He found their behavior "abominably vulgar and I was ashamed to see the theatre shown up by the movies in the person of nice people like Lois Wilson and Florence Vidor."

The heat of New York was quite appalling. For days on end the thermometer stayed near 100 degrees and often climbed above. There were violent thunderstorms and then still more heat. Leslie liked New York only on the crisp clear days of autumn, and the humid boiling weather, coupled with his homesickness, worked him into an absolute fury. Now he hated New York—what a "dreadful specimen of hideousness and din" it was. Never was he going to work there again—absolutely never.

All his thoughts and letters were concentrated on how soon his family would join him. At first, Ruth suggested sending the children ahead, but he vetoed this idea because he hated to think of her being left alone in England. Then Ruth thought Winkie should stay behind and go to boarding school, but Leslie felt he was too young. Money was short, too, by this time, and again rehearsals were long and without salary. On Monday, September 12, Leslie wrote a lengthy letter of love and caution and advice to Ruth.

"Ruthie my darling: I have just got your nice long letter telling me you have been out of bed for the first time. Poor darling, I wish I could have been with you and helped. It must have been awful.

"Do you suppose you would be well enough to sail about October 15th? The play will have started by then and I can get things ready for you. Unless it's a failure when I don't know what I should do. I might even come back to London. Laurette is trying to get Great Neck and Stamford cancelled and open two weeks from to-day at Atlantic City. Great Neck is a bad place to open anyway.

"Tuesday. So far we have not succeeded in getting the date changed but we're still hoping. To-day we have got rid of the Frenchman for a few days and it's much easier rehearsing. The play is beginning at last to come to life. It is still unquestionably charming but a little bit *unusual* for the average audience. However, I stick to my first impression. I do hope it's a big success so I can make some money and we can all have a lovely time. I feel I have so much to make up to you my dearest for all you've been through.

"I do count myself a singularly fortunate person that my little family is just as it is—I wouldn't have any of you different. My only fear is my possible inability to provide for them in such a way that they will only see the beautiful in life and little of the ugliness. I just want strength for that.

"Mother wrote me a long letter and told me some sweet little stories about my baby girl which thrilled me beyond words. How she fascinates me. My love affair with her is scandalous! If only I were a poet what sonnets I could inscribe.

"Darling, there is no *real* news, only my thoughts and even they seem to be very repetitious. I seem to harp on one topic—my family—which is remarkable for one who is reputed to be a *devil* with the women!"

All the gentle warmth and love of an extremely sentimental nature went into that letter to his wife. Loneliness and depression may have put a slightly rosy flush on the picture he carried of his little family, but, essentially, he expressed the feelings that he would always have about them—his far-too-protective instincts for his children, which made him so beloved by them; his anxiety to give his wife the comforts and amusements that he felt she had been denied. It is hard to imagine any wife of ten years who would not worship the husband who wrote like that. Ruth was as sentimental as Leslie. She searched to find something to send him that would always remain between them, a talisman of luck and of love. So it was that a few days before the play opened, Leslie found an old gold sovereign in one of her letters. He was infinitely touched, and wrote: "It was so sweet of you my dearest—I feel like saying 'I'll have it stuffed,' like 'Charley's Aunt' but I mean I'll have it put on a chain and wear it and always treasure it." From then on, he never took it off; he wore it to the end of his life.

Rehearsals now went on all day and a great part of the night. "I am awfully tired and heavy from lack of air. I simply live in the theatre and the hotel and I feel quite rotten. Thank God only four days to our opening in Great Neck. I shall be grateful for the change of atmosphere. I don't know

now whether it's morning, noon or night. I suppose it's still 1926!"

On September 27, *The Cardboard Lover* opened for the first of a number of tryouts. Laurette Taylor was still unhappy with her part and had been thoroughly unnerved by the hostile attitude of the author. During the first act, as Leslie reported to Ruth later, she felt very sick, and he was afraid she was going to be so at any moment. In the second act, everything got rather muddled, and few lines seemed to come out as rehearsed, which terrified Leslie. Despite the worry, there was more than enough recompense for Leslie. The part lived up to all his expectations, there was a packed house, and he got a great reception, with applause at every exit. It was the first time this had happened to such a degree, and he described it to Ruth with tremendous excitement. "Quite the best success I've ever had. This all sounds very conceited—but you know me, Al!"

Though Leslie had scored a personal success, the management were unhappy with the play, and Gilbert Miller intimated that he would close it in two weeks for rewriting and recasting. They played a night in Stamford, and then went to Atlantic City. There was still nothing definite and they kept rehearsing. Miller took a look at them in Atlantic City and announced only that he was delaying the New York opening. A. H. Woods, who was producing with him, came down one night and was obviously so depressed that he never went backstage at all. The houses were very bad. "The audience might have been listening to a play in ancient Greek," groaned Leslie. The same thing happened in Washington, where the whole play was received in a stony silence.

Leslie was in a frightful state of worry by this time because his money was running out, and if the play went back into rehearsal, he would be completely bankrupt. It was the more distressing because for some weeks he had been trying to arrange ship passage for Ruth and the children. When he had traveled back on the *Majestic*, he enthusiastically and rather foolishly suggested that Ruth should do the same. Then when she did book on a large ship, the *Homeric*, he was appalled. "Of course, darling, it's largely a question of money. It's a *very expensive* boat. The four tickets at least one thousand dollars and I'll have only been working a week or two."

He hastily suggested a nice one-class ship, and assured Ruth that "The 'Ohio' is quite a big ship—Royal Mail—and a man at the club travelled on the 'Franconia' and said she was a marvellous ship!" He experienced great difficulty in trying to book their passage from New York. He was expected to pay all the fares at once, "and that's impossible." So, crossing his fingers, he left the arrangements to Ruth in Brighton, once more suggesting and recommending a number of charming, cheap, and "very steady" small boats. Fortunately, Ruth took the hint, and, with many financial dickerings, sailed on the *Carmania* on October 16.

Leslie hoped to have opened in New York by the time she arrived, but the Washington experience, followed by an even more devastating week in Newark, convinced Gilbert Miller and A. H. Woods that some serious rebuilding must be done if the play was ever to face a New York audience. Laurette Taylor seemed miscast and still unhappy and unsure of her part. Leslie, although he continued to look upon her as a great and remarkable actress, found performances painful and difficult. He had to admit that his part, André Salicel, was wonderful and popular with the public, but he could not see the play continuing unchanged.

Naturally, he imagined his health to be seriously affected by all the work and worry and traveling. He had not yet decided where his fatal physical weakness lay and imagined heart attacks were still in the future. But he was already convinced that his poor, weak frame could stand very little without complete collapse, and he rather enjoyed the private drama of illness and looked forward with a grim satisfaction to a future as a chronic invalid. "Here I am—a wreck! My nerves all tired out and very bad nights and looking haggard!"

He survived the exhaustion and overwork, nonetheless, and by the end of October, when the family arrived, he was enjoying an unwelcome spot of rest. *The Cardboard Lover* had closed before coming to New York, and plans for its future were vague.

Gilbert Miller brought in no less a light than P. G. Wodehouse to rewrite the script, and, while this went on, he was looking around for another leading lady. Miller might be able to afford the time to look around, but Leslie had by now spent his meager three weeks' salary, earned on tour, and, such was their financial condition, apart from "money at the brokers," there was nothing with which to pay the bills. Leslie did not want to take money back from the brokers, for everyone was full of inside information on the stock market, and huge fortunes were being built up every day. It seemed almost criminally foolish not to gamble when all New York was doing it. If bellboys and elevator operators, stenographers and hairdressers were able to make large amounts of money, surely actors should be in the act. Perhaps fortunately for Leslie, the need for ready money had to take precedence over the desire to invest in the giant pinball machine that the New York stock exchange had become. Leslie was not much of a gambler anyway. This may have been because his own father had always dabbled disastrously in various unlikely shares, or perhaps he agreed with Alexander Woollcott, who later remarked: "In the empty, silly, noisy years which immediately preceded the Wall Street crash of 1929, I used to get hot tips on the market from the Big Shots . . . no good ever accrued from these tips except the potential benefit which anyone can experience by merely losing all his money."

At any rate, the Howards had no money for such endeavors, and once more they settled into their house on East Road and

Leslie took up his pen to help feed his brood. A number of gay and foolish articles were devised, and one or two were accepted by the *New Yorker* and *Vanity Fair*. He wrote a charming spoof on "Holy Hollywood," which the *New Yorker* printed. In it he suggested that the motion picture, already on equal economic terms with oil, steel, and automobiles, was moving into a spiritual and moral dominance that would soon rival the great religions of mankind. This had been drawn to Leslie's attention by a newspaper report that Cecil B. deMille would now only employ actors who lived a moral life and that in future all contracts with him would contain such a guarantee by the actor.

"Imagine the cumulative effect of this in a few years time," Leslie wrote. "The movie actor of the future will pause before the commission of any act which might be construed as improper in any way . . . gradually the desire to do wrong will depart from him through natural atrophy and he will really become a holy person of whom any nice girl could say reverently: 'He's a movie actor, Mother,' just as she said in the old days: 'He's a minister, Mama.' There will be no more wild Hollywood parties. The ghastly spectre of Breach of Contract will have turned them into prayer meetings."

Leslie had a wonderful time poking fun at the Hollywood moguls who, by the production of one or two religious films, now imagined themselves above mankind in spiritual grace. He suggested slyly that: "The Papal authority [in the new Holy City] would be vested in one great leader, possibly Mr. deMille himself, a number of Archbishops will be created among such prominent members as W. S. Hart, Harold Lloyd, John Gilbert, Harry Langdon, Douglas Fairbanks and Chester Conklin." But he assured Hollywood that there was bound to be dissension. "The Fox section for example may get fed up with the high-church ritualism of the deMillites—those hypocritical deMille papists—and set up its own temple in Culver City."

He ended his absurdity by hoping that someone would read his predictions and warn Hollywood, so that forearmed they could continue to lead their wanton existence. Leslie's humor was well exhibited in this bit of drollery; it had a puckish quality, a mock-solemn, gently derisive touch.

While he amused himself writing articles, he also worked hard fixing up his play *Murray Hill*. He had taken it to England, read it to his family, and anyone else who imprudently sat still long enough to be caught, and all had seemed amused. Then he gave it to E. E. Clive, whom he had known in London and who now directed the Clive Players in Boston. To his delight, Clive agreed to put it on, but with the important proviso that Leslie must play the lead himself. Leslie would have been prepared to play the feminine lead in a wig to get one of his own plays on a stage, but he was under contract to Gilbert Miller and was not able to say when he would be free. There was no way of knowing when *The Cardboard Lover* would reappear or for how long.

Finally, after many weeks, which had included Christmas and the New Year bills, Gilbert Miller announced that the play would open once more in March and the star would be Miss Jeanne Eagels, in Laurette Taylor's part. Jeanne Eagels was a phenomenon on the New York stage—an actress who received a top-star billing on the strength of one part in one play, a part she had played for over four years: Sadie Thompson in Somerset Maugham's *Rain*. To interest her in Jacques Deval's play was not difficult, though she insisted that the title must be changed to *"Her* Cardboard Lover" if she was to be the star. The part of Simone, which Laurette Taylor had found unrewarding, attracted Jeanne Eagels. Perhaps after nearly five years of portraying a tough American prostitute, she longed to try her inborn skill at a sophisticated Frenchwoman in a bedroom farce. Nevertheless, the switch from Sadie to Simone was so extraordinary that it amounted almost to schizophrenia for an actress without great experience. Leslie rehearsed long and patiently (rather reveling in the new Wodehouse lines, most of which had been given to him), but Jeanne Eagels, though she played certain scenes well, was a frightened young woman when the curtain finally went up. She had been difficult to manage throughout the rehearsals. Actors and actresses were removed from the company because Miss Eagels wanted just the right inflection.

Never was a play more fraught with friction and dogged by difficulties. Leslie wondered despairingly why he had ever become involved. He longed to get out of the whole thing. He had had more than enough of temperamental female stars, recasting, rewriting, and repetition. He was appallingly bored with the entire performance. Those were his thoughts on the eve of the opening in New York, but he could not see the morrow. The iron that had been heating in a slow fire since 1917 suddenly glowed white hot. Monday, March 21, 1926, was to be momentous for Leslie Howard.

7 / Matinee Idol, Playwright, Father

It was a Monday much like any other; an opening-night Monday that brought the usual flutterings in the stomach. There was nothing to distinguish it from any one of the other dozens of opening nights he had played in. Arthur was waiting at the theater, as he always was; the cars were piling up in front, depositing a brilliant audience. Leslie took a little *sal volatile*. Various members of the cast popped their heads into his dressing room to tell him who was out front—Miss Peggy Hopkins Joyce, Mrs. Vincent Astor, Fannie Hurst, Ring Lardner, Condé Nast, Jean Borotra, the French tennis player, Franklin P. Adams, Jesse L. Lasky and Adolph Zukor, Hollywood, not Russian, generals, the usual first-night audience. Leslie's nerves were as bad as ever, and possibly a little worse, for André Salicel was a very long part and he expected some uncertainty from his leading lady.

The curtain went up on the baccarat room of the Pergola at Hendaye in the south of France. Simone, a jealous, lovesick featherbrain, terrified of the weakness that will send her crawling back to her errant, fascinating former husband, hires a moon-struck young man, André, to stand by to see that she does no such thing. By the end of the second act, even through a vapor of nerves, Leslie realized that this was the success of

128

his career. For Ruth, sitting in the audience, it was the most incredible and exciting evening of her whole life. Loud applause greeted Leslie every time he came onto the stage, and when the curtain fell at the end of each act there was unleashed a perfect storm of shouting and clapping. At the final curtain, after Simone has forgotten her passion for an ex-husband and discovered that her lover is not so cardboard, the house cheered and clapped the fortunate owner of the title role.

In the New York *World,* Alexander Woollcott wrote: "Mr. Howard was a great favorite with last night's audience which wore itself to a shadow trying to say as much. There were tremendous calls for him and, seemingly, it was not enough that Miss Eagels led him forth again and again. It was the notion of the stubborn assemblage that Mr. Howard should come forth alone and because the stage manager lacked sufficient presence of mind to arrange such a testimonial, it came about that again and again the curtain rose on the lovely pink and gold spectacle of Miss Eagels bowing in solitary grandeur to an audience that kept monotonously yelling, 'Howard, Howard, Howard.'"

Ruth, surrounded by such adulation, found tears of excitement on her cheeks and was afraid someone might see her. Leslie would not like her to make a spectacle of herself. But no one was looking at anything but the stage that night. New York had chosen as the star a young man whose name was not to be found in large print in the program. Partly, perhaps, from a mischievous delight in upsetting the star system, the audience hooted for Howard. The critics hurried from the theater to write their reviews, and Leslie and Ruth, opening the papers in the early hours of Tuesday morning, found the notices that every actor dreams of getting. Burns Mantle headed his *Daily News* column: "Cardboard Lover belongs to Howard."

Percy Hammond reported in the *Herald Tribune*: "Although Miss Eagels excelled as the heroine of the event, Mr. Leslie Howard, in one of the richest roles of the season, rather kidnapped the comedy from its rightful proprietor. Mr. Howard as the determined doormat delights the eye as well as the sense of humor. He is selfdeprecatory in a quaint fashion and does the most astounding things in the least astounding way."

Brooks Atkinson, in the *Times,* found Jeanne Eagels not too happily cast, but said: "On the other hand, Mr. Howard as a blind, young fool plays buoyantly with droll flourishes and a sustaining, sardonic intelligence."

As Leslie and Ruth read each review, their elation increased.

"Mr. Wodehouse's fine hand is noticeable in some dialogue, the main ingredients of which are bestowed on Mr. Howard. Howard utters those lines as though he wrote them. And how sweet they are to the ear."

And another: "Howard is triumphant in spite of all. He catches just the spirit of mockery and drollery that is the secret of success in this sort of play. His is a keen, beautifully simple and persuasive performance that should secure the name of Leslie Howard for years to come."

No one could ask for more from the press, and the Howard household was jubilant. They all expected to see Leslie's name in shimmering lights over the theater at any moment, and Ruth, for one, was irritated when it did not happen that way.

The following Sunday, Woollcott commented on the same thing:

"Reverting for the moment to the widely celebrated first night when a handsome and mildly mischievous audience vainly tried to upset the traditional prerogatives of the star system just long enough to see Leslie Howard take one curtain call alone, it is interesting to note that the advertisements which officially recorded the event in Wednesday's papers made no reference to that quickly suppressed mutiny.

"The press on Tuesday burst in to blossoms of tribute to Mr. Howard's engaging performance but, though seven critics were called as witnesses in the advertisements next day, not one of their reports on the Howard demonstration seeped past the managerial censor. The prankfulness and charm of the play itself, the loveliness and aplomb of Miss Eagels, even the managerial sagacity of Gilbert Miller and A.H. Woods—these were all honoured by effusive and costly quotations. But a playgoer would read these signboards from end to end without once suspecting that a wretch called Leslie Howard had been involved in the performance of 'Her Cardboard Lover.' This is known as the star system."

It was not the sort of thing that produced unhappy, sleepless hours for Leslie. Everything would follow now that his initial success had been made. Indeed, within three weeks, a report appeared in *Variety* headed "Leslie Howard as star." It was said that Gilbert Miller was seeking a play for fall production with Leslie in mind. "Howard appearing with Jeanne Eagels in 'Her Cardboard Lover' and without billing, has made a big personal hit, with the elevation next season coming promptly as reward."

When he had dreamed of success—and who but a potato does not—Leslie never thought of a theater audience cheering and calling his name. He was not capable of quite such conceit. At any rate, the idea would have made him rather uncomfortable, as, indeed, the occurrence did. But once it was over, it was an immensely satisfying experience. It seemed he had almost made modern theater history, one critic reporting: "It was the first time I had ever seen a first night audience in America really take matters into their own hands."

The information even seeped through to Leslie's native land, where the previously unenthusiastic newspapers ran the story, admittedly in small type. "The ovation following the decisive curtain was such as has been rarely adventured in a modern playhouse. For ten minutes the salvos, the cheers and the bravos rang against the respectable rafters of the staid Empire. They were for Leslie Howard, the young British juvenile comedian."

Thus it was that he took his place among the senior members of his profession. Out of the murk of a dozen second-rate plays and third-rate parts, he appeared, looking rather surprised, and became what is generally acknowledged as a "star." It had been a long apprenticeship, ten years of work that was hard, tiring, and deflating. Ten years—twice as long, in fact, as he had given himself in 1917. Then, he had told Ruth that if success did not come in five years he would give up the theater and try to become a man of business. Now at last he had a name in his chosen, though somewhat despised, profession. Where would he go from here? The road up had been hard and slow, but, viewed from the top, the road down looked fast and slippery.

To the actor striving for success, the famous names, the great stars look settled and satisfied. Contentedly munching the caviar of fame in the relaxed Valhalla reserved for those at the top, they seem without worry, financial or otherwise. When, after years of scrimping and saving, of being vilified by drama critics and cold-shouldered by producers, the exhausted actor pulls himself to the summit, he finds to his horror, not the rarefied atmosphere he had expected, but a rather lonely hill, swept from time to time by the chill wind of failure. He begins to understand why so many of the well-known people he has worked with were sharp and difficult; why good supporting actors were removed from a company where they might outshine the lead. It is not comfortable on a pinnacle; there is always someone waiting to replace those who slip. It is no longer possible to take everything that comes along, for one failure can start a long downward spiral. Now one must wait without work and with an exaggerated standard of living, looking for the "right" play and hoping to God it will come before the public forgets all about one.

Leslie was either remarkably lucky or clever, or both, for the plays that followed *Her Cardboard Lover* served only to consolidate his position. Nevertheless, he was to spend many nerve-racked hours reading, discussing, and deciding on each play as it appeared.

Her Cardboard Lover survived happily until the great summer heat. And while he drew crowds of devoted female fans to the Empire, Leslie worked on his winter plans.

John Galsworthy's play *Escape* was offered to him for production in October. It had been performed in London the previous year. In it, Galsworthy continued his interest in prisons and penal reform, which had first been revealed in *Justice*. The story of *Escape* was thin. It consisted of episodes in the day of a convict who has escaped from Dartmoor Prison; of the people he met who helped him, and of his final act of submission. The escaped prisoner is a "gentleman" in the very English sense, ruled by the ancient creed of fair play, of not doing anything that is not "cricket." The play could appear ridiculous on the American stage unless the central character were played with infinite taste. It was, however, a major tour de force as a part and well-nigh irresistible to an actor.

To Leslie, the part offered a great opportunity to escape being typecast as a comic juvenile in drawing rooms, ballrooms, and bedrooms. *Escape* would provide a part of considerable virtuosity, and, if he pulled it off, he could create for himself a wider reputation as an actor.

By this time, he was under contract to Gilbert Miller, and *Escape* was to be produced by Winthrop Ames. Fortunately, Miller had no play scheduled for the autumn for which he had Leslie in mind. He, too, must have felt the possibilities of the part in *Escape*. A press release early in the spring announced: "Leslie Howard to appear in principal role in Galsworthy's 'Escape,' " and the choice was made.

Meanwhile, *Her Cardboard Lover* flourished. Though Leslie might grow weary of his long part, he had little chance to grow bored. Jeanne Eagels, emmeshed in her colorful chiffon drapery, was distinctly unusual and erratic in her performance.

Once she settled into the enormous bed in Act II, her attention was inclined to wander.

One evening, after Leslie had made his entrance and given his leading lady her cue, there followed only ominous silence.

Finally Miss Eagels looked at Leslie, smiled charmingly, and said: "I would like a glass of water."

Leslie, trying to appear unruffled by this odd turn of events, smiled back and repeated his opening lines. Undisturbed and oblivious to what he had said, the pink-and-gold confection in the bed replied: "I said I would like a glass of water, please."

The audience had by now sensed that this was a departure from the script and had begun to whisper. Leslie decided that nothing much could be gained by trying to cover up the incident. He politely turned and walked off the stage. To Stanley Logan, who played the part of the husband and who was waiting in the wings to go on, he said: "She wants a glass of water," and with that he disappeared into his dressing room, leaving poor Logan gaping and the stage manager frantically signaling for the curtain to come down.

Another unfortunate occasion found Jeanne Eagels fast asleep in the glorious bed. Leslie felt desperately sorry for the girl. He found her strangely pathetic. He knew the part was a frightful strain for her, and he forgave her her temperament. She had great talent and was a real theatrical personality, but she was not truly a professional. Her success had come too quickly, and she was terrified to admit even to herself that she could not quite live up to it. Though there were rumblings from the management and warnings from Actors Equity about her behavior, she survived the New York run, and then, tragically, was suspended by Equity during the tour. It was only her second major role on the stage, and it was to be her last. Two years later she was dead, unable to take the pace of her own success.

The Howard household, however, thrived and bloomed during this period, possibly the happiest days of their lives. They had enough money to be comfortable without too much luxury, enough success to be contented without too much importance. Leslie still mowed the lawn and painted the garden chairs, and Ruth worked in her own house. They employed a maid and felt rather grand; but there were still many things they could not do, many they could not afford. There was the real pleasure of sitting, as the evenings lengthened, discussing what they would like to spend their money on when they had it. A house in England they placed at the top of the list, and then horses and dogs. (They had not bought a dog since their return because Brit, their Alsatian, left behind when they went to England, had suffered great loneliness and had finally disappeared from the boarding kennels—a family tragedy that the children never forgot.) It is wonderful how imaginative people can be when their finances are slender, and how indifferent they can become when everything is available to them. Not that later Leslie suffered from a lack of ideas for spending his money, but, rather, that the more money he had, the more responsibilities he had, too. In other words, the plant and equipment became so complicated that a slight ennui crept into his life. So much time and worry went into maintaining the various things he bought that he was discouraged from collecting new ones. He was always rather a simple person, and yachts, mansions, and ostentation were to hold little interest.

So it was that the Howards would remember the summer and winter of 1927 as a happy time. Leslie might occasionally be "victimized" by his female following, but Ruth felt immeasurably secure in his affections. She would never learn that a woman's attitude to love and marriage must always be different from a man's. Her husband, her children, and her home, in that order, were all she asked of life, and Leslie was only typical of his sex if he found his world away from them quite important also.

It was a world of interest and excitement that spring; a shrinking world, too, when at the end of May a young American flew alone across the Atlantic and returned a hero. Leslie and Ruth watched the triumphant drive through New York of Charles Lindbergh, and shared the pride of all Americans as the ticker tape cascaded from the buildings. Within a year, Lindbergh's brilliant example was followed by other remarkable flights—the Pacific was spanned and the arctic regions, and, finally, the German *Graf Zeppelin* carried sixty people across the Atlantic. Leslie, though he never learned to fly, was intrigued with the idea of air travel and promised himself a flight somewhere as soon as it could be arranged.

The victories of science and engineering were being recorded every year. From earphones, a crystal set, and a cat's whisker, Leslie had heard the first squeaks and groans of radio in the early 1920's. Now he was appearing on commercial programs in dramatic scenes. The grip of advertising was just being felt on this new medium for the exchange of human thoughts. Leslie, in another of his numerous articles, visualized what could happen if advertising really got out of hand. Little did he know how depressingly prophetic he was! He joked about symphony orchestras subsidized by oil companies playing to twenty people but surrounded by microphones that carried their oil-laden music to the masses. He laughed at the idea of theaters and auditoriums bearing the names of beer and soap and chewing gum companies. He thought it was all a bad dream he had encountered.

"Lucky Strike Inc. presents John Barrymore in
The Cigarette Maker's Romance—It's Toasted."

He chortled with pleasure at his own inventiveness. Perhaps he should have claimed royalties when it all came to pass just as he had seen it.

But radio was still a new toy and a new source of income in 1927, and Leslie dearly loved to listen; he was always one of the first to get the latest and the strongest set available. He

would rush out to announce to his family that he had heard
Chicago or New Orleans, and, in a few years, Tokyo and
London, Berlin and Cairo were at his bedside. "Come and listen," he would insist, and anyone nearby was dragged away
to hear faint and quite unintelligible sounds purporting to be
Ankara or Calcutta. Leslie would watch faces intently, waiting
for the rapturous expression that would mean they shared his
feeling for the magic and romance in the little box. Trying to
please him, his family always said, "Ah, yes—remarkable,"
but, to his sorrow, casual visitors left looking vaguely puzzled.

So with the radio and his other family pleasures, the spring
turned to summer and the hot weather thinned the crowds
who attended *Her Cardboard Lover*. To Leslie's delight, it was
decided to close the play. He had been working fairly steadily
on *Murray Hill,* which he now called "a Farce in Three acts."
E. E. Clive proposed that it should open his season in Boston,
and Leslie, at the end of August, went there to cast and direct
the opening. He was more excited by the chance to direct than
anything else; he felt it was a splendid opportunity to begin a
breakaway from acting. Having just succeeded as an actor, his
attitude seemed incomprehensible to other people. Why take
ten years to prove to the public that you were one of the best
actors around, and then relish the thought of becoming a director? Perhaps even Leslie did not know the answer to that one.

Murray Hill was a rather complicated, jolly old chestnut.
Its plot was difficult to disentangle. The chief characters were
three maiden ladies locked away behind the brownstone façade
of an old house in New York, still living in Victorian gentility
in 1926. They are in mourning for an aunt who has died in
Italy; the remembrance service is about to take place. The
family have employed a fashionable undertaker, "Crumbles'
Polite Funerals—Morticians par Excellence—Cheerful inter-
ments—Happiness in every box." Mr. Crumbles, "the man
who made $5,000,000 by taking the sting out of death," sends a
young fellow along to organize the proceedings. He is mis-

taken for a profligate nephew, and, as it turns out, he is really not from the undertakers but is secretly in love with the young niece of the house. This simple arrangement finally sorts itself out through drunk scenes and slapstick comedy and occasional bursts of highly entertaining dialogue. The boy gets the girl, and the ending is happy.

The play opened in August in Boston and was reasonably well reviewed. So well, in fact, that Mr. Lee Shubert sent an emissary to discuss its possible New York appearance. Leslie was entranced, and within three weeks was back in New York rehearsing for the opening there. He brought Genevieve Tobin with him from the Boston company to play the part of the innocent girl, and Gaby Fay for the part of one of the aunts.

September 29 marked the day that Leslie Howard's Opus No. 1 appeared in New York. The first-night audience greeted it with enthusiasm, and the next day a matinee audience composed entirely of professionals went mad with delight. Every line was thought to be hysterical; every character received rounds of applause for just appearing. Actors are said to be the most responsive audience in the world; they weep more copiously at tragedies and laugh more insanely at comedies than any normal audience. So it was with *Murray Hill*. Leslie was popular with his confreres, and they were determined to "just love" his play. When he finally appeared himself, the noise sounded like Armistice Day. Never had he expected his quietly humorous lines to receive such a barrage of laughter, and it undoubtedly led him to expect rather better reviews than he got in New York. Woollcott, now his normally staunch supporter, praised the first act and called the rest "floundering mendacity." Mr. J. Brooks Atkinson stated with dignified patronage that it was "rather slovenly written."

To make Leslie feel better, one or two critics gave it an excellent review. Burton Davis felt it combined the best features of Leslie as actor and author. "It sparkles, it twinkles, it smiles," wrote Mr. Davis. "What this country needs is more actors like

Leslie Howard, more farce writers like Leslie Howard and even more stage directors like Mr. Howard."

How the author could preen himself over that review! His first *produced* play and his initial fling at production seemed to speak well of his future chances as a stage director and playwright. Strange to relate, though he became expert at the former, he neither wrote nor attempted to write another play for nearly ten years. Authors need time for contemplation, and time was to be scarce for the rest of his life. Possibly he could no longer bear shutting himself away in his spare moments from his children. No one ever gave more unstintingly of his time than he did to Wink and Doodie.

His romance with his daughter continued unabated. He devised games for her amusement and even wrote songs about her. She became known as "little egg," he as "big egg," and, with help from Terence Neil, who had played with him in *Cardboard Lover,* immortal lyrics were composed. They were only vaguely imaginative. After a stirring overture in which "little egg" was repeated four times, the words ran:

All I want is egg—and then some egg—
and then some egg . . .

This, too, was repeated four times. The rhapsody ended with fine enthusiasm:

You may keep your lobster and clam chowder
All I'll ever do is cry out louder . . .

followed by more "little eggs."

As the title and main component part of this touching love song, Doodie was enchanted with it. The piano banged away, and she was more important than all the seafood in the Atlantic.

Leslie relaxed completely, surrounded by the noise that his children made. They never seemed to get on his nerves, though a boisterous three-year-old and an even more boisterous nine-year-old are not recommended aids to peace of mind. Winkie, from a slow start as a shy, small English boy, had developed into a remarkable tough. He darted about the neighborhood in a leather jacket on a fast bicycle, and was the terror of Miss Goss's life. The surrounding country had to be scoured each evening to uncover him in some nefarious pursuit. One night he was found leaping and whooping with his gang in a fiery ring, lighted with Indian enthusiasm and no thought for the surrounding houses. Leslie, true to form, thought it was very imaginative of him; Ruth determined to send him to boarding school.

What difficulty those two words were to cause husband and wife! School was bad enough, as far as Leslie was concerned; boarding school closely resembled Dartmoor or Sing Sing to him. He saw dozens of unhappy, lonely, unwanted little swots sitting in meek, miserable rows. People, heartless people, that is, sent children to boarding school because they wanted to get rid of them. He felt no urge to get rid of his children. Winkie might be a little rough at times, but that was just because he did not want the local boys to think him an English milksop. The only spanking Leslie had ever given his son was because Winkie let some other boys black his eye, so how could Ruth complain that he was too tough? The child was just carrying out his father's instructions. Winkie listened hopefully while his fate was discussed, and probably put his money on Leslie. Delaying tactics took place until it was too late to send him that year, and the small boy returned to his nocturnal wanderings happy in the knowledge that his father would support him.

Ruth may have worried about her son's ability to influence Leslie, but his was at least a direct, male approach. Doodie, even at three, was already practicing every oblique, womanly wile to get her own way. Once she discovered that her father could not resist her winning smile and cosy manner, she set out to circumvent all the discipline of the senior women of the household. With a native cunning that could have been usefully employed in fifth-column activities, Doodie fomented discord and encouraged argument. Ruth would insist that she do as she was told; the terrible infant would slip away to her daddy, pop a grimy paw into his hand, and ask if she really must. The sunniest of expressions coupled with an inability to pronounce the letter "s" were too much for Leslie. Ruth would be asked if perhaps just this time . . . And the fat little madam would dance away tugging at her father's hand and throwing her mother a look of supreme condescension. It became a pattern of behavior and was extremely hard on Ruth. She was quick and impulsive both in love and in anger, whereas Leslie was nearly always quiet and calm and reasonable with his children. It is natural that a child will turn to its quieter parent, a daughter to a father, but Doodie was inclined to exploit her advantage and frustrate her mother to a degree that her reasonable father should not have allowed.

Still, these were only the surface irritations of family life, and there was more than enough love and warmth to go around.

Within a few days of the New York opening of *Murray Hill,* Leslie was rehearsing for *Escape* and working at night in his own play. He spent nearly every waking hour in one theater or another, rushing to fit in a meal, or to get a breath of the beautiful fresh air for which he had such a strong attachment. In his free moments he would hurry up and down the street outside the theater, drawing in long drafts of air and very slowly letting them out again, while he counted carefully to himself. Someone, probably a doctor, had told him this was the best way to return oxygen to the system, and he took it all most seriously.

Nevertheless, he was tired and very nervous by the time *Escape* was ready for the first night. André Salicel had been a long part, but the role of Captain Matt Denant, the escaped prisoner, was longer and incalculably more difficult. To represent the mounting tide of exhaustion as the fugitive is hounded by his pursuers required every ounce of Leslie's energy and skill. With one or two false steps the play could become sham histrionics. Each gesture and inflection had to be kept to the minimum, and yet the audience must feel that the leading character has reached the extreme of a man's endurance. Leslie gave serious study to his lines at home. But his family was not subjected to impassioned rehearsals in the drawing room. In company with most good actors, perhaps to a more marked degree than many, Leslie could now look at his lines and decide almost immediately how he was going to handle them. He never worried about several interpretations; he read the words and there seemed only one way in which they could be read. He had developed a technique, to be sure, and, though he played naturally and without theatricality, he never supported the school of extreme naturalism; he was not a Stanislavsky follower. Acting was a job for which you were trained in the same way as many other jobs, and, though you developed your own specialty, you did not spend hours imagining yourself an empty teacup, an overflowing bathtub, or a limp flower. It was quite possible to be considering what you would eat for dinner and still turn in a creditable performance.

Nevertheless, no matter what the technique, the final polishing of a performance in rehearsal is tiring, and Leslie was enjoying the symptoms of his usual imminent crack-up when the opening tryouts took place outside New York. The play was hailed as a success before it arrived on Broadway, and the notices were splendid. Some New York critics doubted the veracity of the play; it seemed a little foolish to them that any man would give himself up, because he was a gentleman, to prevent someone else from telling a lie. Yet an admission that the play was moving and dramatic appeared in every column. In the final scene of this "episodic play in a prologue and nine scenes," Matt Denant flees into the vestry of a church, where he is found and hidden by the vicar. When the relentless search party arrives to ask if the fugitive has been seen, the vicar prepares to shield Denant, overwhelmed by his feeling of pity and his wish to give sanctuary. To protect the vicar from the sin of his own lie, Denant emerges from the cassocks and surplices among which he is concealed, with the words: "Sorry, sir, I was hidden there. I surrender, constable."

As the handcuffs are clicked on, he turns a white face to the vicar and tells him: "It's one's decent self one can't escape," and walks off slowly while the vesper bells are ringing and the vicar says gently, "God keep you."

Certainly it was dramatic, and deeply touching, too. If it encouraged the cult of "gentleman worship," there were those among the critics who thought this not altogether a bad idea. For Leslie's first starring performance, the notices were in agreement with each other. If those for *Cardboard Lover* had looked good, the remarks about Leslie following *Escape* looked as if he had written them himself. In fact, it is doubtful that he could have thought of as many superlatives.

Woollcott began his review with the words: "One of the fine performances of our day in the theatre is contributed by Leslie Howard," and ended: "Now and then this flawless and charming comedian takes time off to remind us all (and re-assure himself perhaps) that he is also an actor equipped to scale the heights. I hear a good deal from time to time about the decay of the art of acting in our day but for my own part I ask nothing finer than the honest, sensitive and beautiful performance which Leslie Howard gave last night on the stage of the Booth Theatre. I have not often seen anything better."

Gilbert Gabriel wrote: "Leslie Howard gives a performance which, as if for nothing else on earth, he seems to have been born . . . he never had a finer part to play nor played it finer." John Anderson called Leslie's playing superb, "the peer of the best performances in town."

Leslie, who had expected fairly good notices, was overwhelmed by the acclaim. He was grateful, doubtful, and a little puzzled. He could scarcely restrain a giggle or two. "The critics must have had a very good dinner," he told Ruth in amusement.

Escape, which had incurred rebukes in England for its doubtful ethics, was accepted simply as an interesting play in New York. No one questioned the moral problem raised by the show of sympathy and help for an escaped prisoner. It was well received by the public and slipped happily into the position of a box-office hit.

The cast was a large one, twenty-eight speaking parts, one or two of which were doubled by the same actor. Frieda Inescort, who played the role of "The Shingled Lady" (a character which sets the period of the play!) got charming notices and was a delight both on and off the stage. Ruth was as fond of her as Leslie was, which says a lot for a pretty girl. The scene in which she appeared was a bedroom in a hotel on the moors. The fugitive is discovered by the lady, hiding under her bed. As was bound to happen with vague Leslie, when the curtain went up one night on the bedroom, he was in his dressing room. Frightful sawing noises were heard off stage, as the carpenter cut a hole in the scenery so that he could crawl under the bed while Miss Inescort bravely shrieked her lines to the audience.

The various hiding places of Matt Denant appealed to Leslie's sense of the ridiculous. He had to wait in a cupboard in the church vestry in the final scene while Austin Trevor puttered about as the vicar getting ready for evening service and singing "Oh for the wings of a dove." Every time Trevor opened the cupboard door, he would find Leslie, making a comic face, asking some absurd question. Poor Trevor went on every night knowing "the wings of a dove" might dry up if he could not control his laughter at the schoolboy in the cupboard. At least it mitigated the boredom of a long run.

It was not going to be very many years before Leslie became violently opposed to long runs, but during *Escape,* despite minor capers to liven the proceedings, he was still happily enjoying the first fruits of success.

The party season was in full flood. The old "60" Club continued to operate, and Ruth was ever to be seen entering swathed in a huge black cloak, under which were concealed several bottles of bootleg whisky. The liquor, obtained after much labor, smacked more often of Brooklyn than Edinburgh, and on one occasion Cornelia Otis Skinner found Leslie unhappily clutching two bottles of an eccentric red hue. Despite their lethal appearance, he generously offered everyone a drink, and, feeling that they all might be dead, or at least blind, in the morning, Miss Skinner gently removed the bottles and shepherded their owner into another room where her husband was dispensing quite genuine Vat 69.

There were larger and more glorious evenings spent at the Herbert Bayard Swopes' vast estate on Long Island. Alex Woollcott, writing from China, where he was staying with a family who owned eight palaces and had two hundred servants, once quipped, "You see, they live just like the Swopes!"

Though the Howards dreamed of a house of their own somewhere in England, they continued to live at 7 East Road, Great Neck, and enjoy the vicarious pleasure of other peoples' opulence.

As Christmas came and the new bright year of 1928 was blown in on all the hooters of New York, plans were being made for a return to London during the summer. Nineteen twenty-seven had been the turning point in Leslie's career: two superb hits and a play of his own produced, if not acclaimed. In a crowded party at midnight on December 31, Ruth found Leslie beside her, holding her hand.

"Happy New Year, Ruthie darling—it should be rather fun!"

8 / Mr. Howard : The American Actor

In the spring the Howards once more packed their belongings and made ready to sail for England. Leslie was to play his successful old friend André Salicel, in *Her Cardboard Lover,* at the Lyric Theatre in London. The part of Simone had been accepted by probably the most famous female star on the London stage at that moment, no other than the great Miss Tallulah Bankhead. The really interesting development for Leslie was that he would produce the play. In May he and Gilbert Miller signed a partnership contract, and the newspapers reported:

"The producer and the actor are in partnership for the production of plays in which Mr. Howard appears and the billing will read: 'Gilbert Miller and Leslie Howard present.' 'Berkeley Square' will be the first play and Henry Miller's according to present plans will be the theatre. Mr. Howard will be in actual charge of the company and will seek to engage players for a more or less permanent organization. It is known that Leslie Howard vastly prefers such a billing as 'Gilbert Miller and Leslie Howard present' to a 'Leslie Howard in . . .' designation. Mr. Howard dislikes the star system. The Miller-Howard contract is an unusual one in this country and is based on that which the producer has with Gerald Du Maurier in London."

146

The Howard family was to sail on May 21 on board the *Carmania*. They had given up the house in Great Neck, not without a gentle nostalgia, for it was the background in which their success had been achieved. It held many happy memories for them; they said good-by and knew that a part of their life had ended. Leslie would no longer mow the lawn or paint the chairs; his time had become too valuable. Still, with great hopes and enthusiasm they set out on the next stage. Ruth wanted a house of her own where, after twelve years of suitcases and trunks, moving around like a gypsy, she could put down her roots and, as she fondly imagined, spend the rest of her life. It was a pretty faint hope for an actor's wife, but was nurtured all the more strongly because it seemed unobtainable. Leslie, too, wanted his house in the English countryside.

For the last few days before sailing, the Howards moved into the Algonquin Hotel. Leslie was exhausted, but no one paid too much attention; Leslie was always exhausted and was inclined to grow more so if he was encouraged. On the last day, while Ruth and Miss Goss labeled trunks and dashed in and out collecting tickets and passports, Leslie wandered around the apartment in his dressing gown continually prodding his abdomen, refusing all food—even his carefully grilled lamb chops, plain spinach, and nice, safe baked potato. Ruth cast a glance at him occasionally, privately concluded "Leslie is at it again," and hurried on to the next job. At six o'clock, after the children were dispatched to the ship with Miss Goss and all the luggage, Ruth turned her attention to her husband. Eight hours of prodding his stomach had now made it very sore, and, waving aside Ruth's friendly offer of either bicarbonate or an enema, he dramatically announced his diagnosis —acute appendicitis. Absolute chaos then ensued. The doctor was summoned, garbled messages were sent to Miss Goss, friends offered advice, decision departed. Miss Goss on the *Carmania* did not know whether to rush the children from their beds, grab the luggage, and disembark or to sail, with

Leslie obviously lying near death in a hospital. Naturally, no one had thought to explain to her the nature of his sudden illness. The ship was due to leave at midnight, and the hours went past with no information forthcoming.

Meanwhile, the doctor had started prodding Leslie's bruised inside and was rewarded with wonderful yelps and groans. At ten o'clock, Ruth was gravely informed that Leslie could not sail. She immediately said that she would stay and the children could go on. But no—Leslie raised a feeble hand—she must go with her children, he would stay alone. It took some time to persuade her, but finally an old friend, Raymond Hahn, who was traveling with them, suggested that he would stay behind and bring Leslie over when he was fit to travel. Ruth was bundled into a taxi and arrived on board to calm the distraught Miss Goss just before the last gangway went up.

The spare time afforded by a sea voyage did nothing to calm Ruth's mind, and her worry over Leslie turned to dark suspicion when a cable appeared the next day saying he was quite all right again. Marriage to an actor of astonishing attraction to women had made Ruth wary of such last-minute changes. Perhaps this "attack" was intentional. After all, some female had telephoned the day before they sailed. "Just an idiotic fan," according to Leslie, but was she? When the *Carmania* was pulled into her berth at Southampton, Ruth was all but convinced that monkey business was afoot. Fortunately, another cable awaited her: Leslie had sailed three days later on the *Majestic*. A prey not to women but to his old friend hypochondria, he arrived in England looking very fit and rather sheepish.

Ruth and the children were settled for the moment at the new Stainer house in Onslow Square. A typical London house, tall and thin, five floors and a basement, it contained enough space to provide Dorice wth ballrooms and ballet rooms and still take in the Howard family. Dorice had a flourishing business. Except for her old teacher Madam Vacani, Dorice ran the most successful and chic dancing school in London. All day, students trooped up and down the white front steps, opening and closing the red front door of 39, Onslow Square. Every afternoon superior nannies shepherded their children upstairs to the ballroom. There Doodie was taken by Miss Goss to enjoy the first of many such classes watched by a circle of nannies on gold chairs. In a few days, she, too, owned silver dancing slippers and a cashmere shawl like a spider's web and could compete with the small daughters of English society. Leslie often came to the dancing classes, for he adored watching the rows of solemn little creatures holding out their skirts and pointing their toes. He hardly caused a ripple among the nannies, for who in Londen knew this quiet young man from America?

Soon the city life was found to be too restraining. Leslie heard of something for rent in the country, and within a few weeks the family moved to an old house at Godstone in Surrey. There every few days the family piled into the glorious-looking red touring car that Leslie had brought from America and set off to survey the surrounding country in the hope of discovering a house for themselves. Large picnic lunches were packed, and Ruth and Miss Goss spent hours in the kitchen preparing the feasts while Leslie and the children ran about among the flowers in the sunshine. Leslie had his womenfolk very well trained.

After a few weeks at Godstone, the children "must get some sea air." So the center of operations was moved to Brighton and another rented house. There the air may have been invigorating but the atmosphere was not. Occasional days paddling in the water, many brisk walks along "the front" in an even brisker wind, and crowds of other holiday-makers. Luckily, the house had a sheltered and enclosed garden with large areas of fruit bushes and a grass court for tennis. The children scrambled under the fruit nets eating warm furry gooseberries, while their elders tried more graceful action at the tennis net. Leslie was not a player of any brilliance; he had a steady forehand, but was inclined to idleness, and never ran for anything.

"Yours," he would say with a beguiling smile, while Ruth pounded about getting very red and hot and reaching for shots clearly in his court.

Leslie went up to London each day and worked on the casting of *Cardboard Lover*. Tallulah Bankhead was an autocrat with ability, which was a change from some female stars. She liked, nay demanded, that her leading man be interested in more than her performance, regardless of whether or not she was interested in him. Heaven knows, she received more fanatical public adoration than anyone else on the London stage, and must, therefore, have taken for granted that any man working with her would feel the same as the gallery. Leslie was fond of her, and amused, in his withdrawn way, but the baritone voice joined to the sweeping, forceful manner were not his idea of "womanliness" in its most desirable form. Ruth was constantly shocked—quite often into laughter, for Miss Bankhead was witty, if alarming. But Ruth's standards of behavior would always reflect what Leslie had called her "quiet English county town background," and she was suspicious of this beautiful and voluptuous object who treated everyone with a careless affection and wandered in and out of Leslie's dressing room as though it were her own. Vigilance would obviously be necessary!

Before the play began serious rehearsal, Leslie drove his family to the West Country, touring around Devon and Cornwall. Much like any other family on holiday, they bought hideous ashtrays made from Cornish rock, ate their picnics by the sea or cramped in the leaky car in a rainstorm, stayed at good and bad hotels. There was always laughter—at Ruth, who enjoyed it, for her sweeping statements on every subject; at Leslie for his eating habits and continual health phobia. He placed much faith in bottled waters of all descriptions, somehow convinced that local water was prey to the lurking germs of typhoid and dysentery. It was difficult in remote inns to find these rather recherché drinks. On one occasion when he sent for Vichy water, the family was convulsed over the reply. "I'm sorry, we 'ave no bitchy water" became a Howard "local joke" and was good for at least a weak giggle.

In what must have been the greatest house-renting orgy of their lives, the end of the motor trip found the family in another country house, this time at Bramley in Surrey. It was blessed with that most English of pleasures, a walled garden. Pink and crumbling brick surrounded a happy confusion of summer flowers, and supported espaliered fruit trees. A wrought-iron gate showed the passer-by a small section of the house, gentle and reposed in sixteenth-century memories. A fine house for a family.

On August 21, 1928, *Her Cardboard Lover* began its tempestuous run in an atmosphere of wild excitement. Leslie had not experienced crowds or traffic jams of this size even in New York. He had certainly never seen mobs of mesmerized women who collected outside the theater for thirty hours before the curtain went up. The Tallulahbaloo, as this strange malady was called in London, presented a weird study in group psychology. Charles Morgan called it collective hysteria bordering on madness, and wrote, for the New York *Times:*

". . . the premieres which bring Miss Bankhead to the stage breed a peculiar ecstasy in a very odd crowd of people. . . . Round the door a mob is clustered, principally composed of nervous excited women. What they are staring at and why they are there it is hard to tell. Ordinarily, these loiterers outside theatres are there engaged in the curious occupation of watching the arrival of the audience . . . but the crowd outside the Lyric Theatre seemed not to be very much interested in the motor cars or their occupants. They were staring at the theatre itself, at the bricks and mortar, I suppose under the shelter of which Miss Bankhead was to appear. And they were uttering little breathless, squeaking ejaculations, for all the world like mice in a bag."

By the time the curtain went up, these breathless squeaks had become raucous screams. Leslie received a round of applause, but as soon as one hypnotized young woman crowed "Tallulah is coming," the gallery viewers were in danger of falling over the balustrade. A middle-aged woman took up the attitude of a quarterback about to make a forward pass, younger ones poised for the spring, and onto the stage came the object of their flaming passion. To a man, the gallery leaped upon its feet.

"Marvelous," they screamed. "Ravishing, exquisite, Tallulah you're wonderful," and so far not a word had been spoken by Miss Bankhead! The play was a trial by fire. Leslie felt like nothing so much as a Christian thrown to the lions. Every line that Tallulah uttered was greeted with such approbation that it might have been a clear-cut diamond of purest comedy. At the end of the performance, a reported two thousand strong, the worshipers fell upon the stage door. Leslie remained cowering in his dressing room. Nothing would persuade him to put a foot outside the theater until Miss Bankhead and her following went elsewhere. No one among that number was interested in him anyway.

The notices next day reflected the critics' annoyance over the hysteria in the cheaper seats, and some were lukewarm about the play, but on the whole the reviews were favorable. Leslie's performance was given whatever space was left after these gentlemen had expressed their disgust at adulation, their appreciation of Tallulah, and their comments on the plot. But even if few, they were good words.

Hannen Swaffer wrote: "Leslie Howard was wonderful. His comedy is exquisite. In spite of Miss Bankhead's cleverness, it was Howard's evening."

And Charles Morgan thanked him for preserving "a little

island of true comedy in the midst of so boisterous an ocean of farce and cheap emotionalism. . . . You realise very soon that his is the one figure on the stage that is genuinely worth watching."

The *Evening News* remarked: "Good as her [Miss Bankhead's] performance was, the triumph of the evening was won by Mr. Leslie Howard. . . . This was the most skilful piece of comic acting seen for a long time."

And the *Daily Express* said: ". . . it was Leslie Howard's evening. I now understand how this young Englishman, who left London about two years ago, after the failure of Lord Lathom's play . . . should make himself in 'Her Cardboard Lover' a Broadway star overnight."

Leslie was happy about his reviews. He cared not at all that the stage-door crowds brushed him aside in the stampede to get at Tallulah. He rather preferred it that way. He had had his praise, and he now began to think of and plan for something else.

John Balderston was in London at this time; a shy, gentle, and intelligent man, he was the London correspondent of the New York *World*. He was a deeply rooted American, his great-great-grandmother had been Betsy Ross. Seven years in England had given him a keen understanding of the British character, too. He was a journalist and a historian. His special interest was the eighteenth century, from which he had assembled a remarkable collection of newspapers. In the early 1920's, he began a play based on an unfinished story by Henry James called "A Sense of the Past." This play, *Berkeley Square,* had been presented in London and had come into the hands of Alexander Woollcott. Leslie had heard about it from Woollcott. "You should play it, Leslie, it's a part that might have been made for you."

Leslie had become most interested, but Jed Harris, the impresario, had the American rights, and he was not as convinced as Woollcott that Howard was the man. Time passed, and Leslie appeared in *Escape*. Mr. Harris dropped into his dressing room one night, and with a doubtful enthusiasm remarked, "You were not bad, not bad at all. Come and see me sometime. Good night."

"What about 'Berkeley Square'"? yelled Leslie as the producer disappeared through the door.

Jed Harris's thin bearded face reappeared. "What about it?" he asked coldly.

"What about my playing in it?"

"Why not?" was the enigmatic answer.

Nothing more happened for weeks, and then Leslie received a message: "Please see Mr. Harris at his office." When Leslie arrived for the interview, Mr. Harris was in Florida, but he had left behind a proposition: he wanted Leslie for a repertory company he was thinking of forming—"Just like the Moscow Arts Theatre" explained Harris's manager. "You will have the opportunity of playing five great plays in one season."

"But," replied Leslie, staggering under the blow, "I don't want to. You see I really don't like being an actor, even quite mildly, let alone as violently as all that."

The only reason for recording this meeting is because then, at last, Leslie laid his hands upon the script of *Berkeley Square*.

"I wouldn't bother with it if I were you—it's no good," was the manager's parting shot.

As soon as Leslie read the play, he got one of his hunches. He decided he could not rest until he played the part. But how? Jed Harris clearly would not sell it to him, or even to Gilbert Miller.

Leslie tried to forget about *Berkeley Square*. In this he was not successful. "That play is burning holes in my brain," he groaned to Ruth. Practical as ever, she suggested a cable to John Balderston. This produced nothing except another cable telling Leslie to see Jed Harris. That meteoric name began to haunt him until he cursed it. In desperation, Leslie sent another cable, this time to his senior partner, Gilbert Miller, who was then in London. There seemed little hope, but it was worth a try. Leslie was rewarded, astonished, and enchanted by the reply.

"Dear Partner, have bought 'Berkeley Square.' Good luck, but don't blame me. Gilbert."

And so it was by those devious means that Leslie in 1928 was preparing the production of the play. He and Ruth spent hours with John and Marion Balderston, discussing and re-writing. Every night after *Her Cardboard Lover,* the Howards stopped at the Balderstons' Georgian house in Trevor Square, and the two men worked together, refreshed by beer and large amounts of Stilton cheese. This diet, so late at night, gave Leslie fearsome "heart attacks," but his concentration on the play was such that he returned again and again to the same fare. A good ripe Stilton and a bottle of beer are *very* condu-cive to nocturnal thought. The remainder of 1928 was occupied by this pleasant endeavor.

Christmas was a family gathering at 39, Onslow Square. Happy in their first united celebration, the various members peered at Leslie's camera—a group of rapt smiles crowned by incredible paper hats. All Leslie's relations were together with the exception of Jimmy, once more planting tea or in some other way adorning the British colonies. Lilie missed him, but Frank Stainer was greatly relieved to have this problem out of his life. Leslie's success, surprising though it had been, was more to his taste, even if it was encouraging foolish ideas in Irene and Arthur. Poor Frank Stainer, diligent and serious, be-lieving implicitly in the holy state of big business, was now troubled by two more would-be actors.

Leslie was asked by his mother to help Arthur. "Poor dar-ling, he hates the office." And Leslie, though for once he agreed with his father, could not disappoint his mother. On a piece of paper thrust under his nose, he wrote to Ackerman May, the agent who had given him his first job.

Arthur rushed off, sure that these magic words from his

famous brother would produce immediate results. But dear, vague Leslie, who never kept up with the times, had sent him to see a man who had been dead for five years!

Leslie was never greatly helpful to his aspiring young brother and sister; he was kind and interested, but quite elusive. It puzzled him that anyone should *want* to act. Ruth stated flatly that it was his fault they idolized him and he should not encourage them. "If you were a carpenter, I suppose they'd sit around sawing wood."

Leslie simply smiled, agreed with no one, and went about his business. A brief visit to Vienna and Budapest with Gilbert Miller, a short holiday at Cap Ferrat with Ruth and Doodie, and then rehearsals for *Berkeley Square* began.

9/ "Berkeley Square"

"Any greengrocer will tell you peaches should not be handled overmuch. 'Berkeley Square' when done at the St. Martin's a year or so ago was a peach of a play."

Thus said the *Sunday Graphic* after the play opened in March 1929, and most of the critics felt the new production had lost some of its earlier bloom. They had a fine time drawing comparisons. After *Her Cardboard Lover,* where they had been uniformly polite to Leslie, many returned to their usual condescension. It seemed almost as though they resented Broadway for its acclaim of Leslie; no Americans were going to influence their judgment of a fellow countryman.

"He does not wear his clothes well or keep his feet at the right angle. He slurs his words modernly but in these very things he is possibly truer to the part of the young American, and he is sincere and obviously understands."

"Mr. Leslie Howard is not the answer to a maiden's prayer."

"Mr. Leslie Howard was far too matter of fact . . . he was 20th Century throughout . . . how undesirable it is to allow the leading actor to be the producer."

The play was elegantly staged. Sir Edwin Lutyens designed the sets, Marion Balderston supervised all the costumes, and much of the Queen Anne furniture belonged to her. Every effort was made to re-create the Berkeley Square house of 1784, the haunting beauty of powder and satins. In this setting the young American from 1928 steps back into the past, changes places with his ancestor and namesake and loves a girl, Helen Pettigrew, already dust in her grave. A strange, pathetic meeting of two spirits, whose love can never be consummated on this earth. Puzzled and despised in the eighteenth century, feared as a devil for his knowledge of what is to come, Peter Standish must return to 1928 to read the epitaph of the woman he loves, and know the early Peter Standish married her sister. For the Peter of the twentieth century there can be no marriage. He is linked indissolubly to the past; his soul and his love are with the lovely Helen—Helen who died a spinster at the age of twenty-three, one hundred and forty years before.

This strange, nostalgic theme was not well suited to the English love of logic. That time is like a winding river and we may go back to look again on the bends we have passed seemed too fanciful for them. Yet even the most scornful critic was touched by the magic; no one condemned the play, no matter how incomprehensible he found it. Jean Forbes-Robertson, as Helen, received her share of applause, as did Valerie Taylor, as Kate Pettigrew, and Marie Lohr, in a brilliant characterization of Georgianna, Duchess of Devonshire.

Leslie was not content with his own performance. This, perhaps, is the price the audience on a first night must pay for an actor-producer, in Leslie's case one still absorbing a new job. One scene, in particular, where Peter Standish reaches the edge of mental collapse, did not ring true to Leslie for many days. He was delighted with a letter from a doctor which John Balderston forwarded to him at the end of March.

"During the war I had to deal at times with mentally afflicted men, and I can assure you Mr. Howard's work was so real that it brought back some of the old scenes and made me feel thoroughly sad."

Leslie, who kept few clippings and almost no letters, stuck this into a scrapbook.

Throughout the London season, Leslie pressed for a New York run of *Berkeley Square*. Gilbert Miller was not sure that America, the great land of practical realists, would appreciate the gently rustling ghosts of this English square. Also, at this moment he had another play that he wanted Leslie to be in. A comedy (Leslie made a face at this), a harlequinade of life below and above stairs called *By Candle-light,* adapted by Wodehouse from the play by Siegfried Geyer. It was to be the first dramatic role for Gertrude Lawrence, who had already made a name and a special place for herself in musical comedy. Gilbert Miller was starring her, and wanted a strong supporting cast. Leslie was not very pleased, in fact, he was rather ungracious, but if by doing this play, *Berkeley Square* would be produced in November, he was prepared to martyr himself. It was agreed to rehearse and open *By Candle-light* in England, though not in London.

In the meantime, spring and summer had touched the garden at Bramley, and Leslie was once more promoting sea air. But not at Brighton, never again at Brighton, surrounded by bricks and cement and hosts of other seaside bathers. This time they would go to Cornwall, to Mullion Cove, and live on a farm by the sea, remote and unhurried.

Charming the farm was, though not prepossessing, resembling a red-and-white railway carriage. It had a lovely view, oil lamps, and a garden full of honeysuckle and brambles. Mushrooms sprang up on the soft green turf, liberally encouraged by the cows that Ruth chased from the garden every morning before breakfast. Leslie used to laugh with glee at this sight of Ruth, her dressing gown clutched about her plump figure, bedroom slippers slapping the ground, and a newspaper slapping the behinds of the disinterested cows. He never went out to help her, but he encouraged in a friendly manner while he ate his boiled egg and giggled with Doodie.

The children had a magnificent summer, and, as usual, they were the important ones. Winkie, who had finally been sent to boarding school in the autumn of 1928, was relishing his first long holiday, and Leslie relished it, too. His small son had grown tall and slimmer than ever, very English, and at first almost tediously polite to his "Mater," though the appellation "Pater" was more than even he could produce for the whimsical Leslie.

The summer days, bright and fresh with adventure, slid together like a handful of colored thread, all different and yet all the same, joined by peaceful pleasure and comfortable laziness. Mullion Cove, and the little village of Mullion, remained unexploited. No bus loads of tourists had discovered its quiet cobbled streets; no garish cafés studded the hillsides. These were to come, but in 1929 Mullion still belonged to the dark, taciturn Cornishmen who hung their fishing nets beside the sea.

Leslie dreaded the moment when he must go back to work. He resented the theater that pulled him away from his children and the sunshine and Ruthie. He spoke bitterly against "this most embarrassing of occupations." But if it had not been the theater, it would have been the office or the factory. He suffered, as all but the most ambitious do, from that back-to-school feeling after a holiday. When life can be so charming, why must one be forced to work for a living?

From the train that took him away to London, he wrote:

"Darling—I am most miserable—I did so hate leaving you. I need you all so much. I am quite lost without you. I hate other people. I shall be most disagreeable with them all to-day because I'll feel they have deprived me of my family which is infinitely more entertaining than any society I have met. You must try and come to Manchester because if I had you I could manage without the children.

"This is almost like a love letter I regret to say—a thing no gentleman would ever do to his own wife. God bless you all, my darling. Leslie and Daddy."

Ruth, often torn asunder by his casual acceptance of marriage and of herself, held this letter close—carried it with her until it yellowed and fell apart. This was her Leslie—the one that only she knew—gentle, loving, and deeply dependent. He might change in a day, and indeed he could, becoming interested in the people he met, concentrating on his work, friendly, self-possessed, detached. But underneath, there would be these quick flashes of love and his need for her.

Leslie may have been "disagreeable all day" when he left Mullion, but the *Candle-light* company was far too pleasant for continued annoyance. First, there was Gertrude Lawrence, cheeky as a sparrow, and full of natural wit, unpretentious and human and a Londoner like himself. Then, Reginald Owen, another Englishman, dry, noncommittal, and very, very funny. Added to this, it was an easy, undemanding part, and Reggie Owen and Leslie clowned through their work as master and servant with no effort and lots of merriment.

For a short time, the Howards were reunited when the play tried out at Southampton. The daylight hours were spent exploring the Solent, that lovely stretch of water bounded by the green coast of Hampshire and the even greener Isle of Wight. Such are the perquisites of fame that a naval launch took them all to the Isle of Wight to see the airplane that was to win the Schneider Trophy for Great Britain. A seaplane of beautiful lines, it was being polished on that windy day by a man in dirty overalls—a man with an arresting face, quiet, withdrawn, and politely uninterested. Leslie looked at him again, caught by the face, suddenly familiar.

"Is that . . . ?"

"Yes, you're right. Aircraftman Shaw—the extraordinary Lawrence of Arabia" came the soft reply from Leslie's host of the day.

"So that's Lawrence . . . what a strange fellow he is—after what his life has been, to spend his days polishing an airplane . . . odd."

And while Wink and Doodie investigated the plane, Leslie stood aside and watched T. E. Lawrence . . . watched and felt an idea begin to stir and grow in his mind. What a story there was in the life of this man, hidden now as Aircraftman Shaw. Lawrence the friend of the Arabs, Lawrence a figure to be reckoned with so little time before in the dark mysteries of the Middle East—dusting an aircraft.

As they left that day, Leslie glanced behind at the Schneider Trophy winner and its unlikely keeper.

"One day," he thought, "I shall make a film about him."

Fate is a perverse partner to our lives. It was about the airplane that Leslie would make a film—and never about Lawrence.

Leslie sailed for New York on the *Saxonia,* with Reggie Owen for a roommate and deepest gloom for his other companion.

"I was so miserable at going. It is dreadful. It is rainy and wretched up here. . . ." The mixture as before, depression and homesickness in equal parts, in fact, Leslie in his usual form. The crossing was interminable—Liverpool, Queenstown, Galway; "this is an absurd voyage . . . always thinking of you all and wondering why I am doing this at all when thousands of people lead happy lives in England."

He was infinitely more unhappy when the autumn gales slashed across the ship. "For the first time on the Atlantic I really felt ill. She doesn't seem to be a very steady ship, and Friday night was awful—like a bad night on the Channel. I got into bed with the assistance of Reggie and sal volatile."

After the darkness must come the dawn, and two days later he was gay again. ". . . am now in what is known as 'rude health' feeling very fit, rising at eight daily, doing exercises with Reggie in pyjamas on the top deck and eating enormously."

But let no one imagine this sunny disposition was there to stay. By the next morning he was writing:

"I am well in body but still rather sick in spirit. I dread landing in 'God's Own Country' and long for 'the little isle set in the silver sea' and my little English family. The principal consolation being that it is for them that I do it, so that we may eventually shut ourselves up in our small castle in Sussex or Surrey where Wink and I may indulge in the subtle art of literary endeavour to the admiration (I hope) of our women-folk."

Reggie Owen and Leslie actually got a great deal of amusement out of the voyage, Leslie's schoolboy naughtiness rising to meet the humor of his companion.

"Hordes of Roman Catholic priests came on in Ireland, much to Reggie's disgust. He is a violent anti-papist and goes about shouting 'To Hell with the Pope' in a strong brogue. They hold masses all over the place so I felt constrained to attend the Church of England service on Sunday with the rest of the heretics."

The seemingly endless trip was over after ten days in which Leslie had become attached to the ship. "It seemed to be a connection with you all. . . . I have felt very well but to-day feel rotten and depressed on account, I suppose, of the imminence of the Statue of Liberty."

Once more Leslie stepped ashore onto American soil. His burst of anger against that great republic was a passing thing. Leslie occasionally gave way to irrational, unconsidered rage —it was a weakness which he covered quickly. He admired Americans, he was grateful to the New York audiences, he liked to think himself as partly American. When he was in England he often longed for a sight of the New York sky line, and fought against the inborn caution and conservatism of the British. But at heart he was irretrievably tied to the land which had fathered him but refused to recognize him. This was the little piece of grit he had lodged inside, the hurt that often made him fail to understand himself.

Now he was back in the United States, back in its greatest city, and the vitality of that city reacted on him as it always did. Stimulated and excited, convinced again that in America all things were possible, he forgot his nostalgia. Walking briskly through Central Park, rythmically breathing, he positively enjoyed the clear air, sharpened with the coming of the fall. The trees were turning, vivid and gay, so much more intense in their coloring than English trees. Everything about New York was intense, thought Leslie as he went along, brighter and harder than anywhere else, faster and quite unassailable in its progress. Indeed, anything *could* happen here.

Rehearsals took his attention, and the huge city drummed about him, prosperous and wrapped in its own importance, grinding on, oblivious, to the abyss.

10 / Wall Street by Candlelight

The play opened at the Empire Theatre toward the end of September 1929, a most inauspicious moment in American financial history. The title was shortened to *Candle-Light* in keeping with the current fashion for brief, arresting names. There would come a day when playwrights competed to see how many words they could get on a marquee, but in 1929 even the little preposition "by" was felt to be too much reading for the theatergoing public of New York.

The play flickered with charm, possessing a very bright first act and some amusing dialogue by P. G. Wodehouse, the plastic surgeon of the theater, who had adapted this Viennese bit of nonsense.

Leslie and Reggie Owen collected the lion's share of the notices, for they enjoyed that same share of the hilarious opening act. John Mason Brown in the *Evening Post* applauded them for "the most adroit and sauve comedy this town has had the chance of laughing at in many seasons. Yes, it was their evening and they walked away with it."

Other critics called Owen's part "priceless" and Leslie's "as amusing and expressive a bit of pantomime as one ever sees in the theatre." They were both thought to be "irresistibly funny."

Leslie was rehearsing *Berkeley Square* again within days of these notices. Though he had agreed to stay with *Candle-Light* for the first few weeks of its run, it lasted very little longer and was snuffed out by a mighty, chilling wind blowing between the tall buildings on Wall Street.

On October 24, the extraordinary spiraling boom on the stock exchange, in which over a million Americans had speculated, started to collapse. It took only a small leak to crack the marginal walls—frenzied selling began, and, at the end of the first day, thirteen million shares had been sold. Panic took over; day after day the awful drop went on. Small attention was given the eminent bankers who assembled in the stately offices of J. P. Morgan and assured the terrified investors that "business is fundamentally sound." Whose business was sound? Not the shaking men who raced home from Europe, where they had spent their paper profits; not the company clerks who had speculated with company funds. They could only sell anything and everything, sound shares with the trash, it all had to go in a hopeless attempt to cover the daily losses.

Naturally, Gilbert Miller was not encouraging about the future of *Berkeley Square*. Always an uncertain choice for America, how much more uncertain now? But Leslie had developed a very strong obstinate streak. *Berkeley Square* it must be—or nothing else—and they went to New Haven for the tryout. The houses were marvelous, for by chance they opened on the weekend of the Yale-Harvard football game. The performances sold out, and to audiences who were rapt in attention and rapturous in applause.

"See?" said Leslie.

"All right," said Gilbert. "A lot of intellectuals from Harvard and Yale—they're not an ordinary audience. Wait until Washington."

But the story was the same. Perhaps Washington, with its own eighteenth-century history could easily appreciate this wisp of English fantasy. On the last night, curtain calls went on and on; no one could bear to leave the atmosphere the play had created. Finally, the job of dismantling could be delayed no longer, the scenery must go to New York. The curtain went up as the last people collected coats and drifted from the theater. One tiny old lady turned to look at the stage, and her face became drawn with sorrow.

"Oh! how sad. They're taking it all away."

"Don't look," comforted her husband, leading her out. "Just remember it as it was."

Such was the mood and the magic of *Berkeley Square.*

The New York first night was on November 4, 1929, only a few days after the stock market had taken another sickening lurch and slipped again into what seemed a bottomless drop. Pathetic suicides became daily reading in the papers; out of the windows of the huge buildings that were the pride of New York, hopeless souls escaped from the weight of scandal they could not support; in quiet brownstone mansions, once rich and important men sat alone and shot themselves. It was gruesome and frightening. Leslie knew some of these people. He had been in their houses and had envied them the security of their lives based on something more solid than the acting profession.

It was a grim moment to try to fill a theater, yet the house was sold out for the opening. Never for a second did the attention of this audience wander; everyone seemed engrossed and lifted from the cares of the chaotic world around them. "Berkeley Square—I thought it would look like this," said Leslie, the young American seeing the home of his ancestors for the first time. And the American audience went with him into the past, away from the hateful present. There were twenty-five curtain calls before Leslie stepped forward to make his speech. The play was a hit.

"Something of beauty breaks through even the stock market news," headlined Burns Mantle in the *Daily News,* and he went on to talk of the sounds of Broadway, now interrupted by the louder and more distracting sounds of Wall Street. He said it was no longer easy to concentrate on the drama, and so to him it was a relief "that this play and this player should move into the Broadway scene and offer such fantastical yet curiously holding drama as this. How pleasant a theatre adventure it is to feel that it is not necessary actually to believe anything or anybody. Merely to relax and accept this newer romance . . . What is reality? Only a seeming." Of Leslie, he wrote: "An actor with the soul of a poet is a rare joy in a play that was born in the soul of a poet adventuring in the theatre."

Robert Garland reported in the *World-Telegram:* ". . . there is nothing to do but remove your critical hat in the presence of so magnificent a play and so magnificent a performance as the performance of Mr. Leslie Howard. In 'Escape' I pointed to Mr. Howard as the foremost young actor on the English speaking stage. In 'Berkeley Square' I point to Mr. Howard as the foremost young actor on the English speaking stage."

And Heywood Broun said in the *Telegram:* " 'Berkeley Square' has the advantage of dealing with a transcendental theme, and so the spectator doesn't so much forget the price of Nevada Consolidated Copper as gain a mood in which the money doesn't seem to matter. . . . I am only speaking in the mildest manner when I say that 'Berkeley Square' is easily the finest play now to be seen in New York . . . and, among other things, the play contains the finest acting performance of the season, which is given by Leslie Howard."

Ruth, Doodie, and Miss Goss were comfortably installed in an apartment at 14 East 60th Street, and the first of a series of feeble gestures was being made to Doodie's education. A young woman in the *Berkeley Square* company, titian-haired Henry Main, came daily to attempt the assault on the well-guarded citadel of the five-year-old mind. Leslie felt this was quite enough, for he had decided (along with every other parent) that his daughter had a brain far above ordinary mortals.

Doodie, already bordering on a frightening precocity, was introduced to the drama this year. Leslie took her to *Bitter Sweet,* the enchanting Noel Coward musical with Evelyn Laye, and, perhaps a little unsuitably, to R. C. Sherriff's *Journey's End.* Of course, she saw his own play, where she watched the curtain rise to reveal her aunt Irene lighting the candles. Leslie had brought his youngest sister to New York for the small part of the maid, and Doodie dearly loved this gay, amusing, easy-going aunt.

Leslie took his continuing success gently. He was frightfully embarrassed by the superlatives poured onto his head by over-anxious hostesses and a little furtive when pursued at parties by the half-dazed females who worshiped at his pedestal.

"What a lot of silly nonsense," he muttered. "And what am I supposed to answer when some idiotic woman simpers: 'I think you're the most marvelous man'?"

"Get 'em to ask me," replied Ruth grimly. "I'll tell them all statues have feet of clay."

"Oh, Ruth. How horrid you are—don't you think I'm marvelous?"

"Marvelous—certainly not," lied Ruth when the teasing began, and he would giggle and play her like a trout, watching her rise to each ridiculous fly that he laid before her, until she gave in and laughed with him.

There were many parties for Leslie and Ruth to go to, more to be avoided, and a widening circle of friends—the Lawrence Tibbetts, he the opera star and spectacular lead of *The Rogues Song* on Broadway; Dennis King, singing in *The Desert Song,* their old friend Marc Connelly, and, of course, Margalo Gilmore, playing with Leslie again in *Berkeley Square.* It was fun but exhausting, the more so because Leslie was trying to find time to finish the adaptation of a German play by Hans Chlumberg that he had thought amusing and was expecting to direct. Somehow, with all the distractions, of which Doodie was one of the worst, this play, *Out of a Blue Sky,* finally reached casting and rehearsal as *Berkeley Square* passed its one-hundredth performance.

The cast of *Out of a Blue Sky* was a stellar one: Warren William, Reginald Owen, Gregory Ratoff, Tammany Young, and Eleanor Terry, and there were two applicants for a smaller part whose names would one day be world famous: William Gargan and Clark Gable. During the auditions, Leslie and his stage manager, George Fogel, sat together, and, as Gable read the part, Fogel groaned gently.

"I know, I know," said Leslie.

The dark young man labored on. Finally, Fogel could stand it no longer. "Leslie, he won't do. His ears are too big, his collar doesn't sit properly . . . he's got no charm."

The role that the unfortunate Mr. Gable was trying to secure was that of a German play reader—and what, in all that was sensible, was a German play reader? The young North Americans who auditioned had never before met this odd bird. William Gargan, an Irish Catholic boy from Brooklyn, who, to his own amazement, landed the part, had no more idea than the rest. He read the lines to the director, and the director said, "Yes, yes, that's very nice," and dashed away to play *Berkeley Square.* There never seemed to be time to discuss anything, and the most he ever got out of Leslie was a three-dollar loan one day.

A large part of the rehearsals were taken up by the excitable arguments of Gregory Ratoff. Leslie listened politely to these outbursts; he was a patient man, and most fond of this early Russian dynamo. He recognized, too, the futility of losing his temper, for on one occasion he had advanced to the footlights and shouted, "If you yell at me again, Gregory, you can bloody well get yourself another director."

Ratoff had nearly burst into tears. "I loff you, Leslie, I loff you. I do not mean to be rude, I loff you."

"Oh, that's all right, Gregory, that's all right."

"No, no, it is not! I loff you, I loff you."

"Yes, yes, of course, of course—it's quite all right, old boy."

In great agitation and embarrassment, Leslie sat down again, and within three minutes endured the screams of fury once more.

"What," he asked George Fogel, "can I do?"

Rehearsals were, therefore, somewhat disjointed, and most of the cast remained unenlightened about the meaning of anything. The tryouts and opening night of *Out of a Blue Sky* were undertaken without its director. *Berkeley Square* could not spare him, and the best he could do was watch a special matinee performance.

No one seemed to like the play. "Perfectly worthless trash" was the bitterest comment, and yet the idea had amusing possibilities. On entering the theater, the audience was supposed to expect *Camille,* only to find that no one had turned up for the performance. The curtain went up on a bare stage, with the Russian director hurling abuse at the management. The young play reader walks up and suggests that the audience provide actors and produce their own play. The complications grow when it is discovered that these people, who have been selected at random from the audience, have a previous and rather unfortunate knowledge of each other. Leslie had seen something new and original in this play, and perhaps it was a little ahead of current taste. He felt that everyone missed the point, just as they had with *Murray Hill.* Whatever his view, the play closed and lost a certain amount of money for its backers. One of these, a rather sinister gentleman, had sat through every rehearsal frozen-faced and silent with a most unnerving bulge beneath his left arm.

"Is it true," Leslie asked him one day, "that you know the underworld?"

"Know it"—was the reply—"I rule it," and this fearsome creature flipped open his coat to confirm everyone's worst suspicions about the bulge—a wicked black revolver.

"Oh, my dear," said Leslie in horror, and was not really sorry when the play closed. Even the Shuberts were more desirable than this!

Berkeley Square seemed tirelessly popular. Leslie, of course, was bored, and even more fed up with the requests for benefit performances which the company was asked to put on. A benefit, or charity show, at that time had to be short, amusing, and written to include as many of the cast as possible. Leslie, under pressure, wrote a ridiculous piece called *The New Morality,* proving that the wicked upper classes had become solid, dull, and respectable and the workers were now vice-ridden profligates. He played, in this idiotic affair, first a ponderous banker and then a philandering iceman. *The New Morality* was so successful that it became their standard benefit performance, Leslie's iceman with the Anglo-Bronx accent being the high spot.

As the New York run of *Berkeley Square* came nearer its end, talk started about a tour, but nothing and no one could persuade Leslie to go on uttering the same lines any longer. He wanted England again, and in a sudden burst of homesickness had cabled his agents in London to buy one of the houses he had seen the summer before. His recollection of the chosen house was very hazy, but, surrounded by the steel and cement of New York, he saw it as a green and flowery heaven, old and changeless, calm and restoring. As he was to find to his cost, it was not the most intelligent way to buy a house, but at that moment in the spring days of 1930, he owned it and naturally was consumed with anxiety to live in it.

This was not to be immediately possible, for suddenly the motion-picture industry became aware of Leslie's existence. It had all started by a chance question of Stage Manager Fogel's.

"Why are you not in the movies, Leslie?"

"Very simple, old chap. I've never been asked." And the subject lapsed. Leslie forgot about it, but Fogel began to make a few inquiries. The answer to these came back quickly: certainly Howard was a good idea for films, but Louis B. Mayer had him under contract. Even George Fogel, who knew Leslie and his vagueness better than most, found it hard to believe that he could sign a contract and not remember. Leslie, irritatingly, gave small attention to the subject. The cinema, which had obsessed him ten years before, no longer seemed to interest him and he took a rather jaundiced view of most of the Hollywood offerings.

So it was that George Fogel went alone to see the great mogul Mr. Louis B. Mayer, and to discover what sort of contract Leslie could have signed. The document was produced, and George bent his head over it to see that the name was Howard, all right, but Sidney Howard. Mayer had never heard of Leslie Howard, Hollywood being a long way by carrier pigeon from New York. But there were others in that golden metropolis who had been advised about this "young" Englishman with the unexplainable charm, and suddenly cables fell thickly through the door of the Howard apartment. Agents wanted to represent him. Film companies offered parts.

"What an extraordinary business," said Leslie. "I've been around for years."

The best offer, and the part that appealed the most was in *Outward Bound*. It was a chance to play the Alfred Lunt part, which he had always thought a good one. In order to escape from *Berkeley Square* and placate everyone generally, Leslie closed the New York run, agreed to tour in the play the next winter, and signed for the film *Outward Bound*.

The ways and lavish means of Hollywood were still quite strange to the stage actor, and George Fogel once more dashed to the rescue and took him for a walk while his agent discussed terms, for Leslie had been heard to say to his future employers, "Five thousand dollars a week? No actor in the world is worth five thousand a week!"

Going home to England was delayed. Miss Goss and Doodie were sent back; Ruth and Leslie set out for the West Coast. Whether he was worth it or not, it would be madness to refuse —money like that might not come his way again.

11/ *The City of Angels; the Heaven of Stars*

Hollywood, the brilliant oasis, finally appeared after days in a dust-filled train. Green, lush, tropical, exciting. It had a kind of glamour that lived only for a few years, but they were the golden years—the years after the silent movie had been supplanted and before a wicked little box with distorted pictures not unlike those silent movies had changed the face of Hollywood and made everyone dance a frightening measure to a tune piped by a sponsor and a popularity rating.

It was the Hollywood of the great personality, the monumental mansion, the fabulous party, the gigantic production, where "Pickfair" corresponded to Buckingham Palace and at least one of the brothers Warner had a garden resembling Versailles.

To Leslie and Ruth, it was intriguing, incredible, and impossible. What could you make of a place where the largest cemetery flashed with monster neon signs announcing "Sleep beneath the stars," and the most popular restaurant was an enormous brindle-colored bowler hat called the "Brown Derby"?

The inhabitants of this weird place were unusual, too. Their standard of living was so opulent and their public worship so

175

exaggerated that as a matter of course they came to see themselves as not of common clay at all. To succeed and remain successful on the stage, there had to be a technical mastery of acting and a sustained brilliance, or, at the least, intelligence of performance; in the motion picture, acting was a minor consideration. A beautiful face and the ever-honored sex appeal were the essentials. This was most obvious to Leslie on his first visit to Hollywood because of the number of "silent" stars who had never in their lives uttered a line of dialogue and were now helplessly trying to retain their positions in a world of sound.

One of the greatest of these silent stars was John Gilbert, and he lived on Olympian heights, both actual and metaphysical. His house, where Ruth and Leslie spent many days, was on a pinnacle overlooking Hollywood. The patio, heavy with Moorish arches, hung out on the hillside into which his swimming pool had been excavated. His excursions into matrimony were frequent, and at that moment the beautiful, blonde Ina Claire was gracing the mountain retreat as his wife. The parties around the pool and the tennis court were always amusing, and the Howards were sure to find the young author Louis Bromfield, their friends the Lawrence Tibbetts, or other luminaries from the Hollywood scene. It was all very glamorous and interesting, though not really anything they would covet.

Occasionally, the royal summons from "Pickfair" took them to that elegant estate. There they were entertained in feudal English splendor by Mary Pickford and her husband, Douglas Fairbanks, Sr. Leslie was most amused at the regal atmosphere and the solemnity of the servants. "I am sure there are a good many dukes in England who have never seen such awe and respect," he remarked to Ruth with a wicked little chuckle.

Nobody could have been less suited to the accepted and expected standards of behavior in Hollywood at that time than Leslie. He was bored with the nonsense of dressing up and showing off, sure that his face was by no means "pretty" enough for Hollywood, and embarrassed by much of the vulgarity and garish display. His only solace was on the movie set, where he could amuse himself poking about inside the camera or discussing the lights with the technical crew.

Happily, his old friend and stage manager George Fogel had come to Hollywood with him, in the rather grand position of "personal director." Leslie had professed himself frightened of what the movie industry might do to him and unable to face them alone. He had the greatest faculty for getting someone else to shoulder his burdens—if he was late, they must speak to George; if he could not be found when they wanted him, they must speak to George. In fact, when someone had anything unpleasant to say—he must speak to George.

Leslie had a habit of plastering his hair down with water just before a scene was to be shot. No one could remonstrate with him about this, not even George. Disgusting wavy hair was hideous, in Leslie's opinion.

"But his hair looks black when it's wet—I can't photograph him like that" was the cameraman's cry. George Fogel had worked his way around Howard problems before, and, on his advice, a heat lamp was installed on the set and Leslie, all unwitting, asked to confer with the director underneath it, until the signal was quietly given that his hair had dried enough for work to begin. So it went, and a personal director was a very useful thing all around.

There was a young man in the cast for whom Leslie developed a great fondness. He was the son of the laird of "Pickfair," and very like his good-looking father. Young Doug Fairbanks had immense charm and humor, and, being many years younger than Leslie, he became a devoted follower. Ruth remembered Doug Junior as a little boy of eleven, and the fact that he was by now married to Joan Crawford changed her attitude not one bit. The Howards saw the Fairbankses often, and Ruth treated them both rather firmly like two over-demonstrative children.

12 / England, New York, and Hollywood—Again

In London once more, they found a comfortable old hotel, the Rembrandt, in South Kensington. It specialized in a resident clientele, largely made up of elderly ladies, who seemed to suit its dark green interior and darker green shadows. Here the family was installed for June and July, near Hyde Park for riding, and near Leslie's family.

Almost the first day in England, Leslie drove Miss Goss and Doodie down to a small village in Surrey where he now owned his estate. The village was called Westcott, and the estate, "Stowe Maries," was a bare ten acres, but it seemed a great deal to a family who had always lived in other peoples' houses with only pocket-handkerchief gardens. It was with great expectations that Leslie guided his car down the narrow lane, over an old stone bridge, and under the beech trees.

"I did not remember that it was as charming as this," he remarked with pleasure, but the words had hardly been uttered when the house came into view: red tiles hung over yellow stucco, the whole surrounded by a large and disreputable brick wall. At one end of this depressing construction was an antiquated but scarcely antique building, once intended for a coach house but now used as a garage. The paint was peeling from the doors, which hung precariously on rusted hinges. The full

180

extent of the unfortunate architecture was shielded from a casual inspection by a massive growth of yew and laurel.

Leslie, undaunted by this first impression, firmly led the way into his new establishment. "It was quite pleasant inside," he said encouragingly, turning the key in the hideous front door. They walked into a tiled hall of unbelievable ugliness from which were found a series of stuffy small rooms, empty, dusty, and incredibly dreary. Even the garden, which he remembered as full of flowers and sunshine, dogs and children, was a disillusionment. Laid out in orderly lines and squares, cut up into nasty little flower beds shaped like half-moons and circles, it looked like the work of an enthusiastic keeper of a public park. No one spoke; even Doodie's tireless prattle was stilled by the painful expression on Leslie's face. Silently, the three trooped to the car. Ten miles later Leslie turned his head, sighed, and said, "Goss, I'm afraid I've bought a white elephant."

Miss Goss could scarcely disagree. After all the years of longing, it seemed most unfair that they should be saddled with such a monstrosity in a country overflowing with exquisite houses.

The drive to London was continued in silence, and Leslie could hardly bear to face Ruth. This was to be her house, her reward for fourteen years lived in hotels and from suitcases, and it seemed more like a judgment for an ill-spent youth.

But Ruth was always unpredictable, and very good in times of crisis. When everyone else found the vicissitudes of life too much to bear, Ruth suddenly sprang into energetic action. So it was about the house. She was stunned by her first sight of it, but only for a moment; then her great flair for making any house a charming home for her family rescued her from despondency and she was away, planning and compromising, chopping and changing; walls must come down, bathrooms must go in. There was only one bathroom in the house, a *fin-de-siècle* production of rare discomfort, which Ruth dismissed with a wave of the hand—"Rip it out, it's no good at all." They would need what in those days were referred to as "American bathrooms," tiled and colorful, with bright rubber floors and lots of mirrors.

Leslie just looked on glumly, groaned, and took Doodie for a walk. Whenever they arrived to spend the day at their white elephant, Leslie disappeared with Doodie. Ruth would be interviewing builders and plumbers and electricians, trying to decide on the first jobs to be done, and Leslie was nowhere to be found. Surrounded by surveyors and little men from the gas company and the local County Council, she would be going frantic searching for her husband and always without success.

"He's so vague," Ruth said hopefully. But she knew that this was not the answer. Leslie was really just escaping, as usual, from the world's tedium. Why, in the words of an old saw, keep a dog and bark yourself? He let Ruth do the barking and then could grumble at her for any mistakes. What a design for living he evolved, and how comfortable it made him! He looked out on life with a gentle smile touching his thin, sensitive face; no frown marred the high forehead, no petty problems troubled the pale blue eyes. Ruth shouldered the responsibilities; she was, anyway, a brilliant organizer and enjoyed running everything. If this allowed her too much scope, and an unnatural balance in their marriage, Leslie was not yet prepared to worry about it.

In August, after Wink's school closed, Leslie and Ruth took their children to Mullion again. It had been a year-long separation for Wink, though, of course, his parents had appeared for Sports Day and run without distinction in the Mothers' and Fathers' Race. Wink must have envied his small sister and felt rather left out of the family projects. Sometimes it was not worth being the elder and a boy. Doodie adored her brother, but, although he tried to be kind to her, and was always peace-loving, the difference in their ages made close companionship impossible. The result was that Doodie behaved as an only child might, demanding and getting attention, placing her two small feet in the middle of the stage and expecting applause. Wink began to wander off to follow his own pursuits. He was a much more solitary personality than his sister, who thrived only with a group. Leslie wandered with him when he could —generally after Doodie was in bed, for she seldom let her father out of her grip.

While the family was at Mullion, Leslie suddenly went to France for a week with some friends. Ruth was not completely captivated by this idea, but off he went anyway, establishing his unique independence. To the satisfaction of everyone, including Doodie, who had howled dismally at the station, Leslie was at once the victim of his own folly. He was lonely, he was depressed, and, more important than anything else, he was mortally stricken with imaginary complaints, the most serious personally diagnosed as heart trouble.

"I really will have to see a specialist when I get back and see what he advises about my going to America, etc. I imagine I need absolute rest and no worry for six months. If only our house was ready and I could afford it!"

He came home rather quickly and had a thorough medical check. Nothing was found, which did not relieve his feeling at all. The packing was done, and, after a last look at "Stowe Maries," now more depressing than ever, pulled apart and hung with scaffolding, they were ready to sail. Saying good-by to Winkie was awful. Seeing him standing straight and unblinking in his green-and-black blazer, not asking for sympathy, though he had to face another year without seeing his parents, made it even harder. Leslie would have taken him on the boat at the last moment, but Ruth was practical and restraining. After all, a boy's education was vitally important. Helplessly caught in the treadmill of life, Leslie could only pat his son—"You'll be coming out before you know it, old man"— and go away.

New York was buzzing with a dozen plans. There were film offers to be decided on, and possible plays to be read. First, of course, the *Berkeley Square* tour must be completed. Surrounded once more by familiar faces, Arthur, his dresser, George Fogel, and the same cast as before, Leslie was somewhat mollified—but touring was his idea of absolute torture. The thought of Boston, Toronto, Philadelphia, Cleveland, Pittsburgh, and, finally, four weeks in Chicago at Christmas was boring. What a way to earn a living! Meals in restaurants upset Leslie's delicate digestion—or were said to. Miss Goss cooked most of his food, for he was preternaturally fussy. The whole family could imitate Leslie at the dining table, picking over any slightly suspect dish with his fork, his mouth drawn in, and his nose twitching, rabbit-like. Should the offending food be revealed as sweetbreads or oysters, his expression became one of such revulsion that an innocent bystander might presume they were maggot-ridden. The plate was hastily pushed away and all other food refused with a gentle air of martyrdom.

In Chicago, Leslie developed a cold and then laryngitis. The play opened there on Christmas Eve, and its star was hardly audible in the first act and completely inaudible by the middle of Act II. George Fogel rang the curtain down during this act and offered everyone his money back or seats for the next opening on New Year's Eve. Nearly everyone came back, and so did Leslie's voice—for a triumphant four weeks, after which, they closed and traveled nonstop to California, where, with three weeks at the Belasco Theatre in Los Angeles, the tour was to end.

Leslie had signed to make a film called *Never the Twain Shall Meet* in which he played, of all unlikely things, a beachcomber. The plot of this epic production naturally centered on East being East and West being West—but the twain met busily on the sands of a tropical island where East was portrayed by a very pretty Spanish girl, named Conchita Montenegro, in a sarong, and West by Leslie, in dirty white trousers and a heavy growth of whiskers.

After three weeks at the Belasco, Leslie began to grow this beard, but business for *Berkeley Square* was still booming and the run was lengthened. Finally, Leslie's beard could be hidden no longer by grease paint, so he went off to his beachcombing.

Ruth, in the meantime, was house-hunting, which she found most enjoyable, guided every day by a witty New Yorker, Newell Vanderhoef, who ran a successful real-estate business in Beverly Hills. He took Ruth to lunch on many days and explained each house in turn. "My dear, wait until you see this one. I don't mean it for you at all, but I knew you'd just *love* to get inside. My heavens, the things that house must have seen! It's fascinating!"

So she was busy and having a lovely time, and in due course found, on a road that wound up into the hills, a house built of white stucco and roofed with curved red tile. The house was typical of the pseudo-Spanish hacienda that flourished in Hollywood in the 1930's. Inside, it was well adorned with mosaic tile, heavy iron grillwork, Spanish shawls, and balconies. There was no swimming pool, so the Howards could not be accused of going native at once.

Leslie worked away at the studio, making one film after another. As soon as he finished his South Sea island role, he went into *Free Soul,* with Norma Shearer and, of all people, young Clark Gable. Here, to Leslie's amusement, the story decreed that he must shoot Gable in order to get the girl. An interesting switch from the year before in New York when he had not employed the young man because he lacked appeal!

Free Soul, based on a story and play by Adela Rogers St. John, was the most preposterous lot of nonsense, and the only person who managed to fight through the clouds of bad dialogue was Lionel Barrymore. One critic said Leslie was "lost in the shuffle," and one or two others lost him altogether.

But before the reviews were written, he was at work on another film, *Five and Ten,* by Fannie Hurst, starring Marion Davies.

Leslie became very fond of this legendary figure, for Marion Davies was absolutely unpretentious. Surrounded though she was by almost unbelievable wealth, living in a white colossus by the sea, indulged by her friends, and watched over by a great newspaper baron, she had every reason to be impossible, overbearing, completely without values, and entirely self-interested. Instead, she was a most easy, jolly, warmhearted soul, accepting the pleasures and riches that came to her as slightly comic, never pretending to be anything that she was not.

The Howards were often asked to her beach house, the white palace of colonial pillars, steps, and terraces that rose on the sands of Santa Monica like a giant wedding cake. For all its frightening proportions, the atmosphere was informal and the hostess vague, amusing, and undemanding.

Five and Ten caused no stir in the critical world. The cast was surely capable of better things, for such names as Richard Bennett, Irene Rich, Kent Douglas, Henry Armetta, and Ruth Selwyn wandered through its scenes. Leslie's review was a gem of Hollywood patronage and elegant prose: "Howard gives a nice show. He's English and has played before in pictures over here." So much for "the leading actor on the English-speaking stage"!

In March, Winkie had come to America on the *Bremen,* chaperoned by Gilbert Miller. Ruth met him in New York and brought him to Hollywood delightedly clutching an Indian bow bought at Albuquerque from the first American Indian he had ever seen. Now at last they were a family again, and Leslie was completely happy. When he was not working, they all drove off for the day to picnic on the beach or watch the polo games. Leslie's elder sister, Dorice, joined them for the summer, intent on learning the great American tap dance, which was sweeping around the world. Doodie and Ruth went with her for lessons, and the tile floors in the house on Tower Road rang with the rhythm of metal toes and heels. Women were very emancipated that summer, and trousers began to be generally worn, though they were made with enormous floppy legs and called "lounging pyjamas." All the Howard women sported these glories.

The family never missed a swimming pool, for Ruth Selwyn opened her house to them, one and all, and they were able to treat her pool as their own. There Leslie and Wink practiced ridiculous acrobatics, falling off chairs and leaping off each other's backs, and Doodie paddled around learning to swim. Ruth, who practically never swam, waited on the edge of the pool with armfuls of towels and diligently scrubbed dry the three members of her family as soon as they climbed out. She always retained her English conviction that wet bathing suits brought colds in the head, and the children and Leslie were ever to be seen wandering around in public clutching insecure towels around their middles.

Leslie was not always patient in teaching his children sports, and Doodie was lucky to have as an instructor Robert Montgomery, a young man of extraordinary kindness and extreme good looks who spent hours helping her stay afloat. His name was fast growing in importance in Hollywood and he was one of a few male stars whom Leslie really enjoyed. In July, Bob Montgomery initiated the English children into the exciting rites of "the Fourth" by arriving at Tower Road laden with fireworks.

Leslie began work on a film called *Devotion* with Ann Harding. Robert Milton directed, and another good cast did their best, to little avail. "The playing of Miss Harding, Leslie Howard and Robert Williams is a delight . . . film is full of repression, suppression and dialogue . . ."

Leslie looked back on six months of hard labor with really very little achieved. These four films were of a depressingly low standard and had in no way advanced his reputation as an actor. Though pressed to stay in Hollywood and make yet one more, he refused determinedly. Gilbert Miller had sent him a play to read called *The Animal Kingdom,* by Philip Barry, and

this he had every intention of producing in New York that
winter of 1931.

The last day in Beverly Hills was chaotic: it is only worth
recording because it was the *first* time it happened. It set the
pattern for all future Hollywood departures. The studios were
telephoning, Ruth was packing, Leslie was hiding. He would
not stay any longer no matter how tempting the offers. There
had been exciting news from Surrey: the impossible house had
suddenly revealed hidden treasures. After layers of stucco were
pulled off, sixteenth-century beams and frescoes had appeared,
and Leslie agreed to further investigation and, if possible,
restoration.

Nothing could persuade him to remain in California, and
the Howards fled as though pursued by bill collectors, boarded
the train, and sighed with relief when the Los Angeles station
slipped into the distance.

13 / "The Animal Kingdom"

England looked very calm and comfortable after six months of Hollywood life, and the Howards drifted again into the shadows at the Rembrandt Hotel with relief and pleasure. August was almost at an end, Wink would soon be going back to school, and some provision must be made to instruct Doodie. Leslie's eye was caught by the Lycée Française, a venerable institution that occupied a small triangle of land near the hotel. Investigation showed that it accepted small children, and there Doodie was sent, in floods of tears, at the age of seven, to receive the first attempts at a proper education. Leslie was enchanted with the Lycée; he visualized his daughter chattering away in fluent French within a year.

"The only really important things for a girl to learn are French, literature, and a smattering of the arts," he pointed out to Ruth. Doodie remained unconvinced. Never in all her days had she suffered regimentation, and although the kindergarten, where she found herself, was a most friendly and gentle place, it meant having to go at nine every morning, and she objected to rules of this kind. For once her father appeared adamant.

Before the children began school, the house at Westcott was fully explored. It was an enthralling pastime to wander around and watch the workmen searching out the original building.

How much of it was sixteenth century? What sort of house had it been? Leslie's sense of history was piqued and he hunted through old books on the district to discover the answers to these questions. Ruth, meanwhile, was at work on the more practical problems, supervising the alterations in hand and planning an additional wing to house maids and cars. Leslie joined her long enough to choose wallpaper for his own bedroom: a series of murals depicting Kew Gardens.

At the end of September, Leslie started work again, having been talked into making a film by Alexander Korda. Korda was largely unknown in England and the film, *Reserved for Ladies,* was his first job of direction in that country. A Hungarian, dark and slightly sardonic, he had an arresting personality, and, though some people considered him a skillful and slightly pretentious fraud, his supporters viewed him as a genius. Leslie never placed him entirely in one category or the other. Always scornful and skeptical about Korda's omniscience, frequently intrigued and impressed by his mind, Leslie found working with him a somewhat mixed pleasure. It was, nevertheless, refreshing and encouraging after Hollywood, where production remained rather stereotyped and little that was new and experimental had appeared.

Korda's initial choice was not successful. *Reserved for Ladies,* originally a silent film with Adolphe Menjou, made a somewhat verbose "talkie." Leslie played a type of male Cinderella which had been done too many times: the head waiter mistaken for a prince, the old rags-to-riches theme. But the picture held brief glimpses of the brilliance and taste that later made Alexander Korda a force in British films. In England, the film had a slight public; in the United States, none at all. Leslie's review in New York sounded like a recommendation for a good tailor: "Finely cut and intelligently planned performance."

Reserved for Ladies slipped into the limbo kept especially for bad plays and films that actors want to forget, and Leslie and Ruth got ready to leave for New York again.

Their last night in England was spent with the family at 39, Onslow Square—everyone sitting around happily, gazing fondly at Leslie and listening to him as though to the Delphic oracle. He had not been feeling well, and possibly nobody took this seriously enough. Adulation for his work was as nothing when his health lay unregarded. To himself, he represented a semi-invalid, struggling on against frightful handicaps to feed and clothe his wife and children. That this should be ignored, he found incomprehensible. His mother and sisters kept asking him about the play in New York. What was he going to do after that? Work, work, that is all they are interested in hearing, he thought bitterly. Ruth answered the questions because he seemed suddenly silent.

"Work, work, that's all she's interested in talking about. My health is a matter of complete indifference," he told himself furiously. And then he decided to have a heart attack. Brilliantly enacted, with a hand to his heart and an anguished expression, he slumped back in his chair and asked pathetically for a doctor. No one could do this better than Leslie, or believe more completely in his own performance.

Very naturally, this produced immediate results, and his mother and Ruth rushed next door, where the family doctor lived. In their haste, they climbed the low wall separating the fronts of the two houses, and, in the half-light, Ruth slipped. The sickening fall into the basement area was heard rather than seen, as she fell fifteen feet onto a cement floor, splintering milk bottles outside the kitchen door. For once, she had reason to be grateful for a plump figure; it saved her spine from breaking, but it was a semiconscious broken body that Leslie found when he raced out of the house. An expensive cure for a heart attack.

There was no sailing the next day, and for many days Ruth was too ill to care. She had multiple fractures, and what internal injuries could not yet be known. But she was always resilient and courageous and far too busy to be ill. Within a short time, Leslie was sailing to America, alone but assured that Ruth would follow quickly. He left a family looking rather battle-scarred, for Doodie had fallen a few days after her mother and had one arm in plaster.

Ruth recovered determinedly, and in a month was with Leslie in New York, a great feat of devotion to duty and to him, leaving Doodie and Miss Goss at 39, Onslow Square for the winter.

She found him rehearsing *The Animal Kingdom* and not entirely happy with the play. Philip Barry had written this deft, evanescent comedy with a young actress in mind. She was unknown, relatively untried, and her name was Katharine Hepburn. The part that Barry had created for her was, naturally, the best in the play, and Leslie was wondering by now why he had agreed to appear in it. The cast seemed a good one, with, at that moment, the exception of Miss Hepburn, who found her huge role rather a problem.

One member of the company was introduced to Leslie at the first rehearsal.

"We've met before, Mr. Howard. You directed me in *Out of a Blue Sky*," said William Gargan.

"I did? Oh, yes, I remember now. You're the chap who borrowed three dollars."

Bill Gargan was astonished. What a strange man this Howard must be, obviously rich, busy, and famous, and yet remembering three dollars! Bill decided then and there that Englishmen were tight with their money, and he never had reason to change his mind. Strangely enough, he and Leslie formed a devoted friendship, and an odd pair they made. Bill was a great extrovert, the Brooklyn boy with the fiery temperament, the incredible fund of stories, and the heart big enough for everyone; Leslie was the antithesis of all these qualities: self-contained, inhibited, and undemonstrative, very much an Englishman, with that country's dislike of showmanship or a point overstated. But they gave one another a feeling of warmth and represented, too, a little of what each secretly longed to be.

In *The Animal Kingdom* Bill Gargan was playing Red Reagan, the ex-pugilist serving as a makeshift butler, and no one had ever struggled harder for a role or felt more triumphant when it was his. Bill had wanted that part desperately, and he had even dyed his hair red when he had to face Philip Barry for an audition. He got the part because he *was* Red Reagan, but he realized very quickly that his lines were so good that they would never remain uncut. In scenes between Red Reagan and Tom Collier, played by Leslie, Reagan stole the show. Bill waited for the ax to fall. No star was going to tolerate this unbalanced arrangement.

The play opened in Pittsburgh, and, for all the first-night difficulties, the audience applauded the cast time and again, and then Leslie went to take his star call. As he walked downstage a voice cried, "Where's Red Reagan?" The figure on the stage smiled, turned to the wings, and beckoned. For a moment nothing happened, and then, after another signal from the stage, Bill Gargan came slowly out to join Leslie. He was led to the footlights, and, almost before he knew it, Leslie had left the stage and given Bill his more than justified solo call. To Bill this was a revelation—stars did not behave like that in his experience.

When Bill Gargan heard of cuts the next day, he heard also that Leslie had refused to see Red Reagan denied a line. It was Katharine Hepburn's part that must be shortened. Between one tour city and the next, Philip Barry changed and rewrote *The Animal Kingdom*. The job was made easier when Miss Hepburn left the company, for Barry then switched the emphasis from the woman's part to Leslie's. Miss Hepburn, soon to be a brilliant and exciting actress, was not ready for such an overwhelming part, and Frances Fuller was brought in to play it. Confidently expected to be a hit, *The Animal Kingdom* opened at the Broadhurst Theatre on January 12, 1932.

The superlatives rang out for the play, for the performers,

for the production. When Brooks Atkinson wrote of Philip Barry, he took two columns to applaud and explain the playwright's artistry; then he drew actor and writer together and said: "Mr. Howard has in many respects the actor's counterpart of Mr. Barry's talent. He is a luminous actor; he has grace, precision and spirit, and wherever he touches the surface of a part the light of character shines through. His portrait of Tom Collier represents the rarest sort of collaboration between an actor and an author, and this eminently disinterested department takes the liberty of feeling very proud of what Mr. Barry and Mr. Howard have created."

Quite obviously, the play would run for months. Leslie, as usual, once the nice notices were over, thought it a beastly business. "If he is working at his job, an actor has within, say, thirty performances brought all he is capable of to the building and polishing of a characterization, and once this peak has been reached the rest of the journey must be downhill. At least it must be so mentally, even if, physically, the thing continues like an automaton, six nights and two matinees weekly, monthly, ad infinitum."

Time to brood about himself was invariably bad for Leslie. He went off to one doctor after another, seeking always confirmation of his own diagnosis. In New York that winter, someone recommended a heart specialist, an eminent Scottish doctor. It took but a trice for Leslie to be in his office stripped and ready. Tests were made, electrocardiograms produced, and the specialist turned to Leslie with a grave face.

"Mr. Howard, I am sorry to tell you that you have an incurable disease."

"Yes, yes," said Leslie. "I knew it—I knew it—tell me, what is it?"

"Fear" was the brief reply. How Leslie hated that story, and how Ruth loved it! She told it, imitating exactly the Scottish accent of the doctor, at every possible opportunity that year, and, indeed, for many years to come.

Leslie simply went off to another specialist, and his health worsened every day of the run. The play was killing him, this he knew—but what could he do? He wrote acrimoniously:

"Once an actor, particularly an important one, has embarked on the run of a hit play, practically nothing short of death can release him until the bitter end. There he is, winter and summer, sickness and health, eight times a week at the same stand as long as the public will take it. He is expected to drag himself through a performance in defiance of his doctor's orders, possibly imperiling his life and his family's security—and for what? For an insane catch-phrase 'the show must go on,' a manifest hypocrisy concerning which few people ever bother to enquire—'Why?'"

One might imagine that Leslie had spent a year in this play, he grumbled so vociferously. Of course, he found compensations. He was in great public demand, particularly with his female fans. Every few days a different and charming young thing appeared to interview him. No man can really object when asked to unburden his soul to a pretty girl, and Leslie found "interviews" frequently delightful, so much so, that Bill Gargan never let him forget about them.

"Any good interviews this week, Leslie?"

"Shut up, you fool," replied Leslie, laughing nonetheless, and nervously fixing his eyes on Ruth.

In April, Bill Gargan wanted a release from the play to take a leading part in the film version of *Rain*. He was tied to a "run of the play" contract and asked Leslie's advice.

"I'll see what I can do, old boy. I'm sure it's most unfair," said Leslie, and returned later with the advice that the best he could arrange with Gilbert Miller was to let Bill out of the contract for $1,500. Gargan paid because he had to, and thanked Leslie for interceding on his behalf. It was some weeks before he suddenly realized that Leslie, as Miller's partner, would get $750 of that hard-earned money.

"Cheap, chiseling Englishman, I'll get it back if it takes ten years," Gargan said, and meant, and did! It annoyed him the more because Leslie was off himself, leaving the play and heading for Hollywood.

"What gives with that guy? People say he's forgetful. He may be eighty per cent forgetful, but he's twenty per cent deliberate."

Still, somehow he could never be angry with Leslie once he saw him again. That was the mystery of Leslie—he could charm his greatest enemy with no apparent effort, and his friends were helpless in his hands.

The Animal Kingdom went on in New York, and Leslie, having agreed to make the film later that summer, went off to Hollywood with Ruth. He had first to appear in *Smilin' Through* for Metro-Goldwyn-Mayer, with Norma Shearer and Fredric March. And Ruth had to find a house so that their children could be with them again. Doodie wrote every week, laborious epistles, misspelled and in a handwriting that should have alarmed her father into intensifying her education, but, innocent and unaware, he removed her from school and had her shipped to California with Miss Goss. Wink was left behind to be brought on later by his aunt.

Ruth rented another Spanish house, this time with a swimming pool but much the same quantity of tile and balconies as before. Built around three sides of a formal garden with a fountain in the middle, it was a large house, low and rambling, and belonged to Elsie Janis. Miss Janis's taste was obviously good, and the house was well furnished, but for Ruth it needed a little chintz and a few new and less Andalusian-looking lamps; in fact, it lacked the British touch and proceeded to get it almost at once. By the time that Doodie and Miss Goss appeared, the change was complete. The dark and rather lonely drawing room, with its barn-high ceiling and grille-covered windows, wore a somewhat surprised air—roses sprawled on the sofas and a comfortable veneer of an English country house had been laid on the Latin foundations. Here the family were to live for nearly a year with great happiness and companionship.

Leslie's part in *Smilin' Through* had a pathetic, poignant quality. In the beginning he played a young boy about to marry the girl he loves. She dies tragically, and he spends his life remembering her and waiting each evening for her spirit to return to comfort him. Though the film was made in the early years of good trick photography, Norma Shearer as a transparent ghost was both beautiful and intriguing. In fact, though the story was very unlikely and a little lachrymose, the film possessed a certain wispy charm, and Leslie's performance as the sad, old man had women weeping all over the world. His fan mail rose abruptly, and every member of the family was engaged in answering it.

Despite the financial insecurity that haunted the country, people still went to the movies, and motion pictures were making more money than ever for the studios. The gilded personalities of the celluloid empire enjoyed an era of low income tax, high earnings, and incredible spending. Leslie had no particular interest in going to lavish parties, and became impossibly mulish about giving any, but in the natural course of events the Howards were found at one or two. Ruth enjoyed them and, although her husband would never co-operate, she was amused by the fancy-dress parties that were much in vogue. Leslie loathed costumes, but on one occasion he and Ruth went to a party as the King and Queen of Hearts, after much pressure from Ruth. The King of Hearts, thrust into his suit, was a most morose, miscast, and disagreeable monarch, and his only royal action was to decree that never again would he put on fancy dress.

In 1932 the place to go was the Coconut Grove. There were constant parties in the palm-fringed ballroom. The place to spend a weekend was San Simeon, if you could get an invitation. San Simeon (now a state museum) belonged to William Randolph Hearst. It was called a ranch—a misnomer that was not at all descriptive of the soaring buildings brought, presumably, from Italy and rebuilt on a high escarpment looking across a rough California valley. The swimming pool, of such an immense size that it had a boat on it, was surrounded by packing cases still covering statues bought for Hearst in Europe. Where these *objets d'art* were finally to be placed was a mystery, because similar marble figures were as thick as trees on the grounds. The guests occupied separate cottages. There they were left to themselves, providing they followed the printed directions found in each bedroom. These instructions were explicit and dealt with times of meals, facilities for sports, telephones, telegrams, et cetera. Leslie and Ruth could hardly believe their eyes when they first saw the sheet of paper under the glass on the dressing table.

"I wonder what the rate is for this room?" said Leslie. "We'll probably get a bill when we leave!"

Ruth was more struck by the dining room, which was enormous, had a vaulted ceiling and a long refectory table heavy with silver candelabra. Down the middle of this beautifully polished surface stood an army of ketchup bottles and pickle jars. This was the only visible sign of ranch life. The animals that roamed the property were scarcely those found in the average corral, and at night the roar of lions and the snarl of panthers quite chilled the blood.

"Very interesting experience," remarked Leslie. "But I'd certainly hate to annoy my host!" Nevertheless, when pressure was put on him by William Randolph Hearst to make *Peg o' My Heart* with Marion Davies, even a ranch full of wild animals could not coerce him.

Much more Leslie's idea of pleasure was a quiet dinner with Norma Shearer and her husband, Irving Thalberg, at their beach house. Thalberg, head of production for M-G-M, had infinite taste and sensitivity. A small, slight, intelligent man, he was almost unique in the Hollywood of those days, where the movie mogul was interested mainly in the supercolossal extravaganza and had difficulty spelling it. Both Ruth and Leslie admired and grew fond of Irving Thalberg.

The Animal Kingdom began shooting in June with a fine cast: Ann Harding, William Gargan, Ilka Chase, and a movie vamp, Myrna Loy, in one of her first straight roles. Miss Loy was a dark, languorous beauty of almost catlike seductiveness, and in that early film barely resembled the sprightly comedienne who later became synonymous with the "perfect wife."

An interesting play made a good film. To both Leslie and Bill Gargan, who had played their parts innumerable times, it presented few problems, but they found the short, jerky "takes" necessary for a film tiresome. They missed the continuity of action of the play. The most important scene that Bill and Leslie had together was a very humorous, rather drunken sequence, which lasted about seven minutes. Leslie suggested that this be taken simultaneously by three cameras: long shot, medium shot, and close-up. This was absolutely unheard of in Hollywood, but the idea was given a chance. The director, knowing motion-picture actors, was extremely doubtful, and even more skeptical when, after a short rehearsal, the actors said they were ready. The scene was shot without a single error on the first "take." After all, it was, in Gargan's words, "duck soup" to such old hands. To be able to print the initial shot astonished both director and crew, and to print seven minutes was extraordinary. It was not unusual practice at that time to use only a bare thirty seconds of finished film from a whole day's shooting.

While Bill and Leslie worked together, Ruth and Mary Gargan became good friends. Both possessing a sharp sense of humor, they found much common ground, and they helped each other in a variety of ways: Ruth providing advice and leadership where Mary still lacked experience and sophistication, and Mary guiding the far more gullible Ruth in her daily association with people. No one put anything over on Mary; she was quick, shrewd, and businesslike, immediately assessing the sycophant and the "phony," both of whom abounded in the Hollywood terrain. She was also loyal, generous, and affectionate, with a pretty, roguish face that clearly showed her Irish descent.

At this time Leslie was approached by M. C. Levee, Mary Pickford's manager. Mike Levee had started to work at the age of nine, and had become a prosperous member of the "cloak and suit" trade before the silent films attracted him. A bright, sagacious salesman, he had climbed to the top of that industry. Now he proposed that Leslie play opposite Miss Pickford in a Western film. The whole thing was ridiculously unlikely: Leslie in a large black sombrero on a larger black horse, dashing around the desert scrub brandishing a six-shooter. Nevertheless, he played in *Secrets,* though, as the film went along, he was more and more puzzled. Why had they wanted him for the part? It all seemed so palpably absurd that he went to see Mike Levee.

"Why did you want me for this film?" he asked.

"I didn't want you, Miss Pickford did" was the reply.

"Did you think I'd be good?" said Leslie.

"No—I thought you'd be awful—it's a crazy bit of casting."

"And yet you persuaded me to do it!"

"Certainly. I work for Mary Pickford—she wanted you—I got you."

"Anyone who could sell me this part could sell anything! Will you be my agent?"

Thus were their business lives joined for the rest of Leslie's life. Ten years: not a long time, but a very busy and successful time for them both. Mike Levee represented Leslie in America. He became a good friend to him as well. This was another unusual combination, for they battled each other furiously upon occasion.

"All you're interested in is your ten per cent, Mike."

"I'm interested in getting you a good deal," replied Mike sharply.

"A good deal? Do you call being tied to a colossal studio a good deal?"

Leslie signed with Warner Brothers a three-year contract for three pictures a year, and before the ink was dry he regretted it. Mike suffered through hours of recriminations, somewhat baffled by his client. What was wrong with a contract that produced excellent payment for three years? It guaranteed the future.

"It guarantees nothing but boredom and bad films" was Leslie's tart reply. But they remained friends.

"We cover up for each other," Mike would laugh. "And we discuss everything: children, business and infidelity—but mostly infidelity."

After *Secrets,* came a film about the war called *Captured,* with Douglas Fairbanks, Jr., and Paul Lukas—just another in a long line that helped to pay for the English house, and this was a very important reason for anything. Then Leslie began *Berkeley Square,* and enjoyed the rarity of well-written dialogue and a film that was worth doing.

When he had a free moment, he went out to the Riviera Country Club and investigated the pleasures and frustrations of polo. From an onlooker, he quickly became a player, and bought his first polo pony from Bob Montgomery, by name "1.2.3." A prophetic appellation, for within a year he had 2, 3, 4, 5, and 6! Once bitten by the bug, there seemed no cure, and in his unmounted moments he wandered around swinging a lead-headed stick to improve his polo muscles.

Though Doodie spent the riding hours with her father, Wink, too, had his share of Leslie. Confirmed picnickers, every Sunday the family took lunch to a local beach. Now, of course, they looked for deserted stretches of sand, for Leslie's life could be made unbearable if he were recognized. Another favorite spot was in the desert beyond Palm Springs. There, in sight of the mountains and shaded by palm and smoke trees, everyone bicycled and rode horses and swam. The children had a wonderful life, but perhaps too much pleasure and leisure. Their studies were confined to a morning session with a charming elderly English tutor, Hubert Greenwood, who managed to inculcate a desire for learning in Wink but who could only do his best and hope that some of his own interest and knowledge would rub off on Doodie.

Now the Howards had spent almost a year in California, and that long without a change of season was too much for this London boy.

"Those leaves have been on that tree so long they need dusting," he said scornfully one morning to Ruth—and soon she was packing again, to go back to England, back to see what had happened to the endless stream of money poured into Stowe Maries.

14 / The Green Hills of Surrey

London looked the same. England was depressed, too, but nowhere could one see the glaring contrast of luxurious Beverly Hills and the Okie camps that clung like sores to American life.

And London *was* the same. Nothing seemed to shake its impenetrable calm. Thousands were unemployed, but with the dole, a weekly pay check from the nation, public conscience felt appeased; a pyromaniac named Hitler was the new chancellor of a Germany in ferment; the League of Nations, born in hope out of the hell of war, lay sickened and impotent, deserted by Japan and Germany both bent on military domination. But England looked only on its own soft pastures; no eyes were turned to the black fields of hatred abroad.

The Howards, too, turned themselves to England's beauty, for Stowe Maries, lying in the valley below the hills that ringed London, was an enchantment. Many had been the nights when Ruth nervously presented the bills to Leslie. The cost of builders, plumbers, stonemasons, and electricians had seemed an insanity six thousand miles away in Hollywood, and he had fumed and fulminated. Now he knew the pride of creation as never before. The house, shed of Victorian ugliness, stood proudly among its trees—the sixteenth-century beauty it once had been. The Stowe, as it came to be called, was an old English word meaning "place" or "home," and it meant all of that to the Howards, the first home to which no one else but they belonged.

Though it was only half complete, Ruth and Leslie installed the children and themselves in the house for the summer. Leslie had sent his polo pony "1.2.3." to England, so they had a horse for the stables. Before many days, there was a pony for Doodie to ride through the lanes and woods with her father. The country around Westcott was particularly lovely, and still largely unspoiled. From there, through the years, as the stables grew and their inmates multiplied, the whole family would ride forth for a day, taking food and exploring miles of woodland and hill. Ruth was occasionally persuaded to sit on a horse, though never with great pleasure.

"Leslie, Leslie, keep that horrid child away from me," she would cry, as Doodie thundered around, behaving wickedly. Nothing is more upsetting than the small child who outshines its parent in some endeavor, and poor Ruth gave up her limited attempts at horsemanship. She remained on the ground, and yet managed the stables, ministered to sick horses, and was quite fearless when not astride them.

While his children enjoyed the fruits of his labors, Leslie labored anew. He made a film for Columbia in England, their first, *The Lady Is Willing,* with a very good English cast: Binnie Barnes, Nigel Bruce, Sir Nigel Playfair, and Cedric Hardwicke. Columbia, anxious that their initial offering made overseas should be at least a *succès d'estime,* sent American technical experts, and engaged Gilbert Miller to direct.

Leslie's part was the greatest fun. He played a French "private eye," one who wore innumerable disguises. So charmed was he by such an opportunity, that he began inventing situations so that he could hide behind yet another false mustache. His brother, Arthur, aged twenty-three, had a small part in the film, as an ancient Frenchman with a long white beard, and

Leslie suggested that he should imitate Arthur. The resulting confusion on the set caused much levity, but it was doubtful how much Columbia benefited.

The reviews were poor. In New York the critics politely suggested it would appeal in England, and spoke with condescension of the British cast trying to enunciate clearly, though "Howard speaks more thickly than the all-English players"! London critics were simply bored and rude. "On form it would seem the company had designed this film to be bullet-proof. The screen play is by Guy Bolton, then Leslie Howard came over for it. . . . Principal complaint about the picture is Miller's direction. It has all the attributes of stage technique. . . . It is to be hoped that some day Columbia . . . will have another try at British production. But the miss is most apparent."

Possibly somewhat sadder and wiser, Gilbert Miller returned to the theater. Leslie staged with him at the Lyric Theatre in London a play on Shakespeare's life called *This Side Idolatry*. Strangely enough, it was Leslie's first attempt at the sixteenth century. He had never played in Shakespeare, and, naturally, the period attracted him.

The production was fraught with difficulties. Leslie's part was long, the staging was complicated, and the play difficult to pull together. At home he appeared more tired and sickly than usual. Meals were left untasted, and the rule of silence that prevailed until 11 A.M. each day was stringently enforced by Ruth. Leslie's house was run, very properly, for his comfort, and he, apparently the most undemanding of men, was slavishly spoiled. Close to nervous collapse, he retired to the country while the dress rehearsal was played by his understudy, Glen Byam Shaw. Unaffected by this odd turn of events, his performance was perfectly good, but the play failed within a few weeks. Nothing is more tiring and depressing than a flop, and Leslie was hurt again by the critics of his own land. Another chance to live and work in England had evaded him, and, bitterly, he turned to consider the offers from Hollywood.

For months now, the studios had pressed him to return. He had been offered a film with Greta Garbo, which he refused. Hollywood was stunned, and it made headlines. How could he turn down a chance to appear with this magical figure? "It was a tempting offer," Leslie told the reporters. "Like fifty million others I have never seen her in person. Certainly she has a peculiarly dominating personality on the screen, and that is exactly why I declined that part. I should not hesitate to play opposite the most glamorous of stage actresses because a play can be depended upon to materialize as rehearsed. A picture is different. Added to the terrific competition of her personality, which no man has equalled, the film would, naturally, be cut to her advantage, and where should I be?"

Leslie still had one film to make for R.K.O., but his contract gave him the right of story approval. Thus, in an effort to stay in England, he had turned down each suggestion. Now, faced with justifiable annoyance from his studio, he offered a counterproposal. He would be happy to make *Of Human Bondage* if the studio could buy the rights. He rather imagined that this Somerset Maugham classic was unobtainable, and settled back to spend his first Christmas at Stowe Maries. To his surprise, R.K.O. bought the book, and promptly began sending a series of cables asking him to leave at once for California.

When the winter rain brought down the last leaves in the garden, Leslie sailed for America. He had experienced a new difficulty with one of his children. Doodie professed herself no longer interested in the warm climates. She and her father had enjoyed their first days of fox hunting together, and, once exposed to this glorious sport, she wanted to continue. Somewhat condescendingly, she agreed to attend a day school nearby if Leslie would leave her in England. Winkie, as usual, had little choice, for he was now slaving through his last years at an English public school at Tonbridge. Leslie hated these separations from his children, but he would never impose his will upon them. If Doodie wanted to stay at Stowe Maries, who could blame her? He wanted to stay himself, and it would be nice for Winkie in the Christmas holidays.

So, with Ruth to comfort him, the long trek began again. Urged on by cries of "Hurry" from the studio, they arrived in Hollywood to find nothing happening and nothing about to happen. The film was still uncast, and no girl had been found to play the difficult and leading role of Mavis, the Cockney waitress.

For two months Leslie was unemployed, and, although paid, he was furious. Ruth had reinstalled them in their house of the year before, and he even hated this now, writing to Doodie: "I wish you were here. We miss you. Your wing of the house is very deserted and I always hurry past it in case a ghost pops out at me. I hope you are happy at your school. Write and tell me will you. Are they decent to you there?"

He filled in the time by buying five horses. "I am becoming a horse dealer and just do acting in my spare time," he told Doodie. They wrote to each other every week, and he treated her with a wonderful mock solemnity.

"I am glad you are 'convinced' that you are going to be a dancer. I expect you will have a busy life, what with dancing, acting, painting and riding."

And in another: "We got four of your letters the other day, all together; two to Mummy and me—one to Daddy and one to Mr. Howard, the film actor—we had lots of laughs over them and the one to the movie star I sent on to him and he will reply himself. I don't think you ought to write to these movie stars—they are a bad lot I'm told!"

He addressed her as "Blimer," an odd diminutive invented by Doodie and himself from the Cockney ejaculation "Blimey," or as "Nimrod," for her hunting pursuits. His letters were full of ridiculous drawings of his life in California, and occasionally a plain sheet of paper inscribed "To Miss Howard, with the compliments of the management" folded around a pound note.

He wrote also to his son at school: "By the time you get this you will be back in your old gaol again at Tonbridge. I expect you had a good holiday at home and I hope you took advantage of it and enjoyed yourself during your first holiday in your own family house. I am so furious because I find I could have been there as the picture isn't starting for weeks. One tries to be philosophical but I have a growing dislike of so much chopping and changing and would like us to be together a bit more. Your report [from school] was quite good . . . Bravo! Let me know *at once* if you are not happy there in any way. We are only in the world once and we have a right to reasonable happiness, and my children shall have it if I can give it to them."

The hatred of his own school years colored all his remarks to Doodie and Wink, and, not surprisingly, gave them an excellent opportunity to play on his sympathy.

Work on *Of Human Bondage,* produced by Pandro S. Berman and directed by John Cromwell, started in February. After much discussion and weeks of indecison, an unknown young American actress had been cast in the Cockney part. Her name was Bette Davis. Leslie was shocked by this casting—an American in an otherwise English company. Bette Davis had a miserable time the first week of shooting. Frightened and unsure of herself, probably aware that her own studio considered her plain and, in the vernacular of films, "without a good camera angle," she felt all the Englishmen were whispering about her. Leslie was always polite—he tried not to make people uncomfortable if he could help it—but he was disinterested and vaguely disapproving. "Ridiculous casting—shocking!" She overheard the remarks, and the part that she had longed for became a nightmare. Then one day she played a complicated emotional scene with Leslie. At the end, she was quite exhausted, and no longer cared what they thought of her. But Leslie had been completely surprised. Mike Levee watched the scene and, following Leslie to his dressing room, remarked, "If you're not very careful that girl will steal the picture."

Leslie smiled at him. "Do you know something, Mike? If I *am* very careful, she *will* steal the picture."

From that moment on, Leslie, who relished a good performance and respected a performer as good as Bette Davis, did everything he could to help her finish a part that was to bring her world acclaim. He had been wrong and he admitted it happily. Although he was congratulated on his performance by the critics, Bette Davis scored the great success. It never mattered to him; the film was good, and he always felt it was one of his best parts.

A short rest in the desert followed, lying in a sun tent quite unclothed for a whole day lapping up his beloved sun, then back to work. This time a war film again: *British Agent* with Kay Francis and his friend Bill Gargan. Work to provide money so that his family could enjoy the house in which he could not afford to spend much time. He managed polo at the weekends, playing on Walt Disney's "Mickey Mouse" team with Will Rogers, and he allowed occasional parties to cheer Ruth, who found life alone in the house rather sad at times.

"I miss you all so much darlings," she wrote to Doodie and Wink. "And if it were not for leaving poor Daddy alone I would come to see you." On March 3, Ruth and Leslie celebrated eighteen years of marriage by giving a party. "A *huge* gathering, over fifty people," according to Leslie. He gave Ruth a diamond pin shaped like a small temple, with "18" set in rubies inside. It was made to his design, the only piece he ever took any interest in, or really enjoyed giving. He thought jewelry the most absurd waste of money, and any that Ruth managed to collect was bought after passive if not violent resistance. Bill Gargan again teased him, calling him a closefisted Englishman, typical of his breed. Ruth was entirely different, generous in the extreme, always giving presents and almost pathologically anxious to pick up the bill in a restaurant. They probably reacted on each other, Leslie becoming more careful as Ruth expanded.

"Leslie, that's a check," Gargan would say after they had dined well and the bill was presented. "That's the amount of money that we owe here for our dinner. Now, you asked me to eat and the management must be paid. *I* am not going to pay them."

"Oh, I'm so sorry, old boy," and, somewhat flustered, Leslie would put a few dollars on the plate and then push something underneath it. "No, no, Leslie—you can't tip like that. Get out the green, folding stuff or I won't be able to come back," Gargan would instruct, hugely amused. By then Leslie would be most embarrassed and would put an enormous tip on the plate and flee. It was a good thing that he usually left such payments to Ruth, for pushing fifty cents under a plate was not well received in opulent restaurants.

In this respect, too, he was most unrewarding to women—he never spent much money on them, nor, in fact, really seemed to make an effort about them. Rumors were always current that he was "a devil with the women," for he had only to walk into a room and most females gravitated toward him. Men called him "quite an operator." Women helplessly described it as "a sort of magic." His press agent, Ivy Wilson, who admired him but had never seen the so-called sex appeal, rushed to her husband one evening and said: "I've found out what the girls all love in Leslie Howard. It's the way he says 'good night'—it gave me a soft glow—it was like the purring of a cat—a tomcat!"

Actually, his private life was a great deal calmer than anyone suspected—even Ruth. He really could not help his fantastic charm for the opposite sex, and it surprised him somewhat, for as a boy he had been markedly unsuccessful, constantly unrequited.

Just before *British Agent* was finished, Leslie shipped four polo ponies to England. Some trouble was encountered in loading one of the mares. "Send for Leslie," said Ruth. "He can do anything with women and horses—she'll go on board for Leslie." Sure enough, when he came down to the dock, spoke to the mare, and rubbed her face, she walked into the net, all sweet reasonableness.

The homeward journey was a typical Howard performance. Ruth went on to New York by train with Mary Gargan, leaving Leslie to finish a retake. As Leslie hated traveling alone, he persuaded Bill Gargan to keep him company on the train. Once in the East with Ruth and Mary, Bill was pressed to go on to England. The difficulties of no money, few clothes, and no passport were brushed aside by Leslie, but ten minutes before the boat sailed, all Bill had achieved was the passport. He asked Leslie to lend him some money. "Of course, old chap." So they left for the dock, battled through five thousand fans, besieging Leslie for autographs, though Gargan was still without money. Leslie was occupied by the press and photographers —no money was forthcoming. Finally, after shouting in Leslie's ear for five minutes, Bill learned that Ruth had all the Howard money. He might have known. With her help, he paid his fare and both Gargans sailed for England.

Robert Emmet Sherwood, the playwright, was on board the *Majestic*. He and Leslie were both going to London for Alexander Korda: Leslie to make *The Scarlet Pimpernel;* Sherwood to finish the film script. During the voyage Sherwood showed Leslie a play that he had recently written called *The Petrified Forest*. He said there was a part in it just made for Leslie. All the way to England Leslie read and reread the manuscript. It was a tremendous play, and long before he arrived at Southampton, he had agreed to come back to New York for the production as soon as he was free. It was not often that he read a play as potentially important as *The Petrified Forest,* or met a character that was drawn with such skill, and seemingly drawn for him alone.

15 / Family Reunion

The boat tied up at Southampton. Leslie and Ruth stood on deck trying to identify the foreshortened figures on the dock. Suddenly there was a shout and the small purposeful shape of their daughter was seen leaping up and down. As soon as the gangplank was in position, the two Leslies were together, hand in hand, oblivious of everyone else, Doodie talking without pause, Leslie listening with grave attention broken from time to time by a delighted laugh.

"Look at them," said Ruth. "They're impossible once you let them get together."

Her point was well taken, for Leslie forgot everything once Doodie began to drag him along. Back at the Stowe, he was led around to admire all the latest acquisitions. There was a new wing on the stables, with his four California horses already pushing their noses out of the boxes; the addition to the house was complete; a new wall had been built; Doodie had four Angora rabbits, another dog, a hunter mare, and her own patch of garden. Each must be inspected, admired, and discussed. This made him unobtainable, late for tea, and generally unpopular with the other members of the family. Giggling like a couple of conspirators, father and daughter took their punishment together.

212

Now that he had some polo ponies, Leslie must play polo. This warm summer of 1934, therefore, found him traveling around to the elegant London clubs, Ranelagh, Hurlingham, and Roehampton, taking as energetic a part as, in his opinion, his health would permit. He had sent a trainer over from California with his horses, and this kindly man, Harry Sherwin, played with Leslie, rode with Doodie, and became a good friend of the family.

The Scarlet Pimpernel took up some of Leslie's time, but no more than polo did, for its director, Alexander Korda, had a most aesthetic approach to film making. If it were a beautiful day full of sunshine and the song of birds, he would cancel work. He allowed nothing to interfere with the pleasures and comforts of life.

In this atmosphere, a superb film was produced. With Nigel Bruce as the Prince Regent, Raymond Massey as the vindictive Chauvelin, Merle Oberon as Lady Blakeney, and a dozen other first-class English actors, here was a picture made under ideal conditions, a picture that would remain a classic of its kind for twenty-five years. Leslie could not remember enjoying anything as much. With wonderful costumes, ingenious disguises, excellent dialogue, there was no need for hurry as far as he was concerned. It left plenty of time for polo, and for showing the Gargans the amusements of London.

Leslie took Bill Gargan sight-seeing, meeting him at the Cenotaph: "You can't miss that, old chap," and escorted him to various places of interest. In Downing Street, while looking at the home of the prime minister, they were surrounded by autograph seekers. To Bill's complete surprise, no one paid any attention to Leslie. They thrust papers at Gargan, and he signed, needling his host gently all the while. "Never heard of you over here—eh, old man? This certainly makes up for New York, old boy. You don't seem very big in London, kid."

A great many Americans visited the Stowe that summer,

among them, Charles Farrell and Ralph Bellamy and their wives. The Gargans stayed on while Bill made a picture. Ruth ran a full and carefree household. The sun was shining, the film business prospering; no one cared to worry about the future. A few voices in England tried to raise the alarm and warn the country of a rising, arming Germany under Hitler. But those who read the warning correctly and spoke their minds in England were cried down as fools and warmongers. In the House of Commons the Labor Opposition even censured the Government plan for a small increase in the Royal Air Force as "a revival of dangerous and wasteful competition in preparation for war." Winston Churchill called out his eloquent words of caution and impending catastrophe to a nation that refused to hear. What use for the thoughtful to listen, when the unheeding were so many?

In London, Leslie met and talked with some of the few who believed in Churchill's warning, the people who had been to Germany and knew the fierce aggressive power growing there. Leslie went himself, and he, too, was made to fear. Late were the discussions of an evening around the fire at Stowe Maries. But what could individuals do or say that fateful year as Nazi strength rose up to meet and far outstrip a land that only wanted "peace in our time."

Actors, after all, must act, and even world affairs slip out of view in the daily round of dialogue and camera angles. *The Scarlet Pimpernel* drifted on serenely. Korda smoked a leisurely cigar, and Leslie, dressed as an old French hag, sat at the guillotine and watched an earlier aggression re-enacted.

Robert Sherwood cabled from New York: WHEN DO REHEARSALS BEGIN PETRIFIED FOREST? And who, indeed, could answer him? Not Alexander Korda, quite ignorant of time. Not Leslie, planning new glories at his country house. So it was not September, but November, when Leslie found himself once more upon the sea. Ruth and Miss Goss and the children were to follow later.

While he began to rehearse in New York, the film that had delayed him was previewed in London and justified its lengthy birth. *The Scarlet Pimpernel* received superlative notices.

"In point of sheer pictorial enchantment, no other film in 1934 has reached the exquisite quality achieved in this production."

"An extraordinary fine film steeped in adventure and gallantry."

Now, at last, the headlines read: LESLIE HOWARD, THE BEST STAR OF 1934. The *Daily Mail* wrote: "In the title part Mr. Leslie Howard gives the finest performance of his career, particularly in those passages in which he plays the elegant fop to conceal his identity as The Scarlet Pimpernel."

The *Telegraph* said: "Leslie Howard scores the greatest hit of his screen career . . . his scenes with the Prince Regent and Chauvelin are in the great tradition of English high comedy, and it is hard to believe that any actor past or present, could have bettered them."

The British were cautious and slow in giving praise. It had taken Leslie nearly eighteen years of reasonably good acting to finally receive these notices. But once convinced, the critics and the public supported their favorites with extraordinary zeal. Leslie was given the Picturegoer Gold Medal for 1934 by popular vote. He belonged to England now—they proudly claimed him; he was no longer to be "that American actor!"

When the clippings from the London papers arrived, Leslie's mind was fully occupied with matters in New York. Robert Sherwood's play was at the end of rehearsals and ready for its Boston tryout. Produced by Arthur Hopkins and Gilbert Miller, the production had intelligence and authority.

It was almost the first time that Robert Sherwood had written of his native land, and both the theatrical architecture and the dialogue proclaimed *The Petrified Forest* his finest play. Set in the lunchroom of a gas station in Arizona, the play was built around the people who lived there and those who passed through. Alan Squier walks in for a meal, dust-covered and disillusioned, an intellectual searching for something in which to believe, or final proof that there is nothing. Behind the counter he finds a young girl, dreaming unimaginable dreams. They love each other; she with passion, he with "desperate tranquility," knowing there cannot be a future for such a child with such a man as he. The arrival of a gangster and his hench-man solves this problem and provides a change of pace from pastoral to melodrama. In the end, Alan Squier lies dead by his own request, shot so that the dryad in the cheap café can escape from the "Petrified Forest." To clothe these dry and yet dramatic bones, Sherwood gave his characters something to say, gave them time to say it. He "blended humor and blood-shed, romance and taunt and fantasy's privileged thoughts" to present a section of American life, clear, compelling and some-how rather beautiful, for all its dust and clamor.

Leslie played Alan Squier, Peggy Conklin played the girl, Gaby, and Humphrey Bogart, the gangster. The play opened to bravos in Boston on Christmas Eve and stormed New York with brilliant success on January 7, 1935.

In this, Leslie's penultimate Broadway performance, it was fitting that he should be crowned with the ultimate in critical reviews and public enthusiasm. The press applauded unani-mously. The giants in their morning drama columns gave the actor the nicest breakfast of his life.

"Any dramatist who gives Leslie Howard a good chance to cast his celebrated spell is a friend of the playgoers and de-serves the epaulettes of a public benefactor," said Percy Ham-mond in the New York *Herald*.

"Leslie Howard is one of the drama's most eloquent listen-ers," wrote Burns Mantle. "He can, given a stage and a pipe, inspire more interest and express more drama by letting those around him do most of the talking and practically all of the acting than four ordinary actors. . . ."

John Anderson recorded in the New York *Evening Journal:*

"Mr. Howard is, for all his trepidations at returning from the movies, nothing less than superb at every inflection of [the play]. It is a performance of great insight and marvellous flexibility, where every accent is given its full meaning and statement."

Brooks Atkinson of the New York *Times* summed up the performance, and Leslie, too, with "the philosophy is spoken by Leslie Howard and that is transfiguration for almost any sort of dialogue. Mr. Howard is a superlatively gifted actor. Any drama critic who is worth his salt ought to be able to distinguish plausibly between an actor's personality and his artistic design of a part. As an actor, Mr. Howard is intelligent and conscientious enough to approach each part as a task requiring fresh character perceptions; he is one of the most enlightened craftsmen in the profession. But his style of playing is such a lucid expression of his light slender buoyant personal appearance that I confess I am unable to tell how his acting of Alan Squier differs from his acting of Peter Standish in 'Berkeley Square' or Tom Collier in 'The Animal Kingdom.' In my mind all those parts are permanently stamped in the image of Mr. Howard's limpid personality. All that matters in the current instance is his power to make a theatregoer believe in the reality of the part he is playing. Although Mr. Sherwood has written some lofty phrases for Alan Squier to speak and subjected him to ostentatious behaviour, Mr. Howard's shining acting persuades you that every impulse in it is true."

After the opening-night performance, a dense crowd collected at the stage door. They filled the alleyway and blocked the street. Rather fierce-looking women comprised ninety per cent of the number. Leslie's old friend George Fogel had come backstage, and, by linking arms with two other men, he managed to force a passage through the seething mob. Halfway to the car Leslie was attacked from the rear, cut loose from his protectors, and set upon. Under the stricken gaze of these gentlemen, he found himself surrounded. Two robust females worked upon him with scissors, snipping hair and buttons and, as he jumped back from them, a third seized and kissed him. The rest contented themselves with frantic pawing and impassioned words of everlasting devotion. Rescued by the police just before the scissors removed his trouser buttons, Leslie fell into the car and was driven away. He cocked an eye at the theater and remarked: "The last time I played at this theater was in *The Green Hat* with Katharine Cornell. I had a dressing room on the third floor, and I used to watch Miss Cornell battling through this same frightful mob every night and I thought—my goodness me, it would be very exciting to be so famous!—but you know, George, it isn't so pleasant after all!"

That winter in New York was rather irritating for the Howards as a family. Ruth, the children, and Miss Goss lived in a most comfortable apartment, Winkie went to Columbia University, and Doodie had a brief brush with a sedate educational establishment for young ladies. Life looked pleasant enough, but Leslie, unfortunately, was suffering from that most tiresome complaint which afflicts the forty-year-old man— wife-boredom. He suddenly imagined himself enamored of a younger woman, and became quite dramatic on the subject. He even pretended to live in another hotel, which simply complicated his life because, of course, he could not eat hotel food and rushed home for all his meals. This tedious performance lasted until he was stricken by boils, a most unromantic ailment at the best of times. The unfortunate young woman in the case did her best to offer sympathy and assistance, but Leslie was no longer interested. Only Ruth could possibly cope with his condition, only Ruth could nurse him and provide the dear old familiar care that he had known for almost twenty years. Home he went, rather sheepishly, to be forgiven, of course, his one serious attempt at romance squashed by a skin disease, but more than ever aware that his Ruthie was indispensable. When, a few months later, a reporter tactlessly asked him if divorce was in the wind, he shook with self-righteousness.

"Certainly not. No man would throw away the sort of family life I enjoy. My wife and children are essential to my existence." And he meant it—he would not exchange what he had for anyone in the world.

In the spring, Ruth and Wink went to Hollywood. Miss Goss and Doodie looked after Leslie, for the play still ran.

"Leslie Howard shot for the 100th time to-night," reported the newspapers, and he grumbled as usual. What a tiresome thing a successful play could be.

16 / The Might-Have-Been

A big city was a difficult place in which to amuse a ten-year-old who steadfastly refused to go to school. If Leslie was bored, Doodie seemed even more disgusted. In an effort to entertain themselves, they started reading plays together. This was a successful arrangement, for Doodie, firmly professing no interest in the art of acting, secretly considered herself a combination of Duse and Mrs. Siddons. They read the short scene for father and daughter from Barrie's *Dear Brutus,* and Leslie felt it was a perfect opportunity for a Howard production. He had always been charmed by this gently pathetic scene about a man who longs for a daughter and finds her on Mid-Summer's Eve only to discover she is just a shade, a figment of his longing, a might-have-been.

They began to rehearse this scene every morning. Leslie was a hard taskmaster, but Doodie was a mimic. She had little talent for acting, but she could imitate her father's deft style exactly. *"Don't* go into that house, Daddy—I don't know *why* it is, but I'm *afraid* of that house." Over and over it they went, until every inflection was there, just as he wanted it. Doodie could recite the whole scene, and worked herself into tears in bed at night. *"I* don't want to be a might-have-been either, Daddy," she cried, with her face pressed into Leslie's coat.

"You're not, my darling—there, there," and he would sooth her to sleep, stroking her face and whistling softly his own special tune, as he had done since she was a baby. No one was less likely to suffer from intangibility than his rather rotund daughter, but he never laughed at her fears; they vanished in the warmth of his love.

The scene from *Dear Brutus* was presented on the Rudy Vallee radio show on May 16, 1935. It made a considerable impression on its listeners. Miss Howard, who always reveled in her father's stage-door following, now enjoyed a certain prestige herself. On every side she heard of the inherited genius she had displayed. Leslie smiled politely, and Doodie positively gloried in the notices. Siddons, Duse, Bernhardt were as nothing. She would outrank them all! But there was a very well-kept secret between father and daughter, or perhaps only Leslie really knew it: the little genius was simply an imitative, small monkey; she could not read a line unless her father showed her how. Nevertheless, on the old basis that some people can always be fooled, the performance was repeated, and even Ruth, listening in California, wired: DARLING, MUMMY THOUGHT YOU WERE MARVELLOUS. Interviewed by Rudy Vallee, Doodie clung tenaciously to her stand about acting. No, she had no interest in the theater—only the barnyard. She wanted to be a veterinary surgeon. Leslie was highly entertained. The last thing he would ever do was persuade anyone to be an actor.

The summer heat came early that year, and it was not with pleasure that Leslie presented himself each night at the Broadhurst Theatre. He was plagued to lecture and speak to organizations every week. One such engagement was a mass interview on the stage of the Broadhurst by three hundred college and high-school newspaper reporters. What questions they asked him! What did he think of autograph hunters? "Bad manners. They belong to the movies and the typical movie fan is a freak!" he replied.

"What chance have young people to start in the theater?"

"It's pure gamble," said Leslie. "Just as precarious as ever."

"Do you expect to always be an actor or to do something better?" And he answered gravely: "I've always wanted to better myself in life. I will leave when I can do something equally well or better."

Then he was asked a singularly pertinent question. "Do you want to play *Hamlet?*" Leslie parried it with: "Every actor wants to play *Hamlet*," but it was not really a fair answer. Every actor might want to play that part, but he, Leslie Howard, was seriously considering it.

When John Mason Brown in his column "Two on the Aisle" in the New York *Evening Post* raised the subject of Leslie's future as an actor of stature, the actor read the critic and agreed.

"If Leslie Howard had not shown us once what he can do as an actor by giving such a memorable performance as the tortured hero of Mr. Galsworthy's 'Escape,'" wrote Brown, "some of his admirers would lament a little less that quiet, effortless charm of his which he has brought to one play and one movie after another during the last ten years or more. That he is charming and handsome, no one can deny. That he is skillful is equally self-evident . . . but unusual as are his gifts, and admirable as his performances have been . . . they all have been pretty much of one kind. . . . We do not mean to say that Mr. Howard is not excellent in doing what he does, or that we ever really tire of watching him do it again, or that there is anyone else can do it half so well. But with his performance of Matt Denant in 'Escape' still vivid in our mind, we do wonder why it is that Mr. Howard has never bothered to enlarge his field, or to play the truly courageous part in the theatre which could so easily be his."

Farther down in the article appeared an important comment —significantly marked in blue pencil by Leslie: ". . . it leaves one wondering why a man who ought to make an interesting

Hamlet . . . should have elected to be so unadventurous as an actor."

Hamlet—how often had he thought of this part, and how deep-seated in an actor is the urge to play Shakespeare, whether suitable or not. Leslie, always full of plans and ideas for the future, now seriously considered *Hamlet,* encouraged by the views of this eminent New York critic, and intrigued by a new version of the play sent to him by a recent Yale graduate, Schuyler Watts. This young man came to Leslie's dressing room one night and with the audacity of his years suggested *Hamlet* again.

"Why do you think I should play it?" asked Leslie.

"Because you must be tired of always playing yourself" came the impudent reply.

Far from irritating Leslie, the remark arrested his attention. It reflected his own feelings; here was a young man worth talking to.

Later that night, at Sardi's, they discussed the possibilities of *Hamlet.* Leslie was drawn instinctively to Schuyler Watts, entertained by both his wit and his honesty in a world not renowned for either. In the young man, Leslie recognized, too, a real erudition, a knowledge of Shakespeare, and particularly of *Hamlet,* that sparked his own interest and enthusiasm.

The decision had been made, though at first only subconsciously, when they parted that night. From then forward, Leslie and Schuyler Watts worked together on the preparation of a *Hamlet* version for production in the winter of 1935.

In June *The Petrified Forest* closed. There was always the lure of England, and Leslie sent two more horses there, again under the care of Harry Sherwin. In fact, it had been Sherwin's "Come on, Leslie, let's go to England and play polo" that decided the crossing. Harry Sherwin, operating for a year as a kind of personal buffer for Leslie in New York, now went back to his natural habitat, the saddle. The Howards followed him shortly, but first Leslie had become intrigued with Bermuda and a stop was made there.

He had made a friend in William Beebe, the ichthyologist, renowned for his recent descents in a bathosphere to investigate the dark waters of the ocean. Beebe lived in Bermuda, surrounded by his life study, and there the Howard family found him. Leslie's inquiring mind was fascinated by stories of tropical fish and the beauties of the sea bottom. But he never saw much of these glories; he landed in a hospital with another of his boils. But the children followed Beebe every day, and enjoyed the privilege of instruction from this brilliant man. When the time came to sail, Leslie had not inspected the sea bed—he got claustrophobia from a diving helmet—and his closest association with tropical fish was the large bowl of them that Doodie clutched all the way to England. But he had lain in the sun, scantily clad, as usual, and been photographed for papers all over the world strolling on the beach in nothing more than a towel.

England saw Leslie very briefly. A few weeks of relaxation at his house, some work with Schuyler Watts, who was in London to study the second quarto of *Hamlet* at the British Museum, on which he was to base his version of the play, and then a month at Dunster, in Somerset, where he played polo on the wide green fields below the historic castle. Many of the well-known players took themselves there when polo in London ended for the holidays, and Leslie was able to join them in games nearly every day. He sent six ponies down, and, when not playing, he and Doodie rambled across the beautiful and rough country of Exmoor on the horses. But it was over too soon, and he left again to fulfill film commitments in California, and Ruth went with him to establish a base for the family there. As the boat sailed, he wrote to Doodie:

"Darling little Nimrod, how I miss you already. . . . We have the most beautiful suite here, all filled with Stowe Maries flowers. I'm so homesick . . . give my love to each horse . . .

be a good girl. Go to bed early and keep well. Your very loving Dadlet."

The house they found in Hollywood belonged to Lily Pons, and bordered the mansion of Cecil B. deMille. It was large, patioed, swimming pooled, and quite suitable for a movie star. Its drawing room was dominated by a baronial fireplace, which lacked nothing but the coat of arms and the motto. There were many suggestions for these, the best coming from Dwight Franklin: *Honi soit qui* Lily Pons.

Franklin had been a friend of Ruth and Leslie in the old days on Long Island. He was married to Mary McCaull, and was in Hollywood doing set designs. His wife worked for Warner Brothers as a script writer, and she now helped Leslie prepare an outline for a film about Charles Edward Stuart, the Young Pretender, the "Bonnie Prince Charlie" of Scotland. Leslie was attracted to Prince Charlie, that rather touching, romantic figure, and his forlorn hope. The idea of a picture based on his life had been discussed for a number of years. Leslie had suggested it to any and every producer who approached. Now he let Wink work on the background with Miss McCaull. It became a family project. Wink was studying for his university entrance examinations, hoping to go to Cambridge, and using his spare time for writing. He followed his father's bent for prose, but added a quite unusual flair for poetry, spilling out long, heroic works, sometimes charming, occasionally rather turgid, but bearing the mark of a future maturity and style. Leslie continued to be his staunchest ally; it was a strong common bond between these two, and the father, laughing sometimes at the juicy language of seventeen, encouraged his son all the more fervently because he was himself a writer at heart.

The film version of *The Petrified Forest* had been delayed by casting problems. Warner Brothers wanted Edward G. Robinson for the gangster. Leslie was obdurate on this subject. He had given his word to Humphrey Bogart in New

York that no one else should be Duke Mantee. He also believed that no other actor could bring to this part the chilling melodrama coupled with the brilliant sense of underplaying that had distinguished Bogart's performance. Leslie made it plain that if the studio wanted Howard they must have Humphrey Bogart as well, and to no one's surprise he got his way. The success achieved by Bogart in *The Petrified Forest* was an immediate justification of Leslie's stand. The young actor never forgot, which Leslie found a surprising and endearing quality in Hollywood.

Bette Davis was in the role of Gaby, the dreaming romantic, turning in another thoughtful and clever performance. It was a joy to act with her, for she combined professionalism and intelligence. Scenes could be shot without complicated provisions being taken for the lack of talent and overabundance of beauty which characterized the usual in Hollywood movie queens.

Almost before one film was finished, another was in the wind. Irving Thalberg asked Leslie to play Romeo to Norma Shearer's Juliet. He was disappointed in Leslie's reaction, though on evidence it would appear natural and accurate. Romeo was a boy, a rather tiresome, headstrong boy at that, and Howard was forty-two, hardly star-crossed, and quite sophisticated in his odd way. He considered Romeo a second-rate part in many respects, and he felt it had held no interest for Shakespeare. "The poet had his heart and soul in Juliet," wrote Leslie, ". . . his whole interest is so clearly centered in this shining girl. She is the perfection of youth, beauty, passion and unswerving fidelity. Romeo was necessary since you cannot have a love story without a lover. But he seems hardly to be a three dimensional figure; his principal function is to be the object of Juliet's affection. . . . A woman to be interesting does not have to be anything but in love. . . . But a man who does nothing but love! If he is as young as Romeo is reputed to be, we do not take him seriously. And if he is as old as the average actor has to be to have the necessary experience for this role, he is a bore. Furthermore, as the play opens he is in love with another girl, obviously one of a succession of infatuations. The fellow is in love with love (what is more depressing in a man) and even his friends are laughing at him. To make the chap interesting is a task to frighten any actor."

In addition to Leslie's resistance, Thalberg had to contend with the brothers Warner. Leslie was under contract to them, and they would not release him. The negotiations were difficult and protracted, with Mike Levee trying every dodge to persuade his client and the studio. Because Jack Warner refused to bargain, Leslie underwent a dramatic change of heart. He *wanted* to play Romeo, he longed to play Romeo, and the attitude of his studio was a disgraceful infringement of his personal rights as an artist. This part of Romeo, the young philanderer, could be turned to advantage, he suddenly proclaimed.

"After the first youthful raptures are over, and he is banished and waits miserably in Mantua, the stunning news of Juliet's apparent death produces in him for the rest of the play a mood which has some stature and nobility. Then he is overcome by a fine philosophic world-weariness and melancholy which is prophetic of that profound character study which Shakespeare had not yet created when he wrote Romeo and Juliet. Romeo becomes a baby Hamlet.

"One may, therefore, understand why an actor who has ambitious designs upon the Danish prince and who has never spoken a word of Shakespeare, should want to take his first classical steps in this part."

Leslie's growing determination to produce and play *Hamlet* had an important effect upon his decision to play Romeo. Although it would delay the *Hamlet* deadline, he felt it would be worth it both in experience and extra money. All the studio difficulties were resolved in a switch between Metro-Goldwyn-Mayer and Warner. Robert Montgomery and Clark

Gable were lent to Warner Brothers by M-G-M, and Leslie and Paul Muni went to that studio for roles in *Romeo and Juliet* and *The Good Earth* respectively.

The production of the Shakespeare tragedy was magnificent. No expense was considered too great to reproduce the glories of Verona. Whole sound stages were turned into gardens and streets; Juliet's balcony was thirty feet high; George Cukor came to direct, and the cast read like a Who's Who in Hollywood: Basil Rathbone, John Barrymore, Ralph Forbes, Edna May Oliver, Reginald Denny, choreography by Agnes de Mille. Money appeared to be no object and time of even less importance.

The weeks rolled away, and Leslie amused himself and Doodie with the model airplane craze that had struck California that year. Reggy Denny, his fellow Veronese chum in *Romeo,* had a shop of infinite joys and delicious delights, selling small airplanes with and without engines, kits for making airplanes, paints and balsa wood, glue and sandpaper. Doodie and Leslie spent two or three evenings a week in the marvelous spot. They owned ten planes of different sizes, Leslie finally buying a glory with a six-foot wing span and a one-stroke engine. Every night they returned from their aeronautical excursions to fly their machines around Ruth's bedroom, regardless of her pleas and strongly worded protestations.

The other consuming interest was in trailers. These beautiful things—"sleep four, complete kitchen and bathroom facilities" —were inspected and discussed by father and daughter. Ruth, threatened with this new pursuit and seeing herself having to operate the kitchen and cope with the extensive preparations, threw cold water on the idea at once, most unreasonably in the eyes of her family.

It was difficult for her to maintain discipline, harried as she was from every side, but she called her innate dramatic streak into being whenever the pressure became too intense. Wrapped in haughty majesty, tossing rich, if occasionally incorrect, words at one and all, she carried the day, generally by reducing her family to helpless laughter. After a particularly heated discussion when her language had been quite classical in its stature, she would suddenly say with enormous dignity: "And if you don't like it—you can lump it!" On one occasion all opposition was silenced when she drew herself up and witheringly announced: "As far as I am concerned, you may all take a Swedish swan dive from the top platform!" Though most absurd interests were in this way controlled, horses were beyond Ruth. Leslie bought another eight in Texas that summer and shipped six of them to England. This was his idea of economy, because the horses cost only eighty dollars each in Texas. By the time they were unloaded in England, they had cost much the same as race horses.

The winter turned to spring, and Leslie wanted to be away. He had now definitely set the date of his own production of *Hamlet* in New York for the autumn of 1936, and he needed time and peace to work upon it. Retakes, the bane of a movie actor's life, when scene after scene must be shot again, began as the roses were coming out at Stowe Maries.

"This can go on forever," moaned Leslie. "Norma is wonderful but too serious about this part. The public won't mind whether she says 'Wherefore *art* thou, Romeo,' or '*Wherefore* art thou, Romeo,' and who cares, anyway?"

He never took his work too seriously, except in front of the camera, and Mike Levee found him a happy change from the more dedicated members of the profession. Paul Muni, at work on *The Good Earth,* was also a client of Levee's, and this fine and clever actor was deeply involved with his serious part. "I go to see Muni first," said Mike Levee. "And he is bearing the sorrow of the Chinese famine on his own shoulders; then, depressed beyond words, I go take a look at Leslie. First you can't find him—then when you do catch sight of him he's up a forty-foot ladder taking photographs from the catwalk. It drives the studio nuts—he could break his fool neck, but it's very good for the spirits." Leslie refused to be cautioned about his climbing activities. "Tell them I'm rehearsing for that balcony scene, Mike; it's so high I need the experience!"

When a suitable number of retakes had been produced, Ruth suddenly took matters into her own hands.

"Leslie can do no more work after next Thursday—we're sailing for England."

The studio was aghast. They threatened and pleaded, begged and beseeched.

"My wife, you know," said Leslie sweetly. "I can't do a thing once she makes up her mind."

Ruth's reputation as "that terrible Ruth Howard" became blacker by the hour. Poor Ruth—she said all the things that Leslie longed to say but cleverly realized he could get said for him and still keep his unblemished reputation as a charming, easygoing fellow. Ruth was his "front man," his Charlie McCarthy.

In the inevitable fine flurry, the Howards prepared to quit Hollywood. This time a great effort was made to keep their movements secret because of a kidnaping threat to Doodie. For months the house had been under a nightly guard after reportedly suspicious-looking men had been seen hanging about and asking questions. Doodie thought she would quite like the importance; for a long time she had gazed with envious eyes at Marlene Dietrich's daughter, Maria, followed by detectives and surrounded by iron bars and burglar alarms. But the actuality was rather less pleasant, and when a man sneaked into her bedroom one evening and was only routed by screams and the whole family in pursuit, she began to hate the feeling of being watched. For this reason, if no other, Leslie was desperately anxious to leave America and put his children out of harm's way in the secure, disinterested village of Westcott.

The cloak-and-dagger attempts at a mysterious departure were relatively unsuccessful. There were last-minute importunities from M-G-M, emissaries from that studio, travel agents, friends, and reporters. In the chaos, Ruth forgot to watch Leslie, and, left to his own devices, he weakly agreed to take the butler back to England. This rather gentle individual had developed a crush on his employer and longed to follow him anywhere. Leslie, too good-natured to be firm, finally admitted to Ruth that the man was going to England with them. The muddle by the time they reached New York exceeded even former Howard records, and Ruth had to cope with 129 pieces of luggage, her unpunctual family, and a butler. As ever, she managed it all.

17 / "Hamlet" - a Life's Ambition

"A curious study in morbid psychology is offered by the fatal attraction which the name of Shakespeare exercises upon persons connected with the theatre," a drama critic once wrote. ". . . managers, actors, variety artists, musical comedy stars, all alike flutter for a dozen years or so and then plunge blindly into the detestible man."

The attraction for Leslie was no less intense than for other members of his profession, but his plunge into *Hamlet* should not be thought a blind one. For over a year he had studied and considered, worked at and dreamed about the play and its central figure. He recognized that Hamlet had been played more often than any other Shakespearean part, and that each actor had expressed something of his own intelligence and personality through his performance. From the "vivacious enterprising Hamlet of Betterton" and the "fixed and sullen gloom" of John Philip Kemble, there had been many visions of the character: Edmund Kean, criticized for not seeing Hamlet as a whole, but, rather, as a "sequence of impressive moments," Macready, "lachrymose and fretful," and Edwin Booth playing the Prince as "sane, natural, graceful, melancholy, supersensitive, restless and wildly impetuous." In the memory of some still living remained the dramatic power and glory of

232

Henry Irving's Hamlet and the later, most beautiful performance of Johnston Forbes-Robertson.

There could be as many interpretations of the role as there
were actors with imagination to play it. Leslie knew, or thought
he knew, his own limitations. He was largely without experience in Shakespeare, lacking the great dramatic power of
many previous Hamlets, but able to bring intelligence and
sensitivity to his portrayal. He wanted to speak the glorious
language in a way that would be understandable to everybody;
to widen the audience for Shakespeare, and to reach those people whose only knowledge of the dramatist had been enforced
study at school or attendance at performances where the sense
had been sacrificed to the poetry, and both lost in bored in-
comprehension.

The version prepared by Schuyler Watts took due consideration of Leslie's strengths and of his type of acting. The solilo-
quies were not staged as a dramatic showcase for virtuosity, but,
rather, as the quiet, thoughtful discourse of a student, caught
between ordered revenge and his own instability. In the year
or more in which Leslie prepared for his production, he had
searched out and studied a vast amount of material on the
play. The source to which he went most often and in which
he found the most satisfaction was that of Professor J. Dover
Wilson, of Cambridge, the Shakespeare scholar. Dover Wilson
had published three monographs on *Hamlet,* and his edition of
the text, based also on the second quarto, had appeared in 1934.

Through the soft summer days in Surrey, Leslie worked at
his production. Ruth had never seen him so engrossed in anything as he was in this; hidden away in his room with his
books and his radio, he was completely happy. There were
more friends from Hollywood to stay, and one, Eda Gershgorn,
went with Leslie for long, tranquil, country walks listening to
his plans for *Hamlet* and marveling at the capacity for concentration of this quiet, absent-minded man.

Throughout that summer Leslie made the final arrangements

for casting, and for set and costume design. Stewart Chaney had prepared drawings and models. This was to be a Viking Hamlet, and the eleventh-century designs, of stark simplicity, were unusually beautiful and accurate. John Houseman was to collaborate with Leslie in the direction, and he had brought in Virgil Thomson to compose a fascinating score for the play. Agnes de Mille was doing the choreography for the players scene. From all this intensive work, Leslie could still disentangle himself when he chose and spend afternoons playing polo and relaxing with his children, but time was getting short and his sailing for New York approached.

Leslie's production of *Hamlet* had excited great interest in New York. There was an almost unfortunate amount of publicity in every newspaper and magazine. In an article he wrote for *Stage Magazine,* he said: "When a modern actor, one who is completely lacking in the remotest form of classical training, attempts the preparation, production and performance of a Shakespearean chef d'oeuvre, he saddles himself with a responsibility which is both dangerous and formidable. It is dangerous because he may be revealed (after many satisfactory years of deception) in his true colours as no actor at all in the 'important' sense, or at best as one whose claim to attention has been based on an attractive personality, a pleasing voice, or some originality or bearing." He went on to explain his own approach to *Hamlet,* and the existing traditions that surrounded the play. "The die-hard school . . . insists there is one way and one way only to do Shakespeare and that is the way it has 'always been done', the classical way, with rhetorical-poetical acting in a background of rich realism. The way it has always been done refers, one presumes, to the Shakespeare of living memory, the latter nineteenth century methods of Booth and Irving and even Forbes-Robertson. It ignores completely the lack of reverence of the eighteenth century, in particular that of David Garrick who admits to 'the most imprudent thing I ever did' in his complete alteration and re-writing of 'Hamlet'. On the other side we find parked defiantly the modern radicals—or such of them as have any use at all for Elizabethan drama. With them it is held that nothing should be retained of earlier methods. The play should be cut, re-arranged, scenes and lines transposed, characters modified, new meanings discovered, settings made abstract and significant and symbolic. I must confess to a lack of sympathy for either of these extremes. . . . No, for myself, in order to find a way of approach to the problem I have gone to Shakespeare as one man of the theatre to another. I have tried to understand the methods of his craftsmanship and the conditions under which he worked. I have been governed by a spirit of reasonable humility, but not of slavish reverence. I have had the nerve to consider the two of us co-workers in a theatrical enterprise and have tried to forget that my partner is separated from me by over three hundred years of time and ringing fame."

In the early fall of 1936, into the hullabaloo of advance publicity, Ruth and Leslie arrived. Mike Levee met them in New York and tried to persuade Leslie to postpone his production because Guthrie McClintic had suddenly announced his intention to present *Hamlet* that same season in New York, with John Gielgud. Mike was anxious that Leslie should not attempt any new concept of the play in competition with one the critics and the public knew and accepted, but Leslie was determined. The McClintic production was a surprise and a shock to Leslie. He was puzzled by this seemingly last-minute decision to present a rival *Hamlet.* There were even those who said the plan was a deliberate one, but Leslie felt that he had worked too long on his *Hamlet* to postpone its production again. Possibly, every man having his vanity, this was Leslie's piece of egotism. He backed the play with his own money and he believed in it. He told Mike Levee, "Sometimes it is necessary to disregard the economic aspects. You're a practical re-

of the endless day before the opening. He was beset with advice about revisions in his own interpretation, urged to broaden his performance, to give Hamlet more fire and excitement. Into a head already whirling with words and problems, this mistaken counsel added nothing but more chaos. Everyone brought problems to him. Twenty minutes before the curtain went up, he was trying to sort out the priority seating plan for the theater. Leslie was about to play the longest and most demanding role of his life, and even a few minutes alone were denied him.

Ruth did her utmost to keep him quiet, to fend off the bearers of ill-judged advice and picayune problems, but he was so much the heart of this body of production that he could not rest or relax.

The curtain rose on scenes of great splendor, the pace and the pageantry remained, but Hamlet was not the figure he had been in Boston or Philadelphia. He was a tired man. He was striving too hard to please his critics. Leslie had conceived the character as sensitive, mordant, clever, and restrained. It could not be and should not have been changed to compete with the almost pathologically excitable and exciting Hamlet of John Gielgud. Fortunately, it was a one-night aberration; unfortunately, it was the one night that really mattered.

The New York critics fell upon the play with a fiendish zeal. It was almost as though they had said to each other, "We have already stated what kind of Hamlet we like, who is this movie star to change our minds?"

Douglas Gilbert in the *World-Telegram* likened Leslie to a "petulant schoolmaster" in an "excellent production by the senior class of the South Bend High School," saying in conclusion, "comparisons are not inevitable—they are impossible." John Anderson felt it ". . . quite unnecessary to discuss his performance with any idea that it is an interpretation of Hamlet," and closed his review with the encouragement: "It seems a pity that Mr. Howard ever gave rein to the notion that he could play Hamlet, but since he had completed one of the finest housing projects of that drama that our stage has ever seen, I propose that he leave it standing until someone with size enough comes along to inhabit it."

John Mason Brown called the production "Hamlet with the Hamlet left out," and informed Gielgud that he was at liberty to drop the Giel from his name and call his "the Gud Hamlet."

There were, on that unhappy morning after the first night, a few critics who, though not able to praise Leslie's performance, searched for a crumb of consolation for the actor. Burns Mantle called it "an honest performance, carefully studied, read with a casualness that achieves a pleasantly colloquial expression," and Brooks Atkinson did his best to be kind with "a gracious figure, a beguiling personal beauty, a winning manner, a pleasing voice, an alert intelligence." How nicely even they damned with polite words.

For Leslie and Ruth, tired and overtense, these notices represented heartbreak. Too many months of work and too many hopes had gone into the play. Leslie, in the pain of bitter disappointment, announced to his collaborators that there would be no second night. "There's no point in dragging out the agony."

Luckily, he was persuaded to change his mind. The applause that greeted the final curtain of this next performance was long and encouraging. At any rate, it encouraged Leslie to step forward and, advisedly or not, ask the audience for its help. He made a quiet appeal to them to go from the theater and engage in a campaign of word-of-mouth advertising for the play. Though he affirmed the critics' sacred right to their opinions, he, nevertheless, asked the audience to save the production from the irreparable damage the reviews might do. "I don't think," he ended gently, "it will do Broadway any harm if we stay around here a little while longer."

Though box-office revenue was low in the next week, rallying cries came from many sides. The audience each night, warmly partisan, refused to leave until he had spoken to them. The critic of *Cue,* wrote: "Vicious, critical attacks to the contrary, this department thinks the Howard 'Hamlet' is in no way less distinguished than the other, although it apparently came as a shock to the Gielgud-conditioned critical gentry. So shocked were some of them that they lost all sense of decorum and discretion. . . . Another thing which might be added to the objections to the undignified howls raised by the daily press critics, is that only occasionally were two of them agreed on the merits or faults of any of the supporting cast. The Ophelia was the best ever seen by one veteran and she gave another the 'jitters'; the same difference of opinion applied to each character from Polonius to Osric, suggesting that they all ate of the same ptomaine dish before the play and wrote their reviews while suffering with various degrees of peloric spasm." The opinion of this avenging critic was equally warming. He said of Leslie: "He is a noble prince, intellectual, cultivated, possessed of considerable charm, therefore more potent and full of tension as the forces of the tragedy carry him remorselessly on to vengeance. . . . Mr. Howard's gradual change from a prince suspicious of his king to a tormented but nevertheless implacable bearer of bloody justice gives a crescendo to the play which the usual interpretation lacks."

It was not surprising that a large amount of newsprint was given to the fascinating sport of comparing the productions. The "Howard Hamlet" and the "Gielgud Hamlet" were contested at every dinner party, both in the thin air of the Shakespeare devotees and the hot air of the uninitiated. Neither Howard nor Gielgud could feel as bitter and didactic as their supporters, and the constant flow of odious comparison was merely wearing on them. A fair and intelligent appraisal appeared in the *Herald-Tribune* dissecting the strengths and weaknesses of both *Hamlets* and making it almost impossible for the serious theatregoer to miss either performance.

Both having announced "limited engagements" before a tour,

Leslie removed his production early in December. Despite increasing box-office receipts, he was exhausted by the unhappy situation. He went to rest in Florida before the tour began, and wrote from the train to Doodie in England: "We are on our way to sunny Florida on the 'Orange Blossom Special' if you can imagine such a name for a train. And we are glad to get away—even though everyone in N.Y. was begging us to continue our run. I'm a wreck and the idea of a beach, a palm tree and a spot of sunshine looks pretty good to me. Only I wish I had you with me, honey, and old Wink, because this is a hell of a life for a decrepit English actor. No children, no horses, not much fun and Christmas in dear old Chicago. You will have to come to California where we shall be in March unless you want to come to Detroit, Pittsburgh, St. Louis and one-night stands through Texas!

"We had such excitement here over our late lamented King. It must have been terrific in England. Mummy and I are still arguing—she against him and me for him—I suppose you and Wink do the same."

His reference to the abdication of Edward VIII was an indication, at least, that something more important was debated after theater hours than the relative merits of the two Hamlets.

Florida was a complete change, and Leslie was returned to good humor and optimism when he spoke Hamlet's first line, "A little more than kin, and less than kind," on the stage of the Grand Opera House in Chicago on Christmas night. It was the beginning of a triumphal tour. Leslie had arranged this tour with care and attention, insisting sometimes on missing larger cities in order to play near universities and schools. This gave him much satisfaction, for his reception by the students was full of enthusiasm, and each night after the performance they would come backstage and hold a discussion of the play.

The cast on tour was largely unchanged. Leslie's old friend Denis Green, formerly playing Rosencrantz, now replaced

Joseph Holland as Horatio, but the other major roles remained the same. It was a big traveling company of over sixty people, including their own electrical unit and orchestra and a Scotsman, complete with bagpipes, to play the lament on the death of Hamlet.

Ruth, longing to get her hands on the costumes, became wardrobe mistress and assistant stage manager, and pressed and sewed to the limit of even her enthusiasm. Her main job was still the care of Leslie, and, as the private train drew into a new town, she would put him to bed in a hotel while her work of unpacking the costumes went ahead. During the tour she became a self-appointed mother to the whole company, ministering to their health and advising them firmly on their private lives.

Every company together for a long period develops small feuds and larger love affairs, and Ruth never doubted her own ability to straighten them out. Her greatest interest was in young men who showed reluctance to appreciate the opposite sex. It became her mission to see them happily married, and she propounded the merits of women and matrimony to them at long evening sessions. These usually took place under the stage during the performance, and, in the graveyard scene, heavy drifts of cigarette smoke floated up when the grave was opened. Leslie, seriously extolling the virtues of Yorick, looked upon a sea of heads, playing cards and listening to Ruth's nightly lecture.

The troop played in every manner of theater, local hall, and auditorium. Birds flew chippering across the audience in the most tragic moments, and the smell of the stable rose from the floor in those places where a cattle sale had been the previous engagement. "It's like traveling with Barnum and Bailey's circus," groaned Ruth, but she loved it. To work with Leslie in a joint enterprise was her idea of earthly paradise, and they were never closer or more devoted. When she developed pneumonia and had to be left behind in Kansas City,

Leslie flew back to her after his Wichita performance, because only he could watch over her properly. They celebrated twenty-one years of marriage in the wastes of the desert, and Leslie wrote on her present, "This is a hell of a place for it darling, but we're still going strong—the best is yet to be."

San Francisco welcomed the production in February. The audiences were large and enthusiastic, the critics divided and uncertain. One or two, purposely or accidentally, cribbed their comments from New York. It seemed unfortunate that Leslie's performance could not be judged on its merits, without a constant harking to the earlier notices, but when these had been so unbelievably bad they cast long shadows before them. Yet the sum total of the notices, like this one, congratulated Leslie for his "acting of the Dane which must be greeted with loud huzzahs. There were moments . . . when experienced 'Hamlet goers' actually knew what motivated Hamlet to do certain things."

This, presumably, was the keystone of Leslie's idea in presenting the play, and in his closing speech, on the last night, he remarked that he felt no regret over his venture because his object had been to produce and perform *Hamlet* so that audiences might get an intelligent understanding of the character, as well as enjoyment from the play.

Though his tour had not been able to undo the financial damage of New York, it had restored Leslie's faith in himself. Right across the country the crowds had come out—students, shopgirls, cowhands—to appreciate Shakespeare made intelligible to everyone.

Now the need to earn a living made Hollywood follow closely upon Elsinore. After *Hamlet* closed in San Francisco, Leslie began filming.

The children arrived to find their parents inhabiting a glamorous house, complete with electrically operated gates and a large swimming pool. Their father had gone from the soaring exultation of Shakespeare's verse to the roaring humor of slapstick comedy. His film, *It's Love I'm After,* followed the current fad for wild and zany pictures. His costars were Bette Davis and Olivia de Havilland, and a more complete rest from the months of work and worry would have been hard to find.

The Howard household relaxed with its master, now gay and cloud free. Large dinner parties became the rule and not the exception. Ruth was an accomplished hostess, and worked hard to look after her guests. Leslie was charming to them, but never made the slightest effort for their comfort. No one would have had a drink if he had waited for his host to offer it. "Leslie," remonstrated Ruth, "you behave just like a guest in your own house." He would smile and do nothing. He did not need to—Ruth did it for him.

Leslie had the happy faculty of never looking back. His mind was already occupied with two new projects: the direction of Shaw's *Pygmalion,* to be made in England that year, and the script outline for "Lawrence of Arabia." Though never to be realized, this story had tantalized him since the day on the Solent years before when Leslie had seen Aircraftman Shaw polishing the Schneider Trophy winner.

It's Love I'm After was followed by *Stand-In* with Joan Blondell. Perfectly ridiculous, quite funny, and largely undistinguished, the two films helped to stoke the financial furnace and provide a restful interlude in a constantly migrant life.

Leslie sun-bathed with his children, read aloud to Doodie from R. S. Surtees, or from Damon Runyon, the modern American chronicler of another sporting life. Doodie would roll about the grass convulsed with laughter while her father imitated the accents of Harry the Horse or Nicely Nicely Johnson.

Father and daughter solemnly rehearsed a dance together— imagining their abilities resembled those of Ginger Rogers and Fred Astaire. It was a huge success whenever performed, because Leslie wore a most serious expression throughout, busily counting the steps like a small boy at dancing school.

Wink worked every day preparing for his Cambridge entrance but found moments for pleasant dalliance with the sundry pretty young girls so prevalent on the Hollywood scene. For all this, it was a life that varied only in locale from that led by any other nineteen-year-old boy. Neither he nor his sister was made uncomfortably aware of their father's position. Within the family, each person assumed his proper place, received his share of admiration and respect. In a business where many famous parents appeared to give their children a feeling of inferiority, these two were oddly different. Leslie admired their gifts, real or imagined, considerably more than they admired or envied his. They were proud of their father, but in a proprietary way, more as if they had created him than he them. Wink was in a serious-minded phase of his life, quiet and scholarly, and seemed somewhat older than Leslie. Doodie, the family manager, considered that her father needed guidance.

After their months of frolic, the Howards left for England and Stowe Maries.

18 / Film Director

The rich treasure of George Bernard Shaw's plays had never been made available to the motion-picture public. G.B.S., with his acrimonious wit and his didactic self-importance, considered movies a mental stimulant for idiots. He ignored, insulted, or repulsed every offer from the film industry. Thus it was with incredulity that the news was heard that an unknown and inexperienced European producer had obtained the film rights for one or more Shaw plays. Gabriel Pascal, small, swarthy, and as ingenuously self-important as Bernard Shaw was consciously so, had established a rapport with the tall bearded Irishman that confounded everyone. Leslie, too, had been influenced by Gabby Pascal. This extraordinary little man now collected a brilliant group around him: Anthony Asquith, sensitive, intelligent, and witty, son of a famous family, was to co-direct the film with Leslie; the script writers were W. P. Lipscomb and Cecil Lewis; the film editor, David Lean (later to be the director of *The Bridge on the River Kwai*).

Daily conferences went on throughout the autumn of 1937. Asquith spent hours at Stowe Maries with Leslie and the other people involved, thrashing out the plans for casting and script. Shaw had to be handled with extreme caution because he re-

mained unapproachable and ready to withdraw his agreement
at every turn. At first, no scenes were to be included that were
not in the play, and this created a grave problem. Then, with
his usual flair for the unpredictable, Shaw gave in and wrote
them himself. The script writers walked on eggs when trying
to cut or change any part of the dialogue. With Gabby Pascal
on the one hand behaving, as Leslie said, "as if he were God,"
and G.B.S. on the other, it was a ticklish business, but it drew
the technical staff closer together.

Anthony Asquith and Leslie made a splendid combination;
both possessing lively minds with wide interests, they appealed
to each other. The drawing room at Stowe Maries became a
fascinating place, and Doodie, curled up in a chair, watched
these two at work: Asquith, never still, pacing to and fro,
pausing to gesture, his motions quick and birdlike, his humor
lighting the room and dissolving difficulties; Leslie, often relaxed in a chair, occasionally wandering vaguely around, his
mind seemingly on other matters, but actually thinking quickly
and clearly at every moment. His powers of concentration impressed his co-director, and later, when shooting began, "Puf-
fin" Asquith discovered that this gift extended to his acting.
Leslie was the continuity girl's delight, for he never made a
gesture or an ad lib that he could not repeat exactly and immediately. This made his constant lateness and forgetfulness
the more surprising.

Punctuality and a slavish adherence to shooting schedules
seemed unimportant to all the *Pygmalion* unit. Leslie, Gabby
Pascal, and Asquith nipped off for a holiday among the mountains of Austria just before they went "on the floor" to shoot
the film. Leslie took Ruth and Doodie and his sister Dorice
with him to enjoy the benefits of the air. How much work was
done on the final script and casting remained a secret. The
three men met occasionally, surrounded by skis and quantities
of other attractions not truly conducive to settled thought.
Leslie, at any rate, learned to ski, rather solemnly but not too

badly. He disliked ski boots, "frightful, uncomfortable objects —I have a *blister!*" and was normally to be seen wandering through the beautiful town of Kitzbühel with a pair of rubbers on his feet and his ski boots dangling from one hand. In the evenings there were long discussions with the residents. Austria was waiting without hope, like a mesmerized bird, to be swallowed by the German colossus. The patriots knew their chances of survival were few, and Leslie felt a deep sympathy for their awful plight. From his discussions came a film, which he was to make at the beginning of the war, called *Pimpernel Smith,* but in 1938 words of comfort were hard to find.

The German *Anschluss* took place in March; Hitler, the house painter, had begun his bloody redecoration of the map of Europe. In England most people shuddered, averted their eyes, and said hopefully: "Austrians are really just like Germans." But Leslie thought of the men and women he had talked with far into the night; patriots, burning with pride in their small country and hatred of National Socialism and the German dictator. He wondered where they were now. Hiding, perhaps, like rats in a cellar or mutilated in concentration camps.

At work on *Pygmalion* in the delightful surroundings of the new Pinewood Studios, Austria was a long way off, and, if not forgotten, certainly displaced by the interests of each day. Pinewood was run like a first-class country club, with excellent rooms and a good restaurant. Most of the *Pygmalion* unit stayed there, and foregathered every night to discuss any difficulties and present new ideas. Suggestions from each member of the production staff were encouraged, the atmosphere was informal, and in this way a routine was developed which, though quite unique up to that time, showed its value in the finished film.

Although script changes were technically not allowed, Leslie always liked last-moment inspirations; in his later films, where he had complete power, he used to rewrite entire scenes on the set. On *Pygmalion,* while rewrites were frowned upon, sly pieces of "business" could be slipped in. One particularly apt example of this took place in a scene between Leslie, as Professor Higgins, and Wendy Hiller, as Eliza, the flower girl. The professor of phonetics is supposed to pop marbles in his pupil's mouth as part of her speech training. Wendy Hiller, trying to talk through the marbles, suddenly gasped, "I've swallowed one, Leslie." "That's all right," he replied cheerfully, "we have plenty more." Everyone on the set laughed so long at this sally that it was sneaked into the finished film, and, later, when *Pygmalion* became the musical *My Fair Lady,* the same two lines remained and still got a great laugh from the audience.

At home for the weekends, Leslie was planning a new building in the garden. He had been sold an enormous pair of movie projectors for sound film. No one had any idea why he had bought them, but he spent several hours assembling the wretched things in the hall. Since they stood six feet high, it became apparent, even to Leslie, that they could not occupy a permanent position at the foot of the stairs. Ruth made it plain that she thought her husband a sucker for salesmen, and, nettled, he went off to his room to brood. The outcome of this concentrated thought was a playhouse, set in one of the paddocks, with a forty-foot room, a large fireplace, a bar, dart board, piano, and gramophone, and, naturally, a projection room. This extensive and expensive object was Leslie's answer to family criticism. Ruth never let him forget it. "Yes," she would say airily, showing someone the "Cabin," "Leslie built it for his projectors." Actually, it became a wonderful spot for parties, and every Sunday there were film showings, dart games, and dances.

Leslie stepped into another costly field that year when he ran his first and last race horse. Bred at the Stowe from one of his own mares, the filly Lipstick proved fast, but quickly tired. She raced only a few times, without distinction, but gave her owners much excitement and interest. There were lots of foals that spring wandering around the fields at Stowe Maries.

Each weekend the family could spend together in the quiet enjoyment of a normal life they counted a great fortune. Wink came home from Cambridge occasionally; Doodie, fighting the last battle of her inadequate education, could barely wait for Friday night to free her from the monstrous boredom of school. Leslie arrived and friends appeared and every penny that had gone into their house was returned in happiness a hundredfold.

At Pinewood, *Pygmalion* was almost finished. It still clung tenuously to life, though threatened every day with financial collapse and constantly in danger of being cut off. Each disaster was averted at the last second, and the final film reached the public in the autumn of 1938.

That autumn Europe quailed again before the growing demands of the German dictator. The horror of war hung over the English people. Hitler gazed upon the small, industrious, and rich Czechoslovakian nation with greed and malignity. On the pretext that the German minority must be protected, he claimed the Czech Sudetenland. His excuse was flimsy, his intention plain. The small but powerful Czech army must be removed before he turned upon France. That this was not recognized constitutes what came to be called the tragedy of Munich. There Britain and France acceded to the frightful desires of Hitler and, in the interests of peace, dismembered the proud Czechoslovakian Republic.

The British Prime Minister came home from Munich waving an agreement with the dictator. To a cheering crowd, Chamberlain announced his belief in "peace in our time." Winston Churchill, in a hostile House of Commons, cried: "We have sustained a total and unmitigated defeat." Time was yet to prove which man had fully realized the ferocious appetite of Adolf Hitler.

During the Munich crisis, England had made last-moment attempts to ready for war. The fleet was mobilized; in London simple air-raid shelters were built, and gas masks were distributed throughout the country. Stowe Maries, too, had tried to prepare itself for the fray. In co-operation with a neighboring house, a huge shelter had been dug. It was later found to be quite inadequate, being far from the house, very damp, and not a spot that could be reached in dressing gowns and bedroom slippers without the greater fear of pneumonia. But working on it gave everyone a fine feeling of doing something useful and contributing to the country's state of preparedness. Leslie and Doodie were photographed inside wearing their gas masks as proof to America that England was on her toes.

With the fate of Czechoslovakia settled, the war clouds were pressed back for another year. Into a city sighing with relief, *Pygmalion* made its first appearance, opening at the Leicester Square Theatre. It seemed just what the critics liked and the public wanted.

" 'Pygmalion' as a technical piece of film craft is one of the most brilliant jobs ever turned out of a British studio," wrote the *Observer*.

"This film is a remarkable indication of what directorial skill and really inspired acting can make of third-class film material," said *Time and Tide*. "There can be no doubt that with slightly less assured treatment this once brilliant play of Shaw's would have made the most tedious film imaginable. As it is, it must be classed as a tour-de-force, and a vehicle, through the persons of Wendy Hiller and Leslie Howard, for some of the best acting ever seen on the screen."

Wendy Hiller, as Eliza, made a major success. The direction of Leslie and Anthony Asquith received a long burst of critical applause. This, more than anything else, determined Leslie to withdraw from acting altogether. His future plans were to be based on direction, if not alone, then in combination with acting until he could persuade the industry to forget he once was an actor.

Pygmalion, though rather doubtful fare for general audiences, continued its run in England and opened in the United States. Oddly enough, it was there that it found real acclaim; the critics dug deeply into the bag of shopworn superlatives to describe the film. Three thousand people queued in New York to see it. Before many months were past, *Pygmalion* had been nominated for an Academy Award, and so had its stars and its script writers—including Mr. Shaw.

Leslie had another small project under way. For the first time in ten years, he had written a play. It was on a subject that both fascinated and repulsed him: the unlimited power of the press barons. The central character, Lord Southaven, was a composite figure, bearing no similarity to any single newspaper owner, but resembling in some part each of the different ones that Leslie had met on two continents.

Leslie hoped to make a film of this story, if he could get away with it, so he had arranged for the play's production at Bristol in October 1937. It was called *Alias Mrs. Jones*—a last-minute inspiration of Doodie's.

In the lead as the young man who attacks Lord Southaven's impregnable influence, Leslie cast Denis Green, his old and good friend Horatio. The play caused no stir, though it was an interesting idea, and nothing further came of it.

England had now nothing to offer Leslie. No actor can afford to be unemployed, and, furthermore, it was getting rather cold in Surrey. Southern California looked most attractive. Leslie left for America in December, sailing on the S.S. *Normandie.* He sailed alone, and Doodie and Wink saw him off, feeling rather cheated that they were not to travel on the exotic liner. Ruth, too, stayed at home, mollified perhaps by Leslie's parting note found under her pillow.

"I hate leaving you—but it's a very short time. I love you all so much—especially you, dear. I never can do without you —no matter what happens—you must always be at the back of me."

In a way typical of Leslie, this message showed both sides of an unusual character. He alone had made the decision to leave Ruth behind. He alone, and with opposition from his wife, determined to be independent on this trip. He might cite limited money as the cause, but the cupboard was not that bare. He went because he periodically enjoyed freedom, and then he left a letter for Ruth showing how deeply he loved her and was tied to her strength. It was not insincerity—he meant every word—but it was inconsistent.

New York greeted him with rapture. Fans followed him down Fifth Avenue, and he walked along, hat over his eyes, glasses on his nose, still recognized at every turn, signing books as he went, horribly embarrassed. In a letter to Ruth he wrote:

"Everybody asks me when I am coming back to the theatre. I ask myself that too—and a damn' unsatisfactory answer I get. From my window I see the Carlyle Hotel sticking up and think of all the months we have spent there. I would not care for that again. Our home in England seems so much more satisfying. In fact, I am a more confirmed European than ever, really. But it is amusing to be here briefly and one is astounded at the speed and energy and enthusiasm everyone puts into everything. I am doing [Eddie] Cantor's broadcast on Monday and have had several other offers. But nary a film until at least January [1939]—which is worrying."

From New York he rattled out to Hollywood and moved into the Sunset Towers, a building of great height for that city, perched on the edge of Sunset Boulevard. From there he looked down scornfully.

"I have been feeling rotten my first week here and the climate thoroughly disagreeing with me. I have not even wanted to be in the sun much—in fact I have taken a thorough dislike to the place, which now seems to me to resemble a vast village of gaudily painted mud huts inhabited by a huge tribe of pleasant but very, very primitive aborigines."

Mike Levee seemed anxious for Leslie to appear in a film

being made by David Selznick. It was to be based on *Gone With the Wind,* by Margaret Mitchell, probably the most widely read novel of the century. Casting the film version had produced several difficulties. To find an actress for the central character, Scarlett O'Hara, the studio ran a much-publicized campaign. Excitement reached fever height when Selznick selected Vivien Leigh, a young English actress of no particular past fame, who had won the role over a good many famous contestants. With Vivien Leigh as Scarlett, Clark Gable as everyone's idea of Rhett Butler, Olivia de Havilland as Melanie, only Ashley Wilkes was left, and Leslie was David Selznick's choice for this part.

"To-day I am taking a color test for Ashley for George Cukor, but I am not committed yet. I am not keen about it, I'll never read the book, but I've read the script—miles of it— and I don't know what they're all talking about or what's wrong with them—most of all Ashley. However, money is the mission here, and who am I to refuse it?"

Everyone told Leslie that he was the perfect Ashley, which only convinced him that he was not. "I am suspicious that fifty million Americans can't be right!"

But nothing else appeared in the way of a film offer. With the extraordinary quirk of life in the motion-picture industry, no one seemed at all interested in him. In the United States he was the man of the hour, star and director of one of the best English films ever made, nominee for an Academy Award, and unemployed.

Just before Christmas, Ruth cabled that she and the children would join Leslie, and he wrote: "Have had your wire and replied and got your answer. I'm telephoning you to-night. I don't know what to do. I am uncertain what I am doing. I have no deal yet. 'Gone With the Wind' is the only thing under discussion and I have a hunch it is no good for me. I took a colour test and looked too awful. They put a ghastly make-up on me and made me look like the ghost of Larry Semon and then were surprised it photographed too light. They really are such fools here—everything is by numbers. I wanted no make-up." Leslie had not worn make-up for many years, either on the stage or in the films, and this was just one more black mark in his mind against *G.W.T.W.*

Fortunately, he worked steadily on radio programs and was enchanted when he appeared on Bing Crosby's show and Crosby sang a Howard composition called "Without You," the music by Leslie, words by Leslie and Doodie. "They were delighted with the song and I must say, so was I. It sounded marvellous played by the orchestra and sung by Crosby. Crosby said, 'Tell me, Leslie. How do Howard the actor and Howard the director get along with Howard the song writer?' "

The weather in California was a catastrophe that winter, with torrential rain and snow. Leslie became daily more vindictive and cross. He refused to allow the family to come for Christmas. "Personally, I hate Christmas with family or without. I shall miss you terribly but I do that anyway. I always will."

The tests for Ashley dragged on and he wrote: "I hate the damn part. I have done two technicolour tests, both rotten. I'm not nearly beautiful or young enough for Ashley, and it makes me sick being fixed up to look attractive."

Then came an offer from New York for a play by Sam Behrman with Katharine Cornell. Leslie refused. "It's a charming, clever comedy, but it might be a *hit,* which means New York for months."

In fact, he did not want to do anything except direct. He had been dickering with various people about forming an independent film company in England, and now he signed the contracts for it with the intention of making *The Man Who Lost Himself* some time in late 1939. The immediate future remained uncertain. David Selznick suggested a possible deal "by which I would act in certain pictures and produce and direct others. Mike [Levee] nearly fell over backwards and is *finally* convinced that I have something to offer besides cute leading man performances."

Possibly encouraged by this discussion with Selznick, Leslie settled for Ashley Wilkes during the first month of 1939 in a state of deepest gloom. "Yesterday I put on my Confederate uniform for the first time and looked like a fairy doorman at the Beverly Wiltshire—a fine thing at my age."

Nothing could persuade him that this film was worth doing, but, as the new year struggled into life, he sacrificed himself for the good of his family.

19 / "Gone With the Wind"

—and Home for the War

The long period of inactivity did not end with Leslie's agreement to appear in *G.W.T.W.* "The famous production has at last started—but I have done nothing as yet. Gable and Vivien Leigh and O. de Havilland have been hard at it. After seven days shooting they are five days behind schedule so it looks as if this show will go on for ever."

He sat outside muffled in an overcoat, "trying to sop up a little sun," but was driven indoors by a blizzard in February. "My days seem pretty occupied. I don't get up very early. I have my sun bath on the fire escape. I answer telephone calls. In the evenings I dine with the Gargans or the Levees or the Gershgorns. Occasionally I see Bart Marshall, Ronnie Colman, Ralph Forbes and the English contingent."

Leslie was worried about his mother, who had suffered a heart attack, and worried, too, about the worsening international situation; it made him more annoyed with himself than ever for accepting a film that might take a year to finish. Nevertheless, he wrote with humor to his fourteen-year-old daughter: "Is there going to be a war? Please write and tell me—you must know. If there were, I would return at once and desert from the Confederate army. I'm just a British spy anyway. I'm

still waiting to work—my hair growing longer by the minute. . . ."

In March, Ruth and Doodie joined him in Hollywood. Wink
stayed behind, having landed his first job, on a newspaper, the
Sunday Chronicle. Leslie met them at the train, his blond locks
gleaming in the sun. "No cracks from the younger generation.
I do this for a living, God damn it!"

The summer was one long frustration for him. He went
around muttering darkly about *G.W.T.W.* "Terrible lot of
nonsense—heaven help me if I ever read the book." David
Selznick was reported to be furious.

"David says he is going to sue me for spreading alarm and
despondency," giggled Leslie, quite unperturbed. He scarcely
bothered to look at his lines, on the basis that they might be
changed and anyway were rehearsed and shot so many times
that a halfwit could remember them.

He had always thought the movie actor's life a perfect nightmare of boredom. His description of a typical day on the set
reads as follows:

The movie actor rises at 6.30 A.M. or 7 A.M.—dashes to the
studio—makes up and dresses while the assistant director and
his emissaries are knocking on his door urging him to hurry.
He rushes to the set. The moment he is there, nobody wants
him any more. He sits and waits. Electricians, carpenters,
painters, cameramen, property men fall over him as they go
about their duties. It is too noisy to read. If he leaves the set
he will be dragged back instantly. He has no idea what is
going on. He tries to study the scene for the day. Then he is
informed it will not be shot. He studies the submitted scene.
It seems simple. Each of the two characters concerned has
three lines apiece to say. The stage is finally set, but they have
to wait for the leading lady who did not expect to work that
day. By eleven o'clock she arrives, looking radiant, accompanied by a retinue of make-up artists, hairdressers, costumiers

and personal maids. There is an interlude during which the leading lady's appearance is discussed by the cameramen, the director and the retinue. Then the lights are put out and the two rehearse the scene. They rehearse it for a long time. The director is meticulous. They repeat their three lines apiece many, many times. All the technical workers who have been so busy, now sit and wait. After the six lines have been rehearsed fifteen or twenty times, and the actor is on the point of screaming, the director mercifully announces he will shoot the scene. But now the cameraman says he must see the actors under the lights. So they pose for him till both are hot and tired and dislike each other heartily, while lamps are juggled around them endlessly. Then they run through the scene again so the cameraman can see them in motion. This necessitates more changes and finally the cameraman says, "O.K." "We will take it," says the director. But now the sound man would like to hear it exactly as it will be spoken. They do it again. The sound man now juggles his instruments around and finally says, "O.K." "Let's go," says the director. But now the leading lady's make-up has started to run, so she goes off to fix it.

There is a pause. Lights go out. Everybody sits. The leading lady returns. The lights go on. The director says he would like another rehearsal in case they have "gone cold on it." The leading lady says it is very warm. The lights go out. They rehearse the six lines—twice. The director says, "Let's take it." The lights go on. Then the assistant director says it's one o'clock and the men have to have their lunch. The lights go out. Everybody goes to lunch.

After lunch, following a few rehearsals, light tests, sound tests, etc., the scene is actually shot. It is shot eight or ten times, though only one or two will be "printed." But our wretched actor has given his all, eight or ten times. Do not imagine that this ends the matter. This is only the long shot. They are now pulling everything to pieces, and setting up for the medium shot. Our actor tries to read again. He dare not leave the set as, though everybody knows he will not be needed for at least an hour, there is a general pretence that they are "all ready to go." So he sits there in the confusion smoking cigarettes or eating icecream.

Finally they get the medium shot. This is also done a great many times. Then another interlude. Then the whole thing is gone through again and again in a "two-shot," locally known as "two, big, gorgeous heads." And finally they reach the close-ups, in which one player is photographed at a time, the other giving the responses from the darkness behind the camera. By this time the few words, having been given at least fifty or sixty times during the day, have become gibberish and the actors' faces weary and meaningless masks.

Our actor staggers to his dressing-room at seven or eight in the evening, removes his war-paint, dons his civilian clothes and goes home to his wife speechless with fatigue. He eats some food and falls into bed, to be ready for his 6.30 call in the morning, more exhausted from his three immortal lines than if he had played Hamlet in the afternoon and Macbeth at night.

Leslie found this a dreary life, dull because it was uninspiring. "If I am alone in this opinion then I must be unique in my idea of an interesting occupation. The screen is a fascinating story-telling medium, but it is the director who tells the story."

His slothful attitude toward *Gone With the Wind* caught him out upon occasion. Once he was severely criticized by Vivien Leigh for never knowing his lines. He was immediately all injured innocence and fury.

"I won't allow anyone to say that about me," he told Doodie.

For the next hour Doodie had her only chance to play Scarlett O'Hara, reading the lines to Leslie while he rehearsed the tiny scene that would be shot in the morning. He returned the next night in some jubilation.

"As luck would have it, Vivien forgot her lines today," he informed Doodie. "But I was not cross. Oh, no. I was not unpleasant. I just said: 'Never mind, dear, take your time,' and I hope she feels sorry now!"

It was obvious that this kind of irritation would build up when one member of a cast was so bored with his work.

In the late spring, Ruth had to find somewhere else for them to live because Leslie, expecting to leave Hollywood much earlier, had taken a short lease on the house they were in. They saw a charming, yellow-washed house in Beverly Hills, belonging to Hedy Lamarr, and Leslie bought it. For the first time in the many years that they had spent in California, they owned a house. It was small, newly furnished, had a swimming pool and a very glamourous bedroom for Ruth.

"My dear, surrounded by all these mirrors and this blue satin I shall get impossible ideas," she announced vigorously.

Leslie, waiting to finish his small part as Ashley, started to work on another film for David Selznick, with Edna Best. It was called *Intermezzo, a Love Story* and introduced Ingrid Bergman, who was well known as an actress in her own country but had never made an American film. Leslie was delighted with the work of this beautiful girl in *Intermezzo;* there could be no doubt that she would become a future star.

Leslie's real interest in *Intermezzo* lay in his job as associate producer. Though he might suspect David Selznick of using this bait to keep him happy while *G.W.T.W.* finished retakes, he cared not about the reason why so long as he could have a hand in production. His part in the film was another too easy, too Howard piece of acting, but it produced one quite interesting new pursuit, the violin. Because he played a virtuoso of this instrument, he needed several weeks of concentrated lessons. Everyday the charming theme music of the film floated through the house—while Leslie listened to his teacher. His own efforts were halting, and, the violin being a temperamental piece of musical equipment, very rasping. Even devoted

Doodie left him alone when he began to practice. Playing the piano by ear caused him to try the same technique on the violin with disastrous results. He stuck at his lessons, though, spurred on by the information that Miss Bergman had learned every note of the Grieg Piano Concerto for her role as the young concert pianist.

After long and cacophonous hours of practice, he went, rather proudly, to play his few bars for an important scene in the film. It was an exciting moment—the scene a concert stage, a huge audience of extras dressed in evening clothes sitting in rapt attention, and Leslie, violin tucked under his chin, finishing the final notes of "Intermezzo." The cameras were running, the audience spellbound, and poor Leslie could not produce a melody of any kind. Try as he might, again and again, nothing but squawks and squeaks and dismal wails filled the elegant concert hall! As he explained to Doodie later:

"It was frightfully embarrassing—I ended up playing one single note and the audience had to appear quite hysterical with excitement—standing up and throwing programmes in the air while I bowed and smiled—I never felt more of a fool —but it *was* rather funny."

The last summer of peace slipped away; the pleasures unconsciously accepted. There would never be another year for Leslie without the grim duties of a war-locked land, but no one counts the days of peace so fair until they are no more.

Leslie had a great personal sorrow in July when his mother died. She had been ill for a long time, but it was a grave shock, for she was still young. He had seen much less of her than he would have liked in the last years, due to his migrations, but he was a devoted son. Lilie Stainer had been his most enthusiastic fan, and his boyhood years under her loving guidance had left a strong mark upon him.

August increased the fear of war in Europe. Leslie hurried his film work, determined to be home in England before it began. It was obvious that nothing short of armed intervention could stop Hitler. War was only a matter of months away, for never again would England and France be duped into an ignoble agreement for "peace at any price."

In Hollywood there was speculation about the future plans for the "English contingent." Some were on the reserve officers list and would be called back; others were too old or perhaps too far removed by years and space from their native land to feel the urgency. Leslie was in a different category. He never considered any other course than to go to England at once. He did not care if some of his colleagues wished to remain both British and in Hollywood. Every man must make his own choice and calm his own conscience. In a heroic, overdramatic press release, the Levee office flew the flag and thumped the tub for Howard: "typically English, blind, unswerving duty to King and Country, unquestioning response, that's the attitude of every true Britisher."

With the crash of this ridiculous twenty-one-gun salute from his agent ringing in his ears, Leslie left Hollywood at the end of August, and the family sailed for England. The news became darker and more troubled as they plowed out into the North Atlantic, and the ship was made ready for an immediate blackout. All on board felt the unspoken menace of German U-boats lurking in the deep waters, waiting only for the word to attack. Ruth and Leslie thought mainly of their son, aged twenty-one, who would obviously be among the first called up should war come.

Wink was waiting at Southampton with his small sports car, able to take home one fortunate member of his family. Doodie won this honored position, partly, perhaps, because her shocked older brother had not recovered his powers of speech after one look at her. Nothing had ever appeared less like an English schoolgirl than Doodie. Swaddled in black from head to toe and swathed in gray fox, this weird object looked forty rather than fourteen. That her parents should have allowed her to totter about on three-inch heels in extraordinary clothes was regarded with amazement by their friends. But who can say what problems are encountered in the privacy of a family? Ruth, having tried to discipline her daughter for years, with no help from her husband, had given up the unequal struggle. Leslie was distressed at the child's appearance but, other than dubbing her "the French widow," made no effort to curb her unsuitable tastes. He was deeply concerned about his daughter. She was apparently headstrong and largely uneducated, and yet a product of his own overindulgent kindness. Occasionally, he grew outwardly concerned, but these feeble attempts to improve at least the education of his child were constantly thwarted by circumstances and the individual.

In the first few days after the family returned to Stowe Maries, various plans were laid, albeit somewhat halfheartedly. Leslie got ready for his film *The Man Who Lost Himself;* Doodie was informed that she would be going to finishing school in Switzerland. The future seemed miserably uncertain, but no one could very well stand still waiting for the worst to happen.

On the first day of September, as Leslie conferred in London about the film, German armored columns struck into Polish territory; Britain and France mobilized, and the Allied ultimatum to Germany was about to expire. The country waited in anxiety, but not in fear, for the words of their prime minister, Neville Chamberlain, at 11:15 A.M. on September 3, a bright autumn day. When they came, it was almost a relief. "We are now at war with Germany."

There were to be no more shoddy attempts at placating a ruthless nation intent on aggression. Winston Churchill has written: "The glory of Old England, peace-loving and ill prepared as she was, but instant and fearless at the call of honour, thrilled my being and seemed to lift our fate to those spheres far removed from earthly facts and physical sensation."

So, in a small part, felt even the most inarticulate Englishman that day. Leslie, by no means inarticulate, was already wondering how best he could serve Old England. At forty-six, a military career seemed rather unlikely. Never a very good soldier, the prospect of becoming a middle-aged subaltern posted to an interminable desk job, appealed not at all. He felt he had more to offer his country.

He listened to Chamberlain's speech in London and then experienced, with everyone else, the first curious banshee wailing of the air-raid siren that came within minutes of the Prime Minister's broadcast. The public had been warned about, and expected, immediate attack—the Government was prepared to provide 250,000 hospital beds for air-raid casualties in the first few days of the war. Leslie departed to an inadequate shelter, as did most Londoners who had one available, and reappeared moments later when the "all clear" signified a false alarm.

Shortly afterward, he drove home to Westcott to see and encourage his family. There was a tense and rather emotional atmosphere at Stowe Maries. Wink was hastily stowing a few belongings in a bag. His mother, as ever, doing most of it for him and trying unsuccessfully to keep calm. Two friends from Cambridge had arrived to collect Winkie and take him with them to join the Navy.

"It's a yacht," he explained to Leslie. "Signing on hands at Southampton. Should be quite good fun."

There was precious little time to talk, no chance at all to discuss the advisability of this sudden plan. Ruth, typically feminine, kept herself from crying by giving detailed instructions about warm clothing, and the two men barely had a chance to say good-by in the flood of maternal advice. Leslie stood in the road outside his house, trying to look casual for Ruth's sake, while his son went off, still dazzled by the patriotic fervor of that first day. Leslie tried to remember how he had felt in 1914; to recall the wonderful pride and excitement of standing in line to join the Army, to be a part of the fight against tyranny and "do one's bit." Yet that had been so different, that bright unquestioning bravery of 1914; no one knew then the horror he would be asked to face. The bloody struggle of four years had left the remnants of that generation determined to shield their sons at any cost, to make sure that they would have "a broad, clean, secure pathway through life." They had been wrong; peace with Hitler was a price that nobody could afford to pay. Leslie waved until Wink was out of sight. And, when he was gone, Leslie still stood in the road thinking of his son.

"We are now facing a challenge greater than any civilized history has ever known—a challenge which puts that of the first world war in the shade," he wrote later. "And our children have had to take up that challenge—all our vows on their behalf have gone for nothing. We may reproach ourselves, but they would not have it otherwise. For they are now as we were then, and we were then as our fathers were before us in the Napoleonic Wars and in the centuries before that. They are the descendants of the men who founded the American colonies, who stormed the heights of Abraham and created the commonwealths of Australia, New Zealand and the Union of South Africa. They would not have it otherwise—nor, if we are true to our principles, would we."

He turned from the road to comfort Ruth. Inside their house, the B.B.C. news reported that Winston Churchill had accepted a seat in the Cabinet and was again First Lord of the Admiralty.

"Wink will be all right, Winnie's back," said Leslie with delight, and immediately began explaining to his daughter the background of this man of whom she had scarcely heard, this greatest Englishman in a long history of great men.

20 / London 1940

The first winter of the war brought only surface changes to England. Its subjects had watched with anguish the swift subjugation of Poland, and cheered the magnificent and forlorn stand of the capital, Warsaw. Leslie had listened to reports from this proud city on the short-wave receiving station at Lord Beaverbrook's property in Surrey. Here the latest information was translated by a staff of interpreters and sent to the Beaverbrook newspapers. Leslie spent many evenings in the building that housed this radio equipment, with his friend and neighbor Jonah Barrington, then radio critic for the *Daily Express*. It was here one night that a thin, nasal English voice was heard for the first time.

"Jarmany calling, Jarmany calling," and the man, whom Barrington at once dubbed "Lord Haw-Haw," began his daily broadcasts of misinformation and wickedness. Leslie and Jonah Barrington laughed a lot at the drawling, affected voice, "the only bit of fun to come out of the war so far," in Leslie's opinion. Once Barrington had made a comic character of Lord Haw-Haw, the propaganda value of these broadcasts was never realized. Along with millions of other Englishmen, Leslie listened, occasionally, for the entertainment value.

The aggression in Poland was followed by a time of quiet

and what later was called "the phony war." Early in the new year Leslie visited the British G.H.Q. at Arras on the Western Front. He enjoyed a pleasant dinner with one or two generals and returned little the wiser. He was constantly at work on ideas to present the Allied cause to the rest of the world, and evolved a plan to make a film based on the Foreign Office Blue Book about the final negotiations with Hitler in August and September 1939. He wrote to Lord Halifax, then Foreign Secretary and soon to be ambassador to the United States:

"I am certain that a film depicting the last days of peace and the efforts of England to avoid war and yet remain true to her pledges is a subject so compelling and dramatic that it would attract an enormous public, particularly in the United States.

"I want to produce this picture. I would gladly put aside all personal plans and give my services to such a project. I can provide the personnel, arrange for the finance and for world distribution of the film."

Leslie was deeply concerned about the attitude of the United States. He felt that in America propaganda for the Allied cause would be far better handled if interpolated by well-known writers, actors, and public men of various sorts than by an official mission to Washington.

"We can be pretty sure where Mr. Roosevelt's sympathies lie and since we, therefore, do not have to convert the administration, I submit that an official or government mission would be unnecessary," he wrote in a long and serious paper, "Notes on American Propaganda," which he prepared for the Ministry of Information.

"I am quite certain that, properly camouflaged, the message we want to deliver can be carried direct to the American people. I regret already the word 'camouflage.' We want to give them the facts, supply them with information. After all, most of them are intensely sympathetic to our cause, they are 'rooting' for us, they want us to win. They are vitally interested, morally and humanly, in the drama in which we are taking part. It does not take much more to persuade them that we are the heroes of this drama."

Leslie outlined his plan for documentary films: "The first of these films should concern itself with placing the war-guilt irrefutably upon the Nazis . . . the second . . . could deal with the outbreak of war, its effect on the ordinary citizen, the evacuation of children, the tremendous and immediate change in every day life, the rush to join the colours, the A.R.P. arrangements, the blackouts, the whole changing face of a great city within twenty-four hours."

It was difficult to get a hearing for his suggestions, let alone an answer. The British Government was involved in the vital, belated, and overwhelming task of preparing the country for war while already fighting that war. There were more urgent matters than propaganda consuming the time of the senior members of the Government, and the film industry was still regarded as an entertainment medium. With only the vaguest assurances that any films he made would have official co-operation, Leslie decided to go ahead on his own, producing not a series of short films, but one feature film in which the cause of freedom and Britain's part in it would be clearly defined.

Ever since his Austrian holiday, the germ of a film script had been in his mind. Now he began to draw the plot together. He asked A. G. Macdonell, the author, to write the first script. Leslie outlined his ideas: the setting should be Austria in 1938; a famous painter who is also a violent anti-Nazi is arrested by Hitler's thugs; he must be saved, and an Englishman, a kind of modern Scarlet Pimpernel, successfully rescues him in a magical manner. On the basis of this, Archie Macdonell produced a film scenario, and then, with Leslie, rewrote it. Another writer appeared and tried his hand, and then another. There were too many distractions that spring to keep any writer for long. Everyone was trying to find work of national importance and all considered writing scripts rather inferior. Leslie, feeling frustrated and useless, agreed with them. He, too, was searching for the job where he could offer his country a reasonable contribution.

He lived in London during the week and drove down to Stowe Maries every Friday night. Ruth was busy at the house looking after two small and very grubby evacuees from the East End of London; Doodie was upsetting the office routine of the local Red Cross, trying their patience and their typewriter as a stenographer; Miss Goss had taken over the cooking in the large and staffless kitchen. There were infrequent letters from Wink, Able Seaman, somewhere at sea. When he turned up in Liverpool, Ruth and Leslie went up to see him and to buy him a splendid dinner in the Adelphi Hotel.

There were many people to see in London, and Leslie saw them but nothing concrete came from the endless discussions he had with them. Each time, for want of something better to do, he returned to his film script, found another writer, and changed the plot again. It was a fascinating business, devising methods of escape and rescue, and might have occupied the summer had not a more extraordinary tale of rescue begun to unfold that frightening spring of 1940—Dunkirk.

The "phony war" had ended in April with the Nazi invasion of Norway. By May the German jack boot was planted triumphantly across the back of Europe. Norway, Denmark, Holland, Belgium; nowhere could the awful tide be stemmed. German Panzer divisions ripped across France, turned the vaunted Maginot Line, and pinned the British Expeditionary Force in a tiny plot of land behind the French port of Dunkirk, to be decimated at will. Then, like a miracle sent to restore the faltering, the British withstood the attacks. Hitler, crowing with the delight of easy plunder, underestimated the fighting courage of these English, Scottish, Irish, and Welsh troops. While a heroic rear guard defended the narrow isthmus, 366,000 men were ferried home in every manner of craft; exhausted, dirty, and hungry, but ironically victorious.

Leslie and his family stood often in the fields beyond Stowe Maries watching the trainloads of returning heroes. They threw them chocolate, fruit, and cigarettes, cheering each group as it passed and marveling at the gay gallantry of these unremarkable soldiers.

But, for all the cheering, these were grim days. No sooner had the British troops been received with cries of joy and relief than more dreadful news was on the way. French morale crumbled fast. Paris fell without resistance, and on Sunday, June 23, the British nation heard a fateful announcement. Leslie, tense and anxious like the rest of his countrymen, turned on the radio:

"This is the B.B.C. Home Service—here is the news."

The announcer's voice was so slow, and the pauses so long that Leslie looked up sharply.

"Hello—something's very wrong."

And then the announcer continued.

"France has fallen. We are now alone."

No one spoke. A feeling of desolation lay over the room. If France had been broken so quickly by the German armor, what chance had little England, unprepared and hopelessly weak? And yet each member of the family sitting around the radio remembered the faces and the smiles of the soldiers from Dunkirk and was strangely warmed.

"Most of you, I'm sure, will know what I mean when I speak of the curious elation which comes from sharing in a high and mysterious destiny. The destiny of Britain we cannot know for certain, but we can guess at it and pray for it, and work towards it as we find ourselves singled out of all the nations of the world for the rare honour of fighting alone against the huge and ruthless forces of tyranny."

These were the words that Leslie wrote and spoke that summer to America. It was his first broadcast to the North American continent in a weekly series, "Britain Speaks." He was introduced by J. B. Priestley, and afterward continued on his own once every week. Here, at last, he had found an important place for his talents and his pride in the British cause. His broadcasts began in the fiercest moments of the Battle of Britain and were still going on after London had suffered and won its trial by fire and explosion.

During these violent months he told the United States and Canada about many aspects of life in the beleaguered island, told them how in every county men, women, and children were preparing themselves to meet the challenge of Nazi invasion.

"In all our history our countryside never looked like this, dotted over with trenches, machine gun emplacements, block houses, pill boxes, concrete shelters, tank traps and land mines. One feels that the quiet villages of England are the focal point of the world—as indeed they are, for they are in the front line of the battle for freedom."

While Hurricanes and Spitfires of the Royal Air Force defended the sky over England, Leslie described the simple heroism that inspired the young pilots of these machines. He visited one of the airfields of Fighter Command.

"About noon I went down to the mess and met the Hurricane Squadron that was shortly to take off. I wish I could give you a remote impression of the mess of a fighter station at the midday beer hour. I swear it has an atmosphere more optimistic, cheerful and encouraging than you could find anywhere in the world to-day, certainly anywhere in Europe. You feel that if only you could live for the rest of the war amongst these smiling men in blue that you would never know another moment of depression. It seems they never stop laughing. They are on top of the world. Their tails are up. One day the world will raise their glasses to this Hurricane Squadron as I raised mine that noon."

In September the German *Luftwaffe,* never before challenged in their supremacy, was forced to abandon daylight raids. After huge losses at the hands of a gallant few British pilots, the Nazis flung their tremendous bomber strength into night attacks on London. Hitler proclaimed a "war of total annihilation" on his enemies; this last remaining fortress was to receive no quarter.

"To have lived in and around London during the two weeks ending September 21st, 1940," Leslie told America, "is to have lived through the most menacing, dangerous gruelling fortnight in the long, valiant history of this metropolis." He described the nightly horror of destruction that fell upon his birthplace, the unmistakable flash of bombs leaping up across the horizon, the obligato of anti-aircraft guns as the vultures left the local areas of carnage and moved into the heart of London. He tried to bring the daily and nightly life of Britain closer to the residents of the United States, to engage their sympathy, to invoke their aid.

"This is not London as you may have seen it in the first war," he told them. "There are none of the crowds, none of the light-hearted gaiety, no 'Bing Boys' no music halls, no opera, no 'Tipperary.' Here is only a people facing the worst menace in their history, committed to a life or death proposition and knowing full well all the implications. A people without illusions, but with a stronger, I swear it, more profound conviction that no matter what the cost or how long the time, once again they will triumph."

At the Stowe every weekend, the family caught its breath together. Sometimes Wink would manage a day or two of leave, and then the circle would be complete. Wink joined his father on "Britain Speaks"—"because the Navy is our link with North America. . . . I do not know many ratings of the Royal Navy so you must forgive me if the one I present to you happens to be my own son." Then Doodie, obviously rather jealous, appeared on the program inadequately representing British youth.

Leslie, as usual, found the hours with his children a time of real relaxation. He and Wink talked quietly together whenever they had the chance; "ensconced in my room with beer and pipes." Wink was in a Naval Training Establishment at Portsmouth, and his father went down to see him and also to learn about the air raids on this important dockyard. These separate pursuits were forcibly combined by the German air force. Leslie and Wink conducted their tête-à-tête in a shelter during a particularly nasty raid. It gave Leslie another look at the quiet bravery of average people.

"I watched particularly the old people and the girls . . . if one had a few qualms oneself, one had only to look at the courage of these old people. For it does require courage to sit still in a little, dark, airless place and smile and talk when you know that some of the most ruthless devils alive are trying to kill you with some of the most potent instruments of death known. Finally, much later than I had thought, my son saw me off on the train and we smiled to think we had spent our short visit under fire. The sun was setting as the train travelled through the peaceful Sussex countryside and I could not help marvelling at the serenity of the lovely scene. England has passed through the most dangerous time of its history and I have seen the same calmness and serenity of its landscape reflected in the spirit of its people and I feel the better for it."

The landscape around Stowe Maries may have looked calm also, but great activity was going on. Every night the uneven hum of Nazi planes worried the peaceful air, and, inside the house, dance music competed with the drumbeat of anti-aircraft fire. The drawing room was full of young men in uniform, for Ruth ran open house throughout the war.

Doodie, at sixteen, was in her element. The war had brought little but excitement into her life, with numbers of attractive men in uniform. She had skillfully dodged all efforts to evacuate her to America, not unnaturally preferring the local fun to a possible five years at a boarding school in California. Leslie had done his best to send her away to safety. In the summer of 1940, when the fear of invasion was very real, he had begged her to go. With everyone else, he believed the German onslaught was bound to fall on the south of England, and what could stop the final subjection of the whole island? His worry for his family was increased by the information from a film colleague that his own name was on the German black list. This same colleague was boarding a ship at once, and advised Leslie to do the same. "I've seen the black list, Leslie. Both our names are on it. The Germans would shoot us immediately."

Though Leslie was extremely scornful of this man's terrified departure, and had no intention of leaving himself, he did want his younger child to escape. Nothing would move Doodie; youthful infallibility surrounded her, and, anyway, death seemed more pleasant than boarding school. As was his habit, Leslie hesitated before giving a direct order to his child.

The winter gales removed the terror of invasion, and Doodie helped to entertain the troops. She had a wide selection that year, for the Canadian Army was encamped in force about the countryside. Leslie, returning on Friday evenings, found his house surrounded by military vehicles, and every chair occupied by officers from Toronto and Montreal, Winnipeg and Ottawa. He teased Doodie gently but with a hint of malice about these young men. She seemed suddenly more interested in them than in him. It was the natural reaction of a devoted father when he discovers his child growing up with ideas of her own. Leslie greeted anyone he found in the house with friendliness, but, true to his nature, he would suddenly evaporate. Eventually, Doodie or Ruth would track him down in his own room, working on a broadcast, lying under the sun lamp, or listening to a football game from America on his beloved radio.

The film script that had partially occupied him for eight months was nearly finished. He had given it to yet another writer, Anatole de Grunwald, and through many changes it emerged as a tight and exciting story. Leslie and Tolly de

Grunwald found high entertainment in the cloak-and-dagger situations they invented, and seemed to get along well together. If Leslie had learned anything from twenty years of acting, it was how to dissemble. He managed his writers carefully and cleverly, laughing at their comedy, praising rather than decrying every first draft. He was sensitive to the feelings of authors about new work—it could not be criticized immediately without endangering their delicately balanced pride. A freshly written scene appears a perfect thing to its creator, it is like a new spring hat to a woman—no matter how terrible, nothing against it should be said at first. So Leslie found with writers; he waited until they were involved with another scene before he corrected the previous one, and thus developed the best in them without pain.

While the final script of *Pimpernel Smith* was made ready, Leslie arranged the casting and the financing. He was anxious to get the film started, mainly because it had a contemporary theme, but partly to provide some money to keep his family. One year without earning money and with his American assets frozen by the British Treasury had left him uncomfortably poor. Occasionally, when he thought about this, the blackout depressions gripped him and even Hollywood looked attractive.

"About seven o'clock on the Saturday evening of last week I found myself in a very gloomy mood indeed," he wrote in November. "I had been sitting thinking of what I would have been doing if Hitler had never been born—curse him! I would have been in my nice little house in Beverly Hills sitting by the swimming pool dressed in a pair of shorts, the hot California sun streaming down on me, but just pleasantly broken by the leaves of my favourite lemon tree. I would be humming happily to myself and cogitating somewhat thus: Metropolitan Collossal Pictures have just overpaid me atrociously for my last picture, and I gather from my agent that they are going to pay me even more for my next . . . upon which my young daughter would probably have turned up in a fetching Palm Beach bathing suit and dragged me into the pool. Then, I think, a nice drive through the palm trees, lunch with some friends, a game of tennis with my son . . . and then the evening siren howled forth and the voice of the warden announced that a chink of light was showing through one of my windows. I came down to earth—and the black-out—and my gloomy mood. What good was I doing here? My normal work had been interrupted, I had not earned any money. My participation in the war effort, the purpose for which I was here, seemed negligible. The Navy did not want me, the Army did not want me, the Air Force didn't want me—nobody wanted me. Even my family kept away from me that evening. So I went out into the night in solitary state."

Leslie's walk on this occasion took him past the local pub.

"The voices within sounded cheerful, and though in my Russian mood, I resented cheerfulness, they lured me in. It was warm, smoky, noisy and jovial inside. And very English. I did well to go in. I drank beer and talked to many people. You never know who you are going to meet in our village nowadays. Like most villages near to London, it is full of strangers. Among others, I talked to an actor who had lost his job, a shopkeeper who had lost his shop and a Frenchman who had lost his country."

While Leslie talked to these people he realized what they had also found here to be grateful for, and his mood changed.

"I was full of exultation. I knew again what I had always known, that the human soul is a miracle of adaptability, that we can cram as many lives into a lifetime as our courage and ingenuity will let us, and that the measure of a great people is the ability to do these things. I knew that money and the material things are, in these days, being shown up in their true unimportant light as never before. That it did not matter how much property was destroyed, nor how much wealth poured out for our cause, because property and gold had become valueless. I knew what it was to belong to a free nation with a noble motive and that we were headed for ultimate triumph. And as I listened to the enemy sneaking overhead, I knew the real meaning of being an Englishman in Britain in the year 1940."

21 / "Au Revoir"

The new year of 1941 was hardly bright with promise. Though British troops were victorious in the deserts of the Middle East, London was bedeviled from the awful sky, and the coming of spring would surely bring more violent aggression upon the map of Europe.

At Denham Studios, Leslie began his film *Pimpernel Smith*. It had a wonderfully relaxed air about it, for all the pressures of war. Leslie, never punctual, now worked on a rather erratic schedule. Nothing too important happened before ten thirty, and then the "rushes," film shot the previous day, had to be seen. Naturally, there were other hitches: material unavailable, priorities to be arranged, last-moment casting upsets, lots and lots of reasons for Leslie never to be quite ready, always to be well behind the shooting dates set. Scenes had a habit of being rewritten, at best the night before, and often right on the set. The unfortunate men entrusted with technical jobs, or ones involving salaries and finance, went quietly insane. Nobody could persuade Leslie to worry about money. "What is money?" he was heard to say in a tone faintly reminiscent of Alexander Korda. His conviction that gold was valueless, so clearly outlined in his broadcasts, came with him to the studio.

"Nothing must matter except the final excellence and integ-

279

rity of the film." Somehow, no one could refuse him. They would all grumble and fight with each other, complain about their erratic director, threaten to resign, and then laugh and defend Leslie fiercely. He collected a fond following, rather like a lot of old Nannies looking after a wayward child.

He worked hard, if spasmodically, and, though he was physically a little lazy, his quick, inquisitive mind drove him on. He served on an ideas committee at the Ministry of Information where the task was to find and recommend fresh projects for propaganda. Two of his fellow members were his old friends Anthony Asquith and Michael Powell. Leslie appeared in *49th Parallel* for Powell, one of the major semidocumentary films to come out of the early years of the war. In the film he played a tiny part, as did the other famous people who volunteered their services. Raymond Massey, Laurence Olivier, and Anton Walbrook acted briefly in sequences showing the escape of a German submarine crew across Canada. Because some of the film was shot in Canada, Elisabeth Bergner had to be replaced when it was considered unsafe for her to cross the Atlantic. A German of strong anti-Nazi feelings, she was not anxious to fall into Nazi hands. Her part was taken by a very young, very pretty girl named Glynis Johns. Leslie came across this small and nervous child on the set one day crying softly to herself, and, always affected by tearful females, he went over to see what was wrong. The cause of her tears was the hair style she had been given.

"It's my forehead," she wailed dismally. "I hate my hair pulled off my forehead—it's such a big one."

"Never mind," said Leslie gently. "Mine's awfully big too—and do you know, I've done all right."

In another documentary, *From the Four Corners,* Leslie acted with three young men, a Canadian, an Australian, and a New Zealander. It was only a short film, in which he played himself showing these soldiers around London, but it contained much of Leslie's own feelings about the city and the

men who built it. At the end he quoted a few famous words
from the Declaration of Independence, written, as Leslie put
it, "at the behest of an English colonial officer named George
Washington," and he told these Commonwealth soldiers:
"Those words and that spirit were born and nourished here
and your fathers carried them to the ends of the earth. They
are our inheritance from the past, our legacy to the future.
That's why you came here, to defend them."

All Leslie's efforts were directed toward the United States,
his second home, now watching the outcome of a struggle that
as yet they did not recognize as their own. He wrote his
weekly speeches to that country with care, but he told them
roundly that "the happiest peoples in the civilized world today
are those who are fearlessly waging the good fight with all
their might against terrorism and domination."

He had built a large audience in the United States and
Canada, and judging by the reports of German anger at his
broadcasts, his words carried some weight.

The summer of 1941 was strangely peaceful in England.
The Germans, flushed with their victories in Greece and
Crete, concentrated on their armies in the desert, and London
received a respite from attack. Before *Pimpernel Smith* was
finished, Leslie was at work on another idea. He had heard
the story of a man named R. J. Mitchell, a quiet, scholarly aeronautical engineer who had given England the Spitfire and
sacrificed his own life to do it. The idea of this simple, un-
heroic man working himself to death so that his country
should have an airplane capable of meeting the German
attack when it came inspired Leslie. He explained it to Doodie
as they wandered around the garden one Sunday afternoon.

"It has a great appeal at this stage of the war—after all, the
Spitfire saved us in the Battle of Britain," Leslie said, "and this
man, giving his own life, was really the same as 'The Few'
who were killed flying the plane—he was, in fact, the very
first of 'The Few.' "

The film about Mitchell was called just that: *The First of the Few,* and David Niven, serving then in the 60th Rifles, was released for a short time to appear with Leslie in the picture. Leslie needed a production assistant, and his old friend from Minerva Films, Adrian Brunel, came to join him. Brunel, starting officially as a technical guide to Leslie, became much more. He sacrificed his own interest and ability to direct in order to support Leslie completely and wholeheartedly.

"I certainly gave everything I could," wrote Brunel, "for not only did I love him, but he and his job were worth what I could give."

The First of the Few spanned twenty years of aeronautical development, and included scenes of the Battle of Britain, which were shot at an R.A.F. station, using pilots, not actors, to portray their own contribution to history. Doodie took another stab at acting in this film, playing an American nurse with a bogus accent and rather grubby fingernails. Leslie patiently tried to teach her a few lines; he had written a scene especially for her, during lunch in his dressing room. But there was not enough time to produce the earlier results, and she had become a most self-conscious actress. One line, "You're telling me," which she was absolutely unable to say properly, became a bone of contention with her father.

"Just toss it off, dear—lightly—you're not Mae West, for God's sake!"

After two days' shooting, she returned exhausted to her own home, determined never to repeat the indignity again. No one in her right mind could want to be an actress. Leslie laughed over her attempt and told her it was mostly on the cutting-room floor.

Events throughout the world moved fast that year, and in December came the news of the tragedy of Pearl Harbor and the entry of the United States into the war. It was received in England with deep sorrow, tempered, very naturally, by an overwhelming sense of relief. The British had survived eighteen months under the fear of invasion, and with their forces spread thinly across the world. Now they turned gratefully to this strong, fresh nation.

During these early war years, Leslie developed an odd design for living. Inhabiting a small house near the studio all week, he returned solemnly to his family life on the weekends. There he was waited on and babied, there everything was organized for the maximum comfort of the head of the house. He drove away on Monday, full of advice from Ruth, to operate his rather gayer existence as a free man at Denham. But no matter what the pressures at that end, regardless of the amusements, he came home every Friday to reaffirm his love for wife and family.

His family had changed in 1941. Wink, married in March, was on the point of being sent to the Far East; Doodie was engaged at seventeen to one of the Canadians Leslie had suspected when he saw them so often in his house. He had tried to argue his daughter out of what he considered an absurd decision. He may have been injured at her affection for another man, but basically he worried, as every father would, about a determined headstrong child apparently intent on her own destruction. His arguments were hardly successful.

"Miss Howard," he remarked sadly, "the first time you ever smiled, you smiled at me, and I have never since been able to argue with you. I've spoiled you all your life—it's too late to start saying 'no.' Go ahead, ruin your life; I can't stop you."

Doodie had the will power of her mother, and he had never controlled it. With that singleness of purpose that always defeated him, she announced the date of her wedding. Ruth and Leslie, divided by constant attack, gave their consent.

The wedding preparations consumed the time and energy of his household, but Leslie remained aloof. He suddenly developed a new, unique, and convenient attitude toward the whole business—it smacked of a tribal custom!

"I will not be a part of this awful rigmarole," he announced to Ruth. "I do not approve of trousseaux—dressing up the child like a central African native to be delivered to the highest bidder—it's positively pagan!" Ruth, caught in the crosscurrent between a daughter who expected a whole new wardrobe and a husband who would not contribute to it, had a most difficult time. Leslie decided that his own wedding arrangements had been ideal.

"We didn't need yards of white satin and dozens of expensive flowers," he said. "We didn't have to fill a lot of bored people with champagne—the religious service is completely overwhelmed by all this commercial nonsense."

Defense of religion was a strange role for Leslie. If not an agnostic, he had certainly shown small interest in the teachings of his own church. His children were never either encouraged or discouraged to attend or belong.

"What is money?" jibed Ruth. "It's the artistic integrity that matters!"

Extraordinarily obstinate when he wanted to be, his womenfolk knew better than to drive him. There were other methods, and they were experts in manipulation.

Fortunately, he was engrossed once more in a film, *The Gentle Sex,* about the A.T.S.—the women's army. While he concentrated on these hard-working and courageous females, his own militant women attacked stealthily on the home front. Ruth and Doodie achieved their objective, and the wedding took place in May.

Leslie could not be persuaded to view the whole affair seriously. He put on a bright blue tie—"It's a wedding, not a funeral"—and suggested at the door of the church that he and Doodie should go home and play cards, "Everyone will come back for champagne later." Then in the church he forgot his only line, and fluffed badly. It seemed ridiculous to him that his still young child should be taking such an irrevocable step.

For all his mood of nonsense, he was sad that day and stood

quietly in her room while she dressed to go away, fiddling with inanimate objects, as he always did when his mind was full of unspoken thoughts. The two Leslies looked at one another, both realizing that in an intangible way this was the end of an association for them. Doodie would always be his child, but somehow, when two souls had been as close as theirs, life could not be quite the same again. Leslie said very little—a few words of love and God speed—but Doodie was crying when the car took her away with her young husband, her eyes turned to the road behind, where Leslie stood with Ruth, a diminishing figure, sadly waving.

Leslie put his arm around his wife's shoulders. "Well, old girl, we're back where we started, eh?" Then he disappeared to his room to work on the next week's scenes for *The Gentle Sex*.

There was a special attraction about this film, for with it he had reached a long-awaited goal—he did not have to act in it. As the producer and codirector, his interest was purely technical. "Nothing is more pathetic than middle-aged actors hanging on to their fading youth and playing romantic leads." It would take some years to convince critics, used to the easy, happy atmosphere of his performances, that he had equal talent for direction. But the style and intelligence of the films that he had produced or directed gave promise of a brilliant future for him. Other actors found him considerate and highly sensitive to work for. Unhurried and understanding with them, he encouraged, rather than demanded, a good performance. This alone gave him a great advantage as a director. The films that he made after the war began, though full of compromises and short of money, were to him significantly better than anything else he had achieved.

The Gentle Sex, which marked the new course of his career, was, strangely, a last-moment decision. Originally undertaken by Derrick de Marney, Leslie stepped in to direct when major problems of finance and studio space immobilized the production. He did so because he agreed with De Marney that here was a tale worth telling, and he made of it, for all its documentary exterior, a picture with charm, both touching and humorous.

He enjoyed a type of freedom in his work that he had never known before. A member of the board of Two Cities Films, as a production consultant, he had a strong influence on the films they undertook. Fillipo Del Guidice was the head of the company, but he listened unusually seriously to Leslie's comments. In effect, Leslie's was the voice of authority, and it was something he would never have given up for the far fields of California. He had realized the ambition of his youth —to work for and improve British films.

For Two Cities, Leslie supervised the production of a picture about the nursing service. It was another semidocumentary—indeed, most films had a serious background in the war years—but produced as a feature film, dramatically entitled *The Lamp Still Burns*. Leslie cast Stewart Granger in the leading part, with Rosamund John as the nurse in training. Stewart Granger was new to films, but Leslie had seen him in *The Man in Grey* and felt immediately that he was a young man with limited experience but exceptional appeal. This opinion was quickly confirmed by the women in the British Isles.

The direction of *The Lamp Still Burns* was in the hands of Maurice Elvey, which gave Leslie less technical work to do. It also gave him more freedom. He had been approached a number of times by the British Council to go abroad on lecture tours as a British good-will ambassador. On each previous occasion he had dodged the request. He had no desire to leave the refuge of England, he absolutely detested traveling alone, and he refused to be cut off from his family and from Ruth, who was, as always, indispensable.

In the spring of 1943 the pressure was put upon him once again. He was asked to lecture in Portugal and Spain. He had no idea what he could talk about in those neutral countries, with their German and Italian residents. He was told that the war was not to be mentioned, but every opportunity must be grasped to put forward the Allied way of life—subtly and amusingly—through the theater, particularly through the works of Shakespeare, and always indirectly, rather than by the Teutonic heavy-handedness of Hitler's propagandists.

Leslie reluctantly agreed to go, feeling duty-bound. He had a brief talk with Anthony Eden, the Foreign Minister, which gave him a certain enthusiasm for the task, and at the end of April he boarded a KLM plane for Lisbon. The last arrangements, clouded in official secrecy, were in the best tradition of Howard departures. Determined not to travel alone, he persuaded Alfred Chenhalls, his chartered accountant, that a breath of summer air would do him great good. The problems involved with priority transport for a nonpriority passenger almost defeated even Leslie. But when the plane lifted from the runway, Chenhalls was beside him.

"Alfred slept happily, but I'm afraid I didn't," wrote Leslie in the first of his usual dire epistles to Ruth. His health deteriorated in the customary fashion as England disappeared behind him.

"When we landed at Lisbon airport, it was as hot as Albuquerque in June. I was dying in my tweed suit and thick overcoat and while waiting for the customs we had a glass of port. This was not such a good idea in that heat and excitement. We were met by all kinds of people—British and Portuguese and then whisked off in a car, and they really go on two wheels here. My face, which had been scarlet, started to turn green and I asked them to slow up before I passed out—when I got to the hotel I had a lot of trouble with my damn' heart. A doctor came who knew a few words of French and said it —my heart—sounded very peculiar."

After a press reception, where, he recorded: "I felt very ill and looked it," he decided to spend the weekend at Estoril to recover. "I have had a bad night only sleeping two hours, and don't feel very well. The doctor came in a little while ago. He says my heart is better but my blood-pressure rather high—this is bad for me as mine normally is low."

From Estoril he admitted to a slight improvement in health, and to taking lessons in Portuguese from the chambermaid—"an extremely dark girl with flashing teeth—obviously of Arab origin." Here he wrote notes for two lectures. One, in a theater in Lisbon, was on films, "A lot of nonsense—I'll just keep talking 'til my time is up." The other was more worrisome, being at the Teatro Nacional on *Hamlet,* "which they are all very studious about and about which I don't know much and have forgotten most. I did not bring out any books on this subject (especially Dover Wilson) and all I have is a Penguin *Hamlet* I found here. Unfortunately, it has been put about that I am the great English Shakespeare expert, which God knows I am not. I think I shall come clean and admit all."

The trip to Spain appealed not at all, and he did his best to avoid it. "In this state of health I don't feel like it—I'd rather get back home than end up in a hospital here. I always get panicky feeling like this in a strange country. My familiar places and faces in England seem very dear. I know how poor old Wink feels."

Parties, receptions, and lectures had been arranged in Madrid, so there was no escape for him, and, groaning about his weak heart, he made the nineteen-hour trip by train. "Only German and Italian planes, full of our enemies which would not be amusing." Everywhere he went he found friends. "Except, of course, the Herrenvolk. They are a grim looking lot, men and women, and they don't like us much. We get dirty looks and they seem to resent the idea that we can have a good time. English laughter is the last thing they want to hear—especially after the North African news. I have to hold Alfred back. He will insist on murmuring 'Bizerte' in a stage whisper as we pass them in dignified silence—they always seem to stop talking when we appear."

In Madrid he gave two lectures at the British Institute, went through a meeting with the press, an embassy reception, a formal call on the ambassador, luncheons, dinners, a bullfight, and a flamenco party, a film opening, and the inspection of film studios. At the end of it all he was surprised that he felt "giddy and exhausted." It was suggested that he should go on to Gibraltar, and he longed to see Seville and Granada before he left, but by this time he detected something wrong with his heart, his nerves and his liver—"It may be the sun."

Despite his failing health—"I had to cancel going to an important dinner for the Duke of Alba"—he made a very good impression on the Spaniards. The British Embassy and the British Council representative in Madrid had few-enough occasions to present a suitable Englishman to the residents, and they competed constantly with superior numbers of German visitors and enormous amounts of propaganda.

Leslie was intrigued with the idea of eventually making films in Spain, where the climate resembled California. He also had become quite enthusiastic about lecture tours, writing to Mike Levee in Hollywood that he expected to fly over to Canada in the autumn for a series of speeches there. But England and sanctuary beckoned him home. He and Alfred Chenhalls went back to Lisbon, and recovered again at Estoril. Since one of his films was due to open in Lisbon, Leslie stayed an extra day or two. There he wrote another letter to Ruth, expecting, as he said, to be home before she got it.

"I shall be glad to see everybody. God bless you dear, and au revoir. Leslie."

That was to be Ruth's last word from Leslie. Twenty-seven years, and *au revoir*. His leave-taking was somehow as she had known it would be—sudden and uncomplicated. In the strict sense of *au revoir,* Leslie would not return. But to Ruth, in a very real sense he had never left, for he had delineated the path of her life and filled it with a kind of magic that was hers alone, for always. The news reached Wink on board an armed merchant cruiser, corkscrewing through the southwest moonsoon twenty-five miles off Cape Gardafui, East Africa. With the quick stab of understanding that pain brings and with the power of description that belonged both to father and son, Wink wrote:

"The plane carrying him had been shot down into the sea three hundred miles off Cape Finisterre. The yeoman of the watch had broken the news. He had heard it just before he came to the bridge on the mess-deck wireless. 'Cape Finisterre . . .' I repeated. Away on the horizon the beacon of Gardafui opened like an eye and went out. In the dark I turned away to the chart table and made a note in the log: 'Finisterre abeam' I wrote without thinking. The ship was three thousand sea miles from Finisterre—but nobody noted the mistake. In a moment I altered course and as the ship swung up into the wind, the sharp, stinging top of a wave swept the bridge. The spindrift struck like a knife. And strangely, in that moment, something of us was mingled. I could taste the salt on my cheek that was both mine and his. . . ."

The Understanding

To come to terms, to grips, to an acceptance of grief,
To force oneself, against oneself, to a last understanding
With truth, no matter how bitter—the thin end of belief:
This for the heart is the hardest, the cruellest thing.

That there will sound no more upon the landing
The creak of the returning feet, the stumbling oath
Upon the stairs, the laughing last "good-night". . . the heart
  stops
Upon a frontier of unbelief that love may be no more
Of substance than the far sea wind that spreads the wave-tops
Frigid as sheets on an empty bed.
A sudden shutting door
Startles with false hope . . . on edge we comb the restless
  track
Of ocean as if our hearts had eyes to seek him out,
And ears to hear him call . . .

But love brings him not back;
Not all our love or our unstinted prayers are stout
Enough to shield his candle from the wind. The flame is out
And this our hearts must understand, this hardest thing:
No more for his home-coming may our love be listening;
But here, within this fading dark, as the last stars dim,
Listen, as the wind lifts on your cheek—for the wind shall tell
  of him.

                       Ronald Howard

Epilogue

In Gratitude: The Assessment Completed

Fifty years was to be his span. He died at a moment when his star had never climbed higher in his own country.

"Probably no single war casualty has induced in the public of these islands such an acute sense of personal loss," wrote the critic C. A. LeJeune. "Howard was more than just a popular actor. Since the war he has become something of a symbol to the British people."

He could not have asked more than this. There were hundreds of people who wrote to us simply to say that they would miss him, too. Though it was miserably upsetting for my mother, she read every letter and felt somehow warmed and comforted by the friendship of men and women she had never seen, who cared enough to remember.

Almost at once, and for years after, the reasons for his death were debated. To us they are not important. That he had died was all that we, his family, knew. It is his life that was important to us, not a collection of sensational and rather dubious stories about his death. I have no patience with superstitious delvings into psychic matters. Certainly in Spain he did sit down twice at a table laid for thirteen, but so have a lot of other people who are still living. It is known that a flamenco dancer refused to perform because she thought she saw a skull

292

instead of his head, but at least one other man was present who flew to England with him, and, perhaps because he was not so well known, he looked quite healthy to the dramatic Spanish woman.

It was my father's misfortune to fly on the same day that Churchill was known to be returning from Algiers. There, I think, is the answer to his death. Every German pilot knew the importance of Sir Winston to the Allied war effort. If there was the slightest hope of shooting down his plane, the lowliest *leutnant* would have been longing to do it. Thus it was, I am sure, that when the eight aircraft sighted the Allied plane on that day of all days, though the chance of it being Churchill was slight, the chance was there and well worth taking. If they caught the British prime minister they would be national heroes; if not, it could be covered up somehow and an excuse found, as indeed there was.

Afterward, the German squadron responsible produced the names of the passengers on my father's plane, with the reasons why they must not reach England. There were indeed a number of influential people on board. But these flights were mainly for priority passengers at any time, and on almost any other day the list could have been as impressive. Perhaps, too, the Germans made the passengers appear more important than they were to clear their own consciences. My father, for instance, was not listed as an actor but as a member of the British Secret Service and a manufacturer of aircraft parts. I can testify to the inaccuracy of the latter and, though secret agents are naturally unknown even to their own families, my father was a most unlikely choice for this role, too. He was certainly not a coward, but, knowing him as I did, I would say unhesitatingly that he did not possess the inner resources necessary for the hazards of the Secret Service; he was never a lone wolf. In fact, I can almost hear him giggling at this odd piece of casting. No, he had a number of useful gifts, but resourceful self-sufficiency was not among them. This is an anomaly really, for he was inclined to a solitary existence, being much better company by himself than in a large group. Where my mother could keep a roomful of people laughing while she told stories with great dramatic talent, my father preferred a quiet conversation with one or two people. During the war, when he was constantly meeting and working with senior people in different phases of the Allied cause, he would occasionally be encouraged to talk about the things he was doing, and he enjoyed discussions about the conduct of the war. Here he might hold the floor for a few moments. Invariably, if he did it was on a serious theme and his thoughts were lucidly expressed but without exaggeration or especial emphasis. His attempts at telling funny stories were without exception catastrophic. He could never remember the point, and long before the halfway mark of a story he was floundering around, usually shaken by laughter, because he *knew* it was a *funny* story but quite unable to recall just why. Considering that he could memorize the beautiful complications of Shakespeare, play one part at night and rehearse another all day, his failing seemed extraordinary. Most actors are brilliant raconteurs. But I suppose if anything set him apart from his profession, it was this difference.

He was a most unlikely sort of person for an actor altogether. He neither looked nor thought like one. He basically did not enjoy the company of other actors; he never relished long discussions about every play he was in, or that anyone else was in. The members of the gilded profession, seemingly so exciting, can be hideous bores when encountered en masse, and no one was more aware of this than my father. We saw few of the great names of the theater in our house. Writers came, and painters and barristers and polo players, but actors were the exception. From this lack of apparent theatricality arose further inconsistencies: when a man seems to resemble a college professor and then does not always behave like one, his actions are thought to be out of character. Leslie occasionally behaved like an actor, and surprised everyone. But it must be remembered that he *was* an actor, and in the words of George Cukor, who has dealt with quite a few: "Actors are a different breed of cat." They do not look on life quite as people outside the entertainment world regard it. Nor are they expected to—which accounts, undoubtedly, for the greater freedom they allow themselves when applying everyday standards of morality and manners to their behavior.

My father was only influenced to a minor degree by his success, but it is difficult for any person to reach a senior position without some desire to call the tune. In this he was often selfish but never self-important. He used his charm to achieve his ends. Such charm can sometimes be a handicap, making it so easy to get one's own way that one expects it all the time. Fortunately, my father was saved from willfulness by his easygoing, kind disposition. If he left something to be desired as a husband, my mother would not have changed him. He was all she had ever wanted, or to this day could imagine, and to the end he had needed her and loved her and she had worshiped him.

In everyone's life there are moments of extreme joy and sorrow. There is always, I think, the flash of attraction from man to woman, no matter how happy your marriage. My father was no less susceptible to feminine charm than the next. He was, after all, in a job where every woman tried to be beautiful. To say he never looked at a woman other than his wife would be to make him a dull shade of himself; to pretend that he was a Lothario endlessly pursuing girls would be a fake. He never had enough energy to run after a woman; it was, rather, that he sometimes lacked the energy to run away. For all the twenty-seven years of their marriage, he never seriously considered life without his wife. She was always the solid background, the protecting wall, his dear Ruthie.

He was a very lovable person, warm and responsive, and capable of arousing great affection in others. Time and again

I have been struck, while trying to piece together his life story, by the same words from the people who knew him: "I loved your father." Man or woman, young or old, from divergent professions, they shared this affection. It is a happy legacy.

Fifteen years have gone since the sunny, lonely, sad day when his aircraft fell, shattered by bullets, into the unremitting sea. Fifteen years to cover the sorrow but never quiet the loneliness.

My father had no strong belief in immortality. It existed, he sometimes said, through one's children. To be remembered always by them and possibly by their children's children almost as a legend, this, I think, will be his true immortality—more important to him, perhaps, than any lasting recognition as an actor.

Frequently an overindulgent parent, constantly an entertaining one, never a bad one. He would not have asked for a better epitaph. From my first memories of bouncing around in his arms to the strains of "Who?" to my last sight of his gaily waved hand as he left for Lisbon—"Good-by, Mrs. Dale-Harris"—he was a quite remarkable father.

*Plays and films in which Leslie Howard appeared